50 Years of Scottish Opera

A CELEBRATION

Scottish
Opera

Published by Scottish Opera

Scottish Opera
39 Elmbank Crescent
Glasgow G2 4PT

scottishopera.org.uk

A CIP record for this book is available from the British Library

ISBN 978-0-9572641-1-3

Compiled and edited by Ian Brooke
Designed by Fiona Gauld

Jacket illustrations
Front: Edgaras Montvidas as Tom Rakewell: *The Rake's Progress*, director Sir David McVicar, 2012.
Back (clockwise from top left):
Alexander Young as Ferrando, Dame Janet Baker as Dorabella, Elizabeth Harwood as Fiordiligi, Peter van der Bilt as Guglielmo: *Così fan tutte*, 1975 revival of the 1967 Anthony Besch production;
Lisa Saffer as Zerbinetta, Dame Anne Evans as Ariadne, David Stephenson as Harlequin: *Ariadne auf Naxos*, director Martin Duncan, 1998;
Susannah Glanville as Tosca: *Tosca*, 2012 revival of the 1980 Anthony Besch production.
Peter Sidhom as Alberich: *Das Rheingold*, director Tim Albery, 2000;

All information in this book is as accurate and up-to-date as possible. However, errors and omissions do occur.
Please contact Scottish Opera at the address above if you would like to submit any proposed amendments.

Typeset in Interface by Scottish Opera Graphics Department.

Printed in Great Britain by J Thomson Colour Printers Ltd, Glasgow.

Scottish Opera is registered in Scotland Number SCO37531 Scottish Charity Number SCO19787

Scottish Opera
is core funded by

The Scottish
Government
Riaghaltas na h-Alba

Contents

From: Her Royal Highness The Duchess of Gloucester

As Patron of Scottish Opera since 1986, I have been fortunate enough to see a variety of productions, mostly at the Theatre Royal Glasgow and at the Festival Theatre in Edinburgh, and to meet many of those involved in the Company.

Since its inception 50 years ago, Scottish Opera has become world renowned. With the addition of educational projects and outreach programmes, Opera has become accessible to so many more people. This would not have been possible without the immense generosity of many individuals, corporate organisations and the core funding provided by the Scottish Government; I do so hope that this will long continue and thus contribute to the ongoing success of Scottish Opera.

No doubt, this book will be enjoyed by many. I am sure we should take pride in all that Scottish Opera has achieved over its first half Century, and we now look towards the next 5 decades; amongst the highlights will be the completion and opening, next year, of the new foyers in the Theatre Royal in Glasgow.

I congratulate all those involved and offer my warmest good wishes for the future to everyone in Scottish Opera.

Introduction

Alex Reedijk
General Director

When Sir Alexander Gibson dreamed of establishing an opera company in Scotland – what became Scottish Opera – he was supported by others who shared the same dream: Ainslie Millar, Ian Rodger, Richard Telfer. That first single week of performances of *Madama Butterfly* and *Pelléas et Mélisande* at the King's Theatre, Glasgow in June 1962 proved that there was a demand for high-quality, professional, home-produced opera in Scotland. Without the vision and dedication of the original founders, we wouldn't be in the position today to celebrate 50 years of Scottish Opera.

Curiously, my own introduction to Scottish Opera – and indeed to opera – was not in Scotland, but on the other side of the world, in New Zealand. It was at the St James Theatre in Wellington in the late 1980s that I attended my first professional opera performance, of Mozart's *Così fan tutte*. Looking back, and browsing through photographs, I realise that this production must have been that originally staged by Anthony Besch for Scottish Opera in 1967 – the famous 'black-and-white *Così*'. By the 1980s the production had already been revived on a number of occasions in Scotland, before being hired out to the Adelaide Festival and then restaged in New Zealand. It was this performance of *Così* that ignited my passion for opera, a passion that has remained with me for more than 25 years.

This book is a celebration of all that is great about opera, and about Scottish Opera in particular. What it is not – nor was it ever intended to be – is a record of Board meetings, funding travails or the administrative 'stuff' that is part and parcel of working in the performing arts. While any arts organisation will have its ups and downs over a period of 50 years, what the vast majority of audience members recall are the unforgettable nights they have enjoyed in the theatre, emotionally immersed in great productions of operatic masterpieces.

In *50 Years of Scottish Opera: A Celebration* we have collected anecdotes, favourite memories and reminiscences about the Company from a whole range of people associated with Scottish Opera: singers, conductors, directors, designers, stage managers, administrators and audience members, plus our three most recent Music Directors – John Mauceri, Sir Richard Armstrong and Francesco Corti – and the wives of three of the original founders.

Armed with hundreds of memories, we have sought to match as many of these as possible to photographs held in the Scottish Opera archive. Inside you will find early triumphs including *Otello, Der Rosenkavalier* and the operas of Benjamin Britten; the revelatory stagings of Janáček operas begun in the 1970s; enduring productions such as *Tosca*; more recent critically acclaimed productions such as the *Ring* cycle of 2003, *La traviata* and *The Marriage of Figaro* ; and world and UK premieres across nearly five decades – to name but a few. There is also full coverage of all our productions during our 50th Anniversary Season and a peek behind the scenes at Elmbank Crescent and Edington Street, our administrative and rehearsal premises in Glasgow.

Of course, we can't include every highlight across 50 years, but we hope that many of your own favourite productions are here. However, we have included a comprehensive listing of Company opening nights, including those of our smaller-scale touring productions, so that you may at least identify the time and the place of your Scottish Opera memories!

As we embark on our next half-century, now is as good a time as any to take stock of the Company's standing. At the conclusion of its 50th Anniversary Season, Scottish Opera is in great order. In fact, I believe Scottish Opera is unique in its commitment to a combination of main-stage performances, smaller-scale national touring, education and outreach, and new commissions. In our anniversary season, we have marked the centenary of the birth of Britten (in our annual co-production with the Royal Conservatoire of Scotland), and the bicentenaries of the births of Verdi and Wagner; we have visited 50 venues from Lerwick to Stranraer; we have taken our innovative education and outreach projects, including the Primary Schools tour, *BabyO, SensoryO* and the heartwarming *The Elephant Angel* across Scotland and the UK (as well as visiting Hong Kong, New Zealand and Abu Dhabi); and our new commissions have received a Herald Angel Award and a South Bank Sky Arts Award, and a nomination for an Olivier Award.

None of Scottish Opera's work, however, would be possible if it wasn't for the sustained support of its key funders, and I would like to record my sincere thanks to the Scottish Government, Glasgow City Council, the dozens of charitable trusts and foundations, corporate sponsors, the Members of The Scottish Opera Syndicate, the Patrons of The Alexander Gibson Circle and The Dame Janet Baker Circle, The Friends of Scottish Opera and the Scottish Opera Endowment Trust, without which the Company would not be what it is today.

I would also like to note my gratitude to HRH The Duchess of Gloucester for her continued patronage of Scottish Opera, and to the Board of Scottish Opera, chaired by Colin McClatchie, for their collective knowledge and insight. And of course to the staff, singers and musicians of Scottish Opera, who plan, perform, play, fundraise, build, stage and market opera with total dedication, year in, year out.

But most of all, I would like to thank our audiences for continuing to attend performances of opera across the country and across the years with such enthusiasm. Without audiences, there is no opera.

As Scottish Opera's 50th Anniversary Season closes, it is right to look back on the Company's achievements. But now is also the time to look forward. In the coming months the Company will introduce its new Music Director, Emmanuel Joel-Hornak, and unveil the fantastic new public spaces at Glasgow's Theatre Royal in time for the 2014 Commonwealth Games. I hope that Scottish Opera's productions – next season and for many seasons to come – will continue to inspire and entertain you, and that you will continue to travel with Scottish Opera on our wonderful operatic adventure.

Enjoy the book!

Acknowledgements

Scottish Opera would like to thank the more than 80 contributors who gave freely of their time and memories – without you it would not have been possible to put this book together. Also, the many photographers across five decades whose work remains as a lasting record of Scottish Opera's achievements.

Richard Telfer's meticulous and comprehensive ledgers of Scottish Opera performances from 1962 until the 1980s have proved an invaluable and irreplaceable record of the Company's earlier years. Thanks to Stephen, Iain and Peter Fraser of operascotland.org, and to Lorna Murray and Paul Maloney, for helping to fill gaps in the listings for later years.

Special thanks to John Lawson Graham, whose direct association with Scottish Opera stretched across more than four decades, and, in particular, Jenny Slack (Director of Planning 1986–2010), for your encouragement and support in bringing this project to a successful conclusion.

Any errors that remain are entirely the responsibility of Scottish Opera.

Above: Claire Booth as Ellida: *The Lady from the Sea*, director Harry Fehr, 2012.

Early Days

'There was opera in Scotland before Scottish Opera': the opening line of Conrad Wilson's book on the Company's first 10 years. The point was that any opera in Scotland pre-5 June 1962 was either imported from south of the border, was staged in only Edinburgh or Glasgow by the cities' respective – and respected – Grand Opera companies or appeared en masse in August courtesy of visiting companies at the Edinburgh International Festival.

Sir Alexander Gibson and his fellow founders – Ainslie Millar, Ian Rodger, Richard Telfer – wanted to establish a professional opera company based in Scotland that would be able to draw on the talents of Scottish performers and creatives, as well as attract the highest-profile names from the rest of Britain and abroad. In their aims, they unquestionably succeeded.

With directors and designers of the calibre of Peter Ebert, Anthony Besch, John Stoddart, Peter Rice and Ralph Koltai, and singers of the stature of Dame Janet Baker, Helga Dernesch, Sir Geraint Evans, Charles Craig and David Ward – all shepherded and cajoled by General Administrator Peter Hemmings – Scottish Opera's productions through the 1960s gloriously paved the way for half a century of treasured operatic memories.

KING'S THEATRE GLASGOW

Manager : Edward Ashley

Proprietors : Howard and Wyndham Ltd.

Managing Director : Stewart Cruikshank

Week Commencing TUESDAY, 5th June, 1962

Evenings at 7 p.m.   Saturday Matinee at 2 p.m.

SCOTTISH OPERA

in association with

Scottish Television Ltd. and the Scottish Committee
of the Arts Council of Great Britain

presents

A Centenary Production of Debussy's

PELLEAS ET MELISANDE

Sung in French with

MICHELINE GRANCHER, EMILE BELCOURT, LOUIS MAURIN, JOSEPH ROULEAU

and Puccini's

MADAMA BUTTERFLY

Sung in Italian with

ELAINE MALBIN, CHARLES CRAIG, LAURA SARTI and JOHN CAMERON

Produced by DENNIS ARUNDELL
Designer : MARK KING

Artistic and Musical Director : ALEXANDER GIBSON
Associate Conductor : JAMES LOCKHART

THE SCOTTISH NATIONAL ORCHESTRA
(Leader : Sam Bor)

Pelléas et Mélisande : Wednesday (Gala Performance), Friday and Saturday (Matinee)

Madama Butterfly : Tuesday, Thursday and Saturday (Evening)

PRICES OF ADMISSION : (All seats bookable) Evenings : Boxes : 62/6, 50/-, 34/- ; Stalls : 15/- (Wed. 17/6), 12/6 ;
Back Stalls : 7/6 ; Grand Circle : 15/- (Wed. 21/-), 10/6 ; Upper Circle : 8/6 ; Balcony : 4/-
Saturday Matinee : Boxes : 45/-, 36/-, 22/- ;   Stalls : 10/6, 9/- ; Back Stalls : 5/6 ;   Grand Circle : 10/6, 9/- ;
Upper Circle : 5/6 ;   Balcony : 3/-, 2/-

The 1960s was a very important time for the cultural blossoming of Glasgow. I think we all felt that things were really moving forward, and by the end of the decade Scottish Opera was really getting into its stride. There was a sense that everyone – the opera, the ballet, the Citizens Theatre, the Scottish National Orchestra – was all marching together. It was an exciting time. I remember that back in 1962 it was considered amazingly daring to put on two operas – would it work, or would it not?

GILES HAVERGAL Director, Citizens Theatre 1969–2003

Alex was working as Music Director of Sadler's Wells Opera Company when I met him. A lot of Scottish singers in London, when they heard that Alex was going to come back to Scotland to conduct the Scottish National Orchestra, said that if he started an opera company they would all come and sing for him. That planted the seed in his head. I don't think he had thought of it before because he was too busy working with the orchestra. When the Managing Director of the SNO encouraged him to find something to fill the gap between the orchestra's main season and its summer prom concerts that was where Alex thought they might be able to do a week or so of opera.

LADY GIBSON Wife of the founder of Scottish Opera

Alex and Ainslie were greatly encouraged by some Scottish singers, like David Ward, Bill McAlpine and Harry Blackburn, who were working in London, about setting up an opera company in Scotland. A crucial point was that the Scottish National Orchestra had a gap in the summer when they had no work. Bill Fell, who was the administrator of the SNO, said to Alex, 'What are you going to do to give the players employment in this gap?' And so the possibility arose of Scottish Opera fitting into that slot.

ISABEL RODGER Wife of the late Ian Rodger

I was at George Watson's College in Edinburgh where the music master was Richard Telfer, who was a great friend and mentor of Alexander Gibson. Richard got Alexander to come to the amateur opera company in Edinburgh to conduct *Nabucco*. It was from that production that the thrust of the idea to have a professional opera company in Scotland really started.

RENTON THOMSON Company Accountant 1966–74

My first awareness of Scottish Opera was when I was at school in Watson's in Edinburgh. One of the music staff there was Richard, or Dickie, Telfer. He cut short a class one day, saying, 'I'm going to Glasgow, it's very exciting, but it's confidential.' Two weeks later, Scottish Opera was announced. Little did I think that 37 years later I would become Chairman of the Company!

DUNCAN McGHIE Chairman 1999–2004

Scottish Opera grew, partly at any rate, from the activities of the Drawing Room Music Society – if only because Ainslie Millar and Hugh Marshall were both actively involved in Drawing Room productions. One night in 1961, getting a lift home with, I think, the Millars, the possibility of something called Scottish Opera was mentioned. Some time later I had a phone call from Alexander Gibson inviting me to be Chorus Master for the opening season of *Madama Butterfly* and *Pelléas et Mélisande* in June 1962 – an offer I couldn't refuse!

IAIN CAMPBELL Chorus Master 1962, Assistant to Chorus Master Leon Lovett 1963–5

Sir Alexander Gibson (1926–95).

Ainslie Millar (1920–90).

Ian Rodger (1914–2007).

Richard Telfer (1909–96).

Sir Alexander Gibson with Professor Robin Orr (1909–2006), the first chairman of Scottish Opera.

Professor Sydney Newman, the first vice-chairman of Scottish Opera.

Peter Hemmings (1934–2002), General Administrator of Scottish Opera, 1966–77.

I was at Glasgow University in the early 1960s and during that time I was President of the Cecilian Society, which had Benjamin Britten as its Patron. It had been founded by a Glasgow lawyer called John Boyle. One evening John called at my parents' flat in Highburgh Road and told me of a plan to form something called Scottish Opera. He asked if I would be interested in using the chorus of the Cecilian Society to go around town putting up posters and handing out flyers to publicise the new company. I went along to a rehearsal of *Madama Butterfly* at St Andrew's Hall. It was almost like an out-of-body experience. As a 19-year-old I had never heard anything like it.

John came up with the idea of having some people queuing overnight for tickets for the opening shows at the King's Theatre. There were a couple of flaws in the plan. No one had really heard of Scottish Opera before so it seemed unlikely that there would be a queue. And secondly, we were all students and there was no way we could afford the 10 shillings and sixpence, or whatever it was, for the tickets! But even so, a group of us got together with a Primus stove and some tins of Cream of Asparagus soup and chatted our way through the evening. The only company we had were the local hookers! But it was a great publicity stunt, and it was picked up by all the Glasgow morning papers.

THOMSON SMILLIE Publicity Officer and Development Director 1966–78

At that time I was singing with Glasgow Grand Opera Society but I was very interested to see Scottish Opera's production of *Madama Butterfly*. Through my connections at the King's Theatre I was able to get in and see the opening night from the electrician's box. I can remember the buzz of excitement and tumultuous applause followed by the hush in the auditorium as Alexander Gibson came on and lifted the baton. It was magical!

ANNE CRUICKSHANK Chairman of The Friends of Scottish Opera Strathclyde branch 1992–2010

Pelléas et Mélisande was an unusual choice. It was the suggestion of Richard Telfer, who had been in contact with Mary Garden, the first-ever *Mélisande*, to see if she would come to the performance. We had a very good director called Dennis Arundell, who had worked a lot at Sadler's Wells in London with Alex. In the middle of the performance, when Micheline Grancher was singing her heart out, I had to leave the theatre in order to have my second son, so I didn't see the end of it!

LADY GIBSON Wife of the founder of Scottish Opera

I was privileged to be asked by Robin Orr and Alexander Gibson when I left university if I would be willing to come back to Scotland in due course to work for the opera company they intended to found. I was more than willing when the time came and started work with Scottish Opera as one member of a total administrative staff of three. One of the most memorable aspects of this period was the incredible partnership of Alexander Gibson and Peter Hemmings. After over 50 years of working in the Arts, I can honestly say I have never come across a more productive, creative and harmonious partnership. Their individual strengths were complementary and their astuteness, perspicacity and generosity of spirit made life extremely exciting and enjoyable in those early years. Add to the mix their two wonderful colleagues — Roderick Brydon and Leonard Hancock — and you have the dream team!

EVELYN BRYSON Arts Administrator

Peter Hemmings was a very experienced and able administrator. He had an amazing memory, it was like a computer. I was very fond of Robin Orr. He gave the impression of being a rather vague person who spoke like a P G Wodehouse character, but in fact he was extremely astute and a marvellous chairman of Scottish Opera.

ROBERT PONSONBY Chief Executive, Scottish National Orchestra 1964–72

When I was in the chorus at Glyndebourne in the early 1960s, one of my coaches was the Scottish conductor James Lockhart. One afternoon, out of the blue, he said to me that I was to sing for Alexander Gibson and to prepare an Italian aria and a French aria. It went well and I was engaged. It was all a bit last minute because I think Scottish Opera had booked Josephine Veasey as their main mezzo but for some reason this didn't happen. When I arrived in Glasgow from Glyndebourne, I thought the place was awful! It rained and it was cold. And yet I was absolutely delighted to be there, because I was doing my job – I was able to sing. I was doing what I had wanted to do all my life. They were the happiest years of my working life. I found that in Scotland, not only did I enjoy the actual work and the way we worked together as colleagues and gave of our best, but that there was always a group of people to be friendly and support us in what we did.

LAURA SARTI Singer

Immediately after the 1962 Season, Alex was on to Peter to see if he would be interested in helping to put together another season, and he jumped at it. But Peter had to ask his boss at Sadler's Wells, Norman Tucker, for permission. Norman was an amazing man with a lot of foresight. Of course, Norman had also worked with Alex and he was all for it. So Peter came to work at Scottish Opera for six weeks. There were no coffee shops or restaurants – only the really expensive Malmaison – so there were no places for singers to go out to. So we helped them, we took them out for lunch, we took them on trips to Loch Lomond, and made sure they weren't left alone. I think because they weren't used to that, they found a completely different set-up which they loved. And that's probably why they came back year after year.

Alex and Peter complemented each other. Peter didn't want to perform. Alex didn't really much care for the business side of things. There never seemed to be any envy or jealousy. And the lunches they had! I don't know how anyone ever did any work in the afternoons. They used to go to the Skandia, along with Thomson Smillie later. But the lunches would create the most amazing results.

JANE HEMMINGS Wife of the late Peter Hemmings

Opposite: Marie Collier as Concepcion, Peter Glossop as Ramiro: *L'heure espagnole*, director Anthony Besch, 1963.

Joseph Rouleau as Boris: *Boris Godunov*, 1968 revival of the 1965 Michael Geliot production.

Johanna Peters as the Duchess of Plaza-Toro, Ian Wallace as the Duke of Plaza-Toro: *The Gondoliers*, director Joan Cross, 1968.

Alexander Young as Tom Rakewell: *The Rake's Progress*, director David Pountney, 1971.

Gordon Sandison as Papageno: *The Magic Flute*, director David Pountney, 1974.

The Company felt very much like a small family. Everybody knew each other. Alex and V, and Peter and Jane nurtured their staff and really looked after them, which made it fun to work at Scottish Opera. Because they were so lovely you didn't mind putting in the extra hours. You very much worked until the product was good enough, rather than clock-watching. It was a very special essence of the Company.

SARAH CHESTER née Chapman-Mortimer, Stage Management 1968–73

I worked with Alex very early in my career in concert with the Scottish National Orchestra, and I got to know his family. When I came up to Glasgow Veronica would invite me to stay in the flat in their basement, which was absolutely wonderful. So I grew up in the Scottish musical scene with Alex and his family, which was really very special. That was quite unique in my experience and it helped me greatly. I welcomed that kind of family security. Veronica mothered me as much as her children, I think.

DAME JANET BAKER Mezzo-soprano

We had parties for the casts in each other's houses – ours, the Rodgers, the Hemmings, John and Denise Boyle. The morning after I would do all the washing up and then put all the plates in my car and distribute them back to their owners.

MORAG MILLAR Wife of the late Ainslie Millar

Scottish Opera had had a successful inaugural season. The Company advertised for singers to audition to make up a new amateur chorus for *Otello* in 1963. I was working in a semi-professional musical called *The Most Happy Fella* at the time. The lead in that show was an Australian baritone called Russell Cooper. He told me he had been engaged to sing in a strange Italian opera called *Volo di notte* being given by Scottish Opera. I was encouraged to audition for the chorus, which I did with my one aria, 'E lucevan le stelle', which I sang in a lower key!

We rehearsed *Otello* in a disused Boys' Brigade hall in the Stobcross area of Anderston, which was filthy with a very poor heating system. The chorus were treated as amateurs for the opera but were in fact the main soloists from all the operatic groups in the area – it became evident pretty early on that they had to be kept sweet! I helped check the register of 75 chorus members for John Boyle, the Chorus Secretary, with my choir friend Kathleen Nesbit. We got ceiling-mounted heaters installed. Ralph Koltai's set had a huge ramp, so when you were high up you were in danger of having your hair go on fire! Some of the costumes were borrowed from Covent Garden. I was Otello's standard-bearer. I wore a pair of bizarre tights, with one red leg and the other yellow. The person at Covent Garden must have been about six foot ten, because I had to double up the tights and fit them into the toe of my shoe – I was in absolute agony the whole way through that opera!

Members of the amateur chorus would sometimes be asked to cover roles. I covered Parpignol in *La bohème* and had to go on. Two days later I had a letter from Peter Hemmings saying, 'Dear Jim, Congratulations on your performance. You have made Company history as the first chorus understudy to go on. Thanks again. How about ten shillings?'

JIM McJANNET Chorus Secretary and chorus member for 42 years

My first experience of Scottish Opera was at the auditions for the chorus of *Otello*. I auditioned at the University for Alexander Gibson and Ainslie Millar. The pianist didn't turn up, so I had the great privilege of Alex playing for my audition aria. I was so nervous that when he put down the chord at the beginning, I didn't recognise it. What a great start! I got through the audition and into the chorus, and then discovered they wanted me to play the Herald in Act III. I had one line to sing, announcing the arrival of the ambassador from Venice, and had to perform with the stars Charles Craig and Peter Glossop. It was all a bit hair-raising. When the production was revived there was a newspaper advertising campaign with the line, 'Take a fresh look at *The Glasgow Herald*'. So in *Otello* I became known as 'The Glasgow Herald'!

JOHN LAWSON GRAHAM Scottish Opera 1963–2005

Opposite: Charles Craig as Otello, William McAlpine as Cassio: *Otello*, 1972 revival of the 1963 Anthony Besch production.

I went to Aberdeen to see Scottish Opera, travelling up from London, and saw *Così fan tutte* on Friday and *Götterdämmerung* on Saturday. It seemed worth the trip to see Elizabeth Harwood and Janet Baker in *Così* and Charles Craig and Helga Dernesch in *Götterdämmerung*! Dernesch was the best Brünnhilde in the world at that time and it was a major coup for Scottish Opera to get her.

SIR BRIAN McMASTER Director, Edinburgh International Festival 1991–2006

Peter van der Bilt didn't just sing. He had a riding school in Holland and was a very good horseman. From the beginning, he always stayed with me and Ainslie in Glasgow. He invited us over to Holland on holiday more than once. He was a very nice man, with a great sense of humour.

MORAG MILLAR Wife of the late Ainslie Millar

When Scottish Opera moved into Elmbank Crescent, Peter was trying to sort who would have which offices. There was nothing for Pip Flood-Murphy except for a space by the water tanks on the top floor. He thought that was fine. One day a man in uniform arrived to say that he had come from the Council to check the lead on the roof. He came back the next day with two mates. On the fourth day Pip went up onto the roof to take a look – no lead anywhere!

JANE HEMMINGS Wife of the late Peter Hemmings

I was a geography teacher in Perth, but I had always been interested in singing and done various courses. On one of these courses I came into contact with two people who were instrumental in pushing me in the direction of opera. One was Ian Wallace, and the other was Joseph Hislop, the great Scottish tenor. I was effectively Joseph's last pupil and in fact sang at his funeral. I became more involved with Tayside Opera, then in 1976 there was an advert in the paper for places in the chorus of Scottish Opera. I auditioned and became one of the basses. I was immediately thrown into the chorus for *The Confessions of a Justified Sinner* by Thomas Wilson, *The Merry Widow* and *Macbeth*.

DONALD MAXWELL Singer

Ainslie set up a Bruce Millar memorial trust for opera singers. It's still running as a singing competition at the Conservatoire. There was also a scheme for drama students and David McVicar was the first person to win that.

MORAG MILLAR Wife of the late Ainslie Millar

Opposite: Patricia Hay, Josephte Clément and Claire Livingstone as The Three Ladies: *The Magic Flute*, director Peter Ebert, 1970.

Charles Bristow was a brilliant lighting designer. His 1972 *Pelléas* was wonderfully atmospheric. He painted with lights. Initially it was thought that he wouldn't be needed for the Edinburgh Spring Season, but then it was decided he was. Someone was despatched to Aldeburgh to fetch him back to Edinburgh – the 'someone' was me, with Peter Hemmings' car. Having seen the show start in Edinburgh and had a few before departure, Charlie fell asleep. He then awoke. 'Where are we?' On learning we were still in Scotland, he said, 'Stop the car! Just time for a drink.' After a quick whisky, we drove on. Soon he asked again. 'Where are we?' Now in England, where the licensing hours were half an hour longer, there was time to down a couple more.

JOHN DUFFUS Scottish Opera administration 1971–8

I will never forget arriving in Glasgow in my old grey Sunbeam Talbot and driving, mesmerised, through streets of indescribable desolation and squalor. Glasgow then was not the café and boutique destination of today! It was a salutary place for a pip-squeak from the South to learn his trade. I remember one of my earliest tasks – appointed no doubt with a certain malicious humour – was during a break in rehearsals of *Das Rheingold*, when I was asked to accompany David Ward to 'make sure he doesn't drink too much'. So the mighty Glaswegian and the wet-behind-the-ears public schoolboy set off across the road to the Griffin pub, where Big Davie summoned his favourite barman with a voice that would have shaken the Parthenon. There was a good reason for his preference: a raddled little man appeared with a violently trembling left hand. Since the left hand held the measure and the shaking prevented it from ever filling up, each dram became a basin. At the end of three of these servings I was a goner, and Davie was in fine voice, chorusing 'Rasteten wir' as if he were on the Parkhead terraces.

DAVID POUNTNEY Director of Productions 1975–80

Opposite: Lawrence Richard as Dr Bartolo, John Robertson as Count Almaviva: *The Barber of Seville*, 1972 revival of the 1971 Ian Watt-Smith production.

Sir Alexander Gibson

Born in Motherwell, from an early age music flowed in the veins of Alexander Gibson (1926–95). By 1957 he had been appointed Music Director of Sadler's Wells Opera Company in London, but in 1959 he was invited back to Scotland as the Principal Conductor of the Scottish National Orchestra. It was a gap in the orchestra's performing schedule that presented the opportunity to stage a week-long season of opera in June 1962. The first production was Puccini's *Madama Butterfly*: it was also the final opera Alex conducted, in 1994. In between, he conducted more than 50 new productions and numerous revivals. He was knighted in 1977.

Quite simply, without Sir Alexander Gibson there would be no Scottish Opera.

Here are just a few of the many heartfelt, affectionate tributes to Alex — as a conductor, colleague and friend — about his time as Music Director of Scottish Opera. They speak for themselves.

Opposite: Sir Alexander Gibson at the piano, 1960s.

Alex had a great gift of accompanying. When you were on the stage, you could tell that his whole *raison d'être* was to encourage and nurture you, and make it possible for you. Alex always knew how far he could push you and what level of support from the orchestra you needed. That is very rare.

DAME JANET BAKER Mezzo-soprano

I had only been with the Company a few weeks but was given one line in *Macbeth*: 'Oh Macbeth, beware of Macduff!' I was at my first sitzprobe and Sir Alex was conducting. I sang my line and Alex suddenly looked up and cheerily said, 'Ah, good afternoon.' It was a tiny moment, but as an unknown newcomer it was a huge encouragement. I somehow felt that one day he might just want to hear me sing more than that one line. My highlight — *The Merry Widow*. No one has conducted it better.

DONALD MAXWELL Singer

Alexander Gibson was a remarkably special musician. The music that flowed out of him was like an umbilical cord to me. The connection between him and me was completely secure and inspiring.

KATHRYN HARRIES Soprano

He was wonderful at Puccini. Puccini was in his bones. He didn't spoon-feed you and he didn't do any unnecessary conducting. He would let people make music. But if things looked like getting rocky he would straightaway be back in charge.

CLAIRE LIVINGSTONE Singer

I always found Alex very inspiring as a conductor. People used to make jokes about his stirring-the-porridge circular conducting but I can't remember any occasion on which I had any difficulty whatsoever following him. He was very lovely to work with. Of course he was fussy and he wanted things to be right, but he made it fun as well. I can remember Alex's pale face. When he was in the pit there was only the light from the music stand hitting his face and everything else was pretty well dark. He was with you all the way.

ANN BAIRD Singer, and Manager Opera for Youth and Opera Go Round

Alex was an inspiring figure, still a bit underrated as a conductor. He was great at doing big projects. The *Ring* cycle and *The Trojans* stand out particularly. He had the gift which is very important in conductors of keeping control of the performance but seeming to give to the principals the opportunity to do their own thing. That's rare. Alex was a marvellous natural musician. I never heard him do anything ugly or unnatural. There was very little that Alex couldn't do well.

ROBERT PONSONBY Chief Executive, Scottish National Orchestra 1964–72

He was very helpful and sympathetic — a tower of strength. He had an enormous reputation in Scotland. It was great to have his support, particularly when I had to deal with politicians and business leaders, with some of whom he was on first-name terms.

JOHN COX General Administrator and Artistic Director 1981–6

Opposite: Sir Alexander Gibson on stage with the cast of *Die Meistersinger von Nürnberg*, including Norman Bailey as Hans Sachs, Patricia Wells as Eva and Alberto Remedios as Walther, 1983.

Initially I was in awe of Alexander Gibson. Everyone regarded him as an extraordinary individual who through the force of his quiet personality had drawn a lot of people together to create the opera company and to develop the Scottish National Orchestra. He asked me if I would catalogue the huge library of his recordings. It was a wonderful exercise in stylistic analysis for me. I would go round to his house in Cleveden Gardens, even if he wasn't there, and get on with the work in the study. He would even leave me his car when he was conducting overseas. We became great friends and I admired Alex more than I can possibly say.

JOHN DUFFUS Scottish Opera administration 1971–8

A great musician and a wonderful human being. He had opera in his soul. He was always very supportive and generous. I was very privileged to work with him.

GRAHAM VICK Director of Productions 1984–7

I was the Sandman in *Hansel and Gretel*. The Sandman sings approximately two pages. Alexander Gibson was conducting. At the dress rehearsal I went on and sang the first bar. Alex stopped me and sent me off. He did this three times. I had no idea what I'd done wrong so afterwards I went to apologise to him. Alex said, 'No, it's OK. It's a public rehearsal and the audience expect something to go wrong, and I knew you'd understand!

LINDA ORMISTON Singer

He was fun, was Alex, and fun was part of what went on. We were rehearsing *Così fan tutte* in Perth and I was in the chorus. Anthony Besch had decided that we should march on graded by size – Richard Angus, who was very tall, John Lawson Graham, myself and three others – and then turn to the front. Alex waited until the first performance, and then when we came on he looked at us somewhat puzzled and leaned to one side to conduct us! That sort of summed him up. He was a very fine orchestral accompanist. He was great at letting the singers get on with it, which is why so many singers enjoyed singing with him. They got to do what they knew was right, rather than having it imposed on them.

JOHN ROBERTSON Singer

He changed the face of music in Scotland completely. He nurtured and encouraged Scottish composers, singers and instrumentalists. He was always there to give support. His legacy is all around us!

JOHN LAWSON GRAHAM Scottish Opera 1963–2005

Opposite: Sir Alexander Gibson introducing HRH The Duke of Edinburgh to the cast of *The Merry Widow* at the King's Theatre, Glasgow on 7 May 1974.

Sir Alexander Gibson

Giacomo Puccini
Madama Butterfly

Puccini's *Madama Butterfly* has been central to the history of Scottish Opera. Of course, it was the first opera produced by the Company in 1962, directed by Dennis Arundell and starring the glamorous American Elaine Malbin as Cio-Cio-San. But by 1965 Scottish Opera had a new production, this time directed by Peter Ebert, with the delightful Felicia Weathers opposite the great Charles Craig, who had also appeared as Pinkerton in the first production.

A new staging by Spanish actress and director Nuria Espert opened to great acclaim in 1987 to mark the Company's 25th Anniversary. Scottish Opera's present production, by Sir David McVicar, premiered in 2000 and to date has had two revivals.

Madama Butterfly has been conducted by all four Scottish Opera Music Directors – Sir Alexander Gibson, John Mauceri, Sir Richard Armstrong and Francesco Corti – and will be conducted by incoming Music Director Emmanuel Joel-Hornak in 2014.

Opposite: Felicia Weathers as Cio-Cio-San: *Madama Butterfly*, director Peter Ebert, 1965.

The one thing that still sticks in my mind after all these years is my first rehearsal for *Madama Butterfly*. Butterfly was played by the American Elaine Malbin, who was a TV star. She looked round and thought, 'What hellhole have I come to? And who are these people?' Charles Craig was among them. He was elderly, bald, rather small, wearing a coat, with a little diamond in his ring. I remember that he opened his mouth to sing and my knees buckled, I swear to you, at the incredible sound of that voice. When she realised that she was suddenly faced with people who could sing, Elaine Malbin got really frightened. She didn't have a big voice, and she wanted to sing to the front. I rehearsed my Suzuki parts a bit upstage from her. She wanted me downstage so that she could sing at me. So she gave me a shove and I ended up sprawling on the floor in front of Alexander Gibson!

I enjoyed very much working with Felicia Weathers. By Act III she would say to me, panting, 'Oh Laura, I don't think I can get through this.' I would say, 'Come on, pull yourself together!' I don't think anyone realises the huge amount of physical and nervous energy singers put into their performances.

LAURA SARTI Singer

The first sitzprobe for *Butterfly* was held in the old St Andrew's Hall, which sounded even better without an audience than it did when full. To hear Charles Craig and Laura Sarti – among others – with the Scottish National Orchestra in that wonderful space was just heaven! Alex Gibson was the perfect conductor for this music, getting a rich and luxurious sound from the orchestra, whose strings never played better for him than on that occasion. I remember the auditions for the part of Cio-Cio-San's child. Several children were tried but, when faced with Elaine Malbin in full voice, disqualified themselves by bursting into tears!

IAIN CAMPBELL Chorus Master 1962, Assistant to Chorus Master Leon Lovett 1963–5

I've sung about 35 roles with Scottish Opera, and I've sung Suzuki with lots of Butterflies. You would get everybody from the very discreet Butterfly-like character to the full-blown Italian soprano who thought that for every top note you had to run to the front of the stage, throw up your arms and bellow out! I quite like the tea-and-sympathy roles where you have to listen all the time and you're interacting. It's much more interesting than singing an aria yourself.

CLAIRE LIVINGSTONE Singer

Lindsay Marshall as Trouble, Elaine Malbin as Cio-Cio-San: *Madama Butterfly*, director Dennis Arundell, 1962.

Felicia Weathers as Cio-Cio-San, Alasdair McLean (now one of Scottish Opera's piano tuners) as Trouble: *Madama Butterfly*, 1968 revival of the 1965 Peter Ebert production.

David Hillman (back to camera) as Lieutenant Pinkerton, Maria Pellegrini as Cio-Cio-San: *Madama Butterfly*, 1976 revival of the 1965 Peter Ebert production.

The Company needed to think a little outside the box in terms of who was going to direct productions. We were in danger of continuing to work with the same people. We all knew of Nuria Espert as an actress but I don't think she had ever done any opera. She had worked as a director, though, and made films. We just approached her. She was one of the most charming people I think I shall ever know. She brought Ezio Frigerio, a very distinguished Italian designer, and his partner Franca Squarciapino, and they came up with the most beautiful idea. Finding Nuria was a treat, because we were working with an actress who really understood how to act on stage. She had an immense emotional feel for the work and the main character. We did very well with it because I rented it twice to Covent Garden and made more in fees than it cost to put on originally!

RICHARD MANTLE Managing Director 1985–91

The 25th Anniversary production was directed by Nuria Espert, and I think she produced the best *Madama Butterfly* I have ever seen. She staged it as if it was in a modern block of flats in Japan. Cio-Cio-San came on in her jeans and then she was dressed by her sisters and friends in traditional wedding robes. Then they took her to a cherry blossom tree in front of the block and shook the petals all over her and she was transformed into Butterfly. I'll never forget that. It was one of my most special moments in the theatre.

LADY GIBSON Wife of the founder of Scottish Opera

Opposite: Anne-Marie Owens as Suzuki, Seppo Ruohonen as Lieutenant Pinkerton, Jonathan Hawkins as Imperial Commissioner, Neil Jenkins as Goro, Yoko Watanabe as Cio-Cio-San: *Madama Butterfly*, director Nuria Espert, 1987.

I remember seeing the Nuria Espert production of *Madama Butterfly* for the Company's 25th anniversary. I was very impressed by it and when I was asked to do a new production I said, 'Well that's a hard act to follow.' But we did something completely different and that was very special because the cast were absolutely wonderful. Natalia Dercho didn't speak very much English and my German wasn't good enough to direct her, so we did it with sign language. We had the most wonderful symbiotic relationship. It was like doing a silent movie, and it worked. When the Japanese theme crashes in at the end it needs some kind of visual counterpart. When Butterfly dies with honour as a woman of her culture, the American flag drops to reveal a golden Japanese screen – it's an apotheosis. I didn't want her death to be 'opera Butterfly', I wanted it to be somehow magnificent. The boys who played Trouble were magical – it was so much fun directing them. They called Jane Irwin 'Auntie Jane' and they called Natalia 'Mummy' and we would give them challenges, such as to draw what they had done that day, because that was a way of getting them to remember stuff. During one run-through of Act II, we had done the waiting scene and the Humming Chorus, and as Butterfly had left the stage we discovered that the little boy had really gone to sleep! That was a special moment.

SIR DAVID McVICAR Director

I got a call from my agent in February 2007 asking if I was free to conduct *Madama Butterfly*. I said, 'Yes.' When I arrived in Glasgow I was impressed by the very friendly people, and this is a fundamental aspect of me working with Scottish Opera. I like Scotland. It's important that if you are away from home, you feel to be in a friendly environment. My first rehearsal with the Orchestra was at the Couper Institute in Clarkston Road. I took the 44A bus! I knew nobody and nobody knew me. After a few bars of *Madama Butterfly*, I realised that the chemistry with the Orchestra was working.

FRANCESCO CORTI Music Director 2008–13

Everybody was enthralled that we had an Italian maestro in front of us who had the verve, conviction, understanding and spirit to bring to life a score [*Madama Butterfly*] that we had known for many years in a different and vital way. Shortly after that first rehearsal the Orchestra had a meeting and felt that they had something in common with Francesco which could be developed and that Francesco would be an ideal candidate for Music Director.

JAY ALLEN Orchestra & Concerts Director

I first worked with Francesco Corti when he came as a guest to conduct *Madama Butterfly*. Acting as someone's assistant is always most enjoyable when there is a sense of true collaboration involved, and I was delighted to find that this was invariably the case with Francesco at the helm, as it had been with Richard Armstrong before him.

DEREK CLARK Head of Music

Opposite: Natalia Dercho as Cio-Cio-San, Jane Irwin as Suzuki, Sam Aschavir as Trouble: *Madama Butterfly*, director Sir David McVicar, 2000.

Wolfgang Amadeus Mozart
Così fan tutte

When asked to name a standout Scottish Opera production, those with longer memories invariably pick Mozart's *Così fan tutte* — otherwise known as 'the black-and-white *Così*'.

Premiered on 12 April 1967 in the intimate surroundings of Perth Theatre, it was directed by Anthony Besch, designed by John Stoddart and conducted by Sir Alexander Gibson. Starting out in a black-and-white world, colour only began to appear in the staging when Guglielmo and Ferrando returned in disguise to woo the other's lover. The effect was startling and original. However, it was the casting, particularly that of Dame Janet Baker as Dorabella and Elizabeth Harwood as Fiordiligi, which turned a fine production into a great production.

But *Così*'s run throughout Scottish Opera's history. Following a number of revivals of the Besch production, there were new stagings by Richard Jones, Jürgen Gosch, Stewart Laing and David McVicar, all bringing their own individual directorial views to bear on this most enigmatic of operas.

Opposite: Alexander Young as Ferrando, Dame Janet Baker as Dorabella, Elizabeth Harwood as Fiordiligi, Peter van der Bilt as Guglielmo: *Così fan tutte*, 1975 revival of the 1967 Anthony Besch production.

Così fan tutte with Janet Baker as Dorabella and Elizabeth Harwood as Fiordiligi was enchanting. I remember Janet's mischievous sense of humour in one performance, confusing Alex by switching beds with Elizabeth in the first Act so that he nearly missed their cues. Janet played a key part in the success of Scottish Opera. To this day people rightly think of Janet as our greatest star and those who saw her many wonderful performances will never forget them.

LADY GIBSON Wife of the founder of Scottish Opera

I trained as an architect in Australia and came to the UK in 1960. After about five years, I met Peter Rice and assisted him on a couple of Opera for All productions. I'd worked with Anthony Besch on a tiny production of *The Mikado*, designing the sets, and he asked me to design *Così fan tutte*. I knew nothing about the opera – I'd never heard it. Anthony had also worked with me on a small animated film which we made at my kitchen table in Notting Hill Gate in 1964 or '65, using animated photographs against an engraved background, all in black and white. There was one colour sequence in which a woman looks out of a window and sees a peacock, and the peacock is in colour. When I came to design *Così fan tutte*, I wanted to use architectural features from a book of engravings. I had the idea that everything would be in black and white, but as the boys came back in disguise, they would be in colour, and the girls would gradually change into colour too, as they each fell in love with the 'wrong' boy. But at the end, everyone is in black and white again. We thought it was a cute idea! The costumes were made in London. I met Jane Bond, who was the costume buyer at that time. I was very particular about the fabrics, because as I didn't know much I thought everything had to be how I had drawn it – I wasn't about to compromise! I met Janet and Elizabeth, who were wonderful. They were very similar in outlook and used to giggle together like sisters, which is why there was such a tremendous spark in the production.

JOHN STODDART Designer

I first heard Scottish Opera on the radio – I think it was Geraint Evans in *Falstaff*. I had done a lot of work with Alexander Gibson and the Scottish National Orchestra in concert. I was in London and as the music came over the airwaves I felt that there was something quite special going on in Glasgow. I don't know why it was obvious over the airwaves, but it was! I thought that I would like to be involved in it – it sounded magical. And shortly after I was invited up and my first role was Dorabella in *Così fan tutte*. I was thrilled that I was in on the ground floor, because it was such an exciting venture. I knew Anthony Besch from Glyndebourne. I think he got a bit of resistance when he first suggested me, because opera wasn't something that I was immediately connected with. I was a straight classical singer and they wondered if I was capable of humour. Anthony said, 'Yes, she'll be fine. You wait and see.' And of course it was a marvellous production. It set a sort of benchmark for *Così*, it was so simple and brilliant – the idea of it going from black and white to vibrant colour.

DAME JANET BAKER Mezzo-soprano

Opposite: Alexander Young as Ferrando, Thomas Hemsley as Don Alfonso, Peter van der Bilt as Guglielmo: *Così fan tutte*, 1975 revival of the 1967 Anthony Besch production.

I was fortunate to be cast as Despina in the 1967 production of *Così fan tutte*, but I almost missed the first night. We were rehearsing in Glasgow, before the show opened the following week in Perth. I was alone on set when I realised that one of the flats was about to fall on me. The stage manager, Pip Flood-Murphy, hurried towards the flat with the intention of holding it up. I ran away from the flat to get out of the way. We crashed into each other centre stage. Pip was knocked out completely. I was close to it. Fortunately the flat had missed us both. I distinctly remember lying on the stage with the cast around me, and Janet Baker saying, 'Look at that bump on Jenny's forehead.' Both Pip and I ended up in the emergency department of the local hospital, and were discharged when it became apparent neither of us had concussion. However, over the next few days the right-hand side of my face turned black and blue and became very swollen. Jane and Peter Hemmings wouldn't hear of me recuperating in my hotel and insisted I stay with them — so began a long and much-valued friendship. It was only with a great deal of help from the make-up department that I managed to perform on the first night. And I still have the bump as proof!

JENIFER EDDY Singer

I started as one of the sopranos in the professional Scottish Opera chorus in 1967 at the Edinburgh Festival, then moved immediately into Opera for All. My first main role with the Company was Cherubino in *The Marriage of Figaro*, but I do remember sitting in the King's Theatre as a student watching *Così fan tutte*. It was the first opera I had attended. Afterwards I said that if I got into the profession one of the things I would like to do was to feature in that production — and that came true. In the revival I got the chance to play Despina with Janet Baker and Elizabeth Harwood, which was the most exciting experience of my life up to that point.

PATRICIA HAY Lyric Soprano

Opposite: Alexander Young as Ferrando, Elizabeth Harwood as Fiordiligi, Dame Janet Baker as Dorabella, Peter van der Bilt as Guglielmo: *Così fan tutte*, 1975 revival of the 1967 Anthony Besch production.

My mother took me to the theatre in Perth. She said, 'We'll go to the opera, it's Mozart.' We were right up in the gods. It was *Così fan tutte*. Of course, I didn't know when I was there that this was one of the all-time great productions. Elizabeth Harwood as Fiordiligi, Janet Baker as Dorabella, Peter van der Bilt as Guglielmo, Ryland Davies as Ferrando, Inia Te Wiata as Don Alfonso. I was perhaps 18 at the time and was exposed to excellence in every way — visually, vocally, dramatically — and was immediately hooked. That's the great thing about Scottish Opera, because by putting on productions of this quality over 50 years it has stimulated people intellectually and emotionally.

DONALD MAXWELL Singer

At its best, opera is magic. At its worst, it's boredom. In 1967, in my home town of Perth, in the lovely little theatre there, the Alexander Gibson/Anthony Besch/John Stoddart team premiered their fantastic *Così fan tutte* with Janet Baker and Elizabeth Harwood as the two leading ladies. With this production Scottish Opera gained international acclaim and I fell in love with magic.

THE HON JAMES BRUCE CBE (1927–2013)
Scottish Opera Board member and Chairman of the Scottish Opera Endowment Trust

Andrew Shore as Don Alfonso, Maldwyn Davies as Ferrando, Elizabeth Gale as Despina, Stephen Page as Guglielmo, Marie Slorach as Fiordiligi, Clare Shearer as Dorabella: *Così fan tutte*, director Richard Jones, 1988.

Terence Sharpe as Don Alfonso, Thomas Randle as Ferrando, Simon Keenlyside as Guglielmo, Jane Eaglen as Fiordiligi: *Così fan tutte*, director Jürgen Gosch, 1990.

Peter Savidge as Don Alfonso, Morten Ernst Lassen as Guglielmo, Katija Dragojevic as Dorabella, Olivia Keen as Fiordiligi, Jeremy Ovenden as Ferrando, Rebecca Cain as Despina: *Così fan tutte*, director Stewart Laing, 2001.

I think *Così fan tutte* is actually my favourite opera. I saw the famous Anthony Besch production in its last outing, with Margaret Marshall and Ann Murray as a very classy pair of sisters. That was followed by the Richard Jones version with the ever-growing volcano and bunny rabbits, which was comic bliss! *Così* is one of the hardest pieces in the repertory to get right and I am continually amazed that managements so often ask debutant directors to take it on. It needs real experience and in-depth knowledge. It also needs a strong cast, which we had. It included a star turn as Despina from Marie McLaughlin, in what was, amazingly, only her second-ever appearance with her home company! Tobias Ringborg was a stylish and refreshing conductor. Raising the pit to nearly house level in the Theatre Royal was a revelation; the orchestra could actually hear and see the singers and the notoriously tricky balance problems of the house were swept away. *Così* is one of the saddest comedies ever written. Da Ponte's 'School for Lovers' is the school of life with all the cruel and painful lessons that implies. A good friend, who is an actor, came to see it and by the end said that he felt sick. I said, 'Good! I want you to!'

SIR DAVID McVICAR Director

The *Così fan tutte* with conductor Tobias Ringborg was fantastic. I've been playing *Così* since 1974 and it felt like he showed me something new when I thought I knew everything about it.

ALAN WARHURST Sub-principal Bassoon, The Orchestra of Scottish Opera

Opposite: Caitlin Hulcup as Dorabella and Ville Rusanen as Guglielmo: *Così fan tutte*, director Sir David McVicar, 2009.

Wolfgang Amadeus Mozart
Don Giovanni

Don Giovanni wasn't the first Mozart opera to be staged by Scottish Opera — that accolade belongs to *Die Entführung aus dem Serail* in 1963. But the Don wasn't far behind, making his first appearance in Peter Ebert's long-lived production the following year — and he has been with Scottish Opera in various guises ever since.

Following David Pountney's late-1970s production, Scottish Opera encountered perhaps its most vociferous critical backlash on 17 April 1985 when Graham Vick presented his radical reimagining of the opera. It certainly had its admirers, but it was a step too far, too fast for some. Such was the uproar that the production lasted a mere seven performances. Yet by concentrating on the production, many forget that the cast included, among others, Sir Willard White, Sergei Leiferkus and Karita Mattila, all on their way to operatic greatness.

Since the 1980s various new productions have come and gone, including a notable John Cox staging designed by the Scottish artist Peter Howson and introducing Peter Mattei to Scottish audiences, and another by Tim Albery. As Sir Thomas Allen and Simon Higlett prepare a new production for Autumn 2013, it seems the Don is never too far away.

Opposite: Henriikka Gröndahl as Donna Elvira, James Rutherford as Leporello: *Don Giovanni*, director Tim Albery, 2006.

Margaret Price as Zerlina, Michael Maurel as Masetto: *Don Giovanni*, director Peter Ebert, 1965.

Norman White as the Commendatore, John Lawson Graham as Don Giovanni: *Don Giovanni*, Opera for All, director Peter Ebert, 1967.

Stafford Dean as Leporello: *Don Giovanni*, 1970 revival of the 1965 Peter Ebert production.

Robert Tear as Don Ottavio: *Don Giovanni*, 1976 revival of the 1965 Peter Ebert production.

I remember working alongside other designers, such as Ralph Koltai. It was customary for the built sets to arrive on lorries late on Saturday night. However, in the case of *Don Giovanni*, there was no lorry – only Ralph and his assistant and large blocks of Polystyrene loaded onto his Landrover. With blow-torch in hand, he set to work on carving the blocks into a huge sculpture that was to be the centrepiece of the set. By the morning the setting was ready, to the delight of the director, Peter Ebert, and later the critics.

PETER RICE Designer

Don Giovanni, Sadler's Wells' opening production at the Coliseum in 1968, had proved critically and artistically unsuccessful. So it was a pleasant surprise when my manager phoned to say that Peter Hemmings had invited me to play Leporello in Scottish Opera's revival the following season. I arrived in Glasgow to find a strong cast had been assembled. The Don was Peter van der Bilt, tall and elegant with a dark baritone – he was ideal casting. Ludmilla Andrew was thrilling as Donna Anna, and as Donna Elvira, Luisa Bosabalian's warm lyric soprano portrayed fully one of Mozart's greatest female creations. Werner Krenn, who had just recorded his role with Sutherland and Bonynge, was Don Ottavio and brought a purity of tone to his great arias. Joseph Rouleau was a chilling Commendatore, and two young company members, Patricia Hay and John Graham, were well cast and excellent as Zerlina and Masetto. The death of Don Giovanni was as effective as any of the 30 or so productions of the opera in which I would later appear.

STAFFORD DEAN Bass

The first Scottish Opera production I saw was a matinee performance of *Don Giovanni* in 1979, directed by David Pountney. I don't know how I knew it was on but I do remember having to shout and scream until my mother finally bought tickets for the second circle. It was an amazing level of casting. It had Alexander Gibson in the pit, Robert Lloyd, Willard White, Felicity Palmer, Norma Sharp, Robin Leggate, Donald Maxwell – people who have become friends and colleagues. David later told me that he didn't like it very much, but I was completely bowled over by it. My mother got a taste for opera following that and took out a subscription.

SIR DAVID McVICAR Director

When I became Director of Productions the first show I was asked to do was *Don Giovanni*. It was supposed to be a revival but it couldn't be a revival, and there was only enough money available for a revival of an original production. This meant I had a rock-bottom amount of money to do a new production, but I found that very liberating. *Don Giovanni* is a great revolutionary, provocative piece and I wanted to set my own stall out. I wanted to attract a new, younger audience to opera. I wanted to follow the tradition in Glasgow of bold, innovative theatre companies like the Citizens and the Tron. I directed a *Don Giovanni* that was very exciting – thrilling for some people and horrifying for others. It divided the audience absolutely in two. I had no idea it would be as controversial as it was! One of the things that made the show so vivid and powerful was the quality of the cast. Sergei Leiferkus completely loved the show. He was brilliant, and was willing to go all the way. Karita Mattila was 23 years old. I could go anywhere with them, and did.

GRAHAM VICK Director of Productions 1984–7

Graham did some very fine productions. At that time he was a key member of the younger directorial talent. He was in demand and it was good that he gave his time to Scottish Opera. But I was absolutely shocked by his *Don Giovanni* – make no mistake! It was very powerful indeed. It did not espouse nobility. Graham was much more interested in the sleazy morality of the Don. Sergei Leiferkus was Don Giovanni. I was very pleased with that bit of casting because he went global after he had been with us. There was a public outcry, and the traditionalists were aghast. But some audience members really took to it, to the extent that the Friends had T-shirts made that said in bold letters across the front, 'I enjoyed Don Giovanni.'

JOHN COX General Administrator and Artistic Director 1981–6

My baptism of fire was inheriting a plan for Graham Vick to direct a new production of *Don Giovanni*. It was fantastic – a distinguished director and a cast that would be beyond many opera companies today. All the names are or have been at the top of the profession: Sergei Leiferkus, Willard White, Karita Mattila making her UK debut, Katherine Ciesinski. But it became a notorious production over one scene. *Don Giovanni* beat up Masetto and forced his head down a toilet. It was an uncomfortable moment – indeed, it's an uncomfortable moment in the opera. I remember saying to Graham that I thought it was unnecessary. But I'm not there to direct shows. I've never witnessed anything like the outcry that it caused!

RICHARD MANTLE Managing Director 1985–91

I saw Graham Vick's toilet. Everyone saw Graham's toilet! It was a brave, often wild, extremely fine production with a superb cast.

CHRISTOPHER BARRON Chief Executive 2000–5

Opposite: Karita Mattila as Donna Elvira, Sir Willard White as Leporello: *Don Giovanni*, director Graham Vick, 1985.

Peter Mattei as Don Giovanni, Yanni Yannissis as Leporello: *Don Giovanni*, director John Cox, 1995.

Alessandro Guerzoni as the Commendatore, Morten Ernst Lassen as Don Giovanni: *Don Giovanni*, 2001 revival of the 1995 John Cox production.

I admired the darkness of Peter Howson's work and that darkness was what I wanted for my production of *Don Giovanni*. Peter had been to Bosnia as a war artist and that had coloured his work amazingly strongly. You sensed in our production that the forces of darkness were all around. Peter was very interested in the implication of sin in the Don and the idea of retribution, and I think he stayed with that idea in a lot of his later work. Peter Mattei was extraordinary, and a new star. He was one of those maverick artists. And I began to understand what Donna Elvira was about by working with Joan Rodgers. Elvira is key to the piece because her love is true, and sensual, and unwavering, and Joan was always such a truthful performer, never demonstrative. She was a rewarding and revealing artist to work with. And Lisa Milne was perfect as Zerlina.

JOHN COX General Administrator and Artistic Director 1981–6

I had been to an auditioning event in Oslo. On the Saturday evening there was a gala concert. Peter Mattei sang. I was looking for a Don Giovanni at the time. On the Sunday I rang Richard Armstrong and said, 'You've got to trust me, I've found the Don.' Fortunately it worked out alright!

JENNY SLACK Director of Planning 1986–2010

When I was a freelance production manager with the Company, I recall being with Peter Howson in his studio when he took a phone call from an art dealer in the US who offered him over £150,000 for his draft model box of 1:25 scale paintings for the back cloths and other scenic items in *Don Giovanni*. I was aghast for two reasons: firstly, the discards had been piled up under the table on which the model box sat, and secondly, the same £150,000 worth of model box had poked out of the boot of my beige Ford Escort as I trundled around London seeing scenery builders looking for quotes to build the set!

ALEX REEDIJK General Director 2006–

I worked on the final revival of the Peter Howson-designed *Don Giovanni*. He came to many of the rehearsals and sat at the back, sketching away. He designed luggage labels for Don Giovanni's cases, one of which had Saltcoats written on it!

DEREK CLARK Head of Music

Richard Wagner

Love him or loathe him, there is no getting away from Richard Wagner. Scottish Opera has had an often exhilarating, occasionally tempestuous, relationship with the operas of the revolutionary composer. The Company first presented Wagner's work as early as 1966, with a production of *Die Walküre* that toured from Glasgow to Edinburgh and Aberdeen. It was the start of an operatic journey that led to a staging of the full *Ring* cycle, with a stellar cast including David Ward as Wotan, at Glasgow's King's Theatre in December 1971.

A Richard Jones-directed *Ring* was curtailed after *Die Walküre* in the early 1990s. However, a partnership between Scottish Opera and the Edinburgh International Festival resulted in one of the most talked-about and acclaimed *Ring* cycles of recent years, as director Tim Albery, designers Hildegard Bechtler and Ana Jebens, and conductor Sir Richard Armstrong built from *Das Rheingold* in 2000 towards five award-winning cycles in Edinburgh, Glasgow and Manchester in 2003.

Scottish Opera audiences have also been thrilled by, among others, David Pountney's beautiful production of *Die Meistersinger von Nürnberg*, *Tristan und Isolde* directed and designed by Yannis Kokkos with Jeffrey Lawton and Dame Anne Evans, which opened the Festival Theatre in Edinburgh and toured to Portugal, and 2013's *The Flying Dutchman*, which relocated the action to the composer's original Scottish setting.

Opposite: Leah-Marian Jones as Flosshilde, Marianne Andersen as Wellgunde, Inka Rinn as Woglinde: *Das Rheingold*, director Tim Albery, 2000.

Der Ring des Nibelungen 2003

When I was initially approached in the early 1990s to see if I would be interested in being Music Director at Scottish Opera, the invitation included continuing the *Ring* cycle directed by Richard Jones, of which *Das Rheingold* and *Die Walküre* had been staged. I took on the role of Music Director but I was concerned that the *Ring* cycle was getting so strung out – there had already been three years between the first two instalments. With *Siegfried* and *Götterdämmerung* still to be staged, it meant that there would be seven years from first to last production. My advice was to stop and instead go about developing a strong base in other areas of the repertoire. Then at a later date that was considered appropriate, we would approach the *Ring* again but I would be involved in all aspects of planning from Day 1.

Tim Albery and Hildegard Bechtler were very aware that I had a background in Wagner and that I perhaps had things to offer. No way was I going to tell them how to do things but I was very interested in what was going on and to give advice. I thought it was very generous of them when they invited me into their creative conversations much earlier than would normally be the case. That was a very interesting and satisfying way of working, and very special. It was a happy and constructive collaboration.

Almost everybody was singing their role for the first time. A handful of players in the orchestra had previously played *Das Rheingold* and *Die Walküre*, but I think no one had played *Siegfried* or *Götterdämmerung* before. So the task of teaching and getting inside this music, honing a view of the style of playing, was enormous. It was a colossal undertaking.

The *Ring* cycle of 2003 illustrated the ensemble approach of Scottish Opera. The values of well-chosen performers, really well groomed and not vying for individual stardom, and keeping them throughout the cycle, were crucial to its success. When the orchestra played *Götterdämmerung* for the first time then went back to *Das Rheingold* they could bring a huge amount more experience to it, like re-reading a book. One of the most significant things about the *Ring* cycle in Scotland was the quality of the playing, which was as good as any orchestra anywhere.

SIR RICHARD ARMSTRONG Music Director 1993–2005

Opposite: Peter Sidhom as Alberich: *Das Rheingold*, director Tim Albery, 2000.

I was asked to direct the *Ring* cycle only a year before *Das Rheingold* was due to open. But of course I had to conceive what form all four operas would take, so there was very little time and I didn't know the piece very well. It became apparent very early on in discussions with Hildegard Bechtler that we were going to set it in the present. There would be some elements of intense realism and others would be quite abstract. So, for instance, there would be a scene with a curved wall, a small mountain and a fridge. Which is where the idea for the Valkyries in their biker gear at a roadside bar came from. Also in *Die Walküre* we had a motorway with broken pillars, but underneath was a completely real hotel room. We played the game of very real and very abstract quite a lot. To express the mythological you have to have banal little details. You can gradually piece together a universe. There are some productions that I can barely remember, but I can pretty much still see the *Ring* moment by moment.

Matthew Best worked and worked and worked as Wotan. It's incredibly hard to sing and physically demanding. It was a very long journey for him, but over the four years it developed into a really accomplished performance. Elizabeth Byrne was incredibly committed and emotionally very honest.

If you can put together a *Ring* cycle that works I can't imagine a more exhilarating way of spending five years of your life. Wagner, in many ways such a hateful man, had such an understanding of human nature, and I wanted to lock into the humanity of the characters rather than treat them as ciphers or representations of mythical ideas. I wanted the relationships to feel real.

TIM ALBERY Director

Elizabeth Byrne as Brünnhilde, Matthew Best as Wotan: *Die Walküre*, director Tim Albery, 2001.

The Valkyries: *Die Walküre*, director Tim Albery, 2001.

Ursula Füri-Bernhard as Sieglinde, Jan Kyhle as Siegmund, Carsten Stabell as Hunding: *Die Walküre*, director Tim Albery, 2001.

Gillian Keith as The Woodbird, Graham Sanders as Siegfried: *Siegfried*, director Tim Albery, 2002.

To start and finish the *Ring* cycle with the same singers, creative team and musicians is a rare achievement – just keeping the diaries going! It meant there was a strong team who knew each other very well. Having Matthew Best there as Wotan was the most important piece of casting and he was just fantastic. He had a thrilling sound, which might not have been expected from a young-ish man from a very different background to some of the more historic German voices.

CHRISTOPHER BARRON Chief Executive 2000–5

I'd just done my first Brünnhilde with an American regional opera company. Out of the blue I got a call from Scottish Opera asking me to go over. But I wasn't quite sure why I was there. I had music rehearsals with Richard Armstrong, who was very complimentary. We were getting quite close to stage and piano rehearsals but I was still a bit perplexed. In the end I forced the issue, and it worked out really well for me. It was a success and I was asked back to do the rest of the *Ring* cycle. I liked working with Tim Albery – we had a great time. He speaks really good German and he understands every word of the text. That was a real A+ in my book because I could discuss something with him if I didn't agree with it or try something in a different way. He was very open to spontaneous ideas.

ELIZABETH BYRNE Dramatic Soprano

The *Ring* cyclewas a wonderful 'once (or maybe twice if you're lucky) in a lifetime' opportunity for me as a Leader. I have been asked on several occasions if it was physically demanding to play the cycle. Surprisingly, it wasn't tiring. I am convinced that Wagner was aware at what point we violinists would need a rest and obliges by giving us a few minutes' break in the music to recover!

ANTHONY MOFFAT Leader, The Orchestra of Scottish Opera

People think that Wagner is loud, but in his orchestration absolutely every single note matters and it needs to be absolutely perfect. Not just the note or the intonation but the way you play it. It's a great challenge. To do the *Ring* cycle in a week, which we did at the Edinburgh Festival, is a particular challenge. There are tens of thousands of articles written about Wagner but nowhere, it seems to me, has there been anything written about the importance of a fish supper before performing his music – it's absolutely vital!

ALAN WARHURST Sub-principal Bassoon, The Orchestra of Scottish Opera

Opposite: Elizabeth Byrne as Brünnhilde: *Götterdämmerung,* director Tim Albery, 2003.

After I retired from singing in 2002 Richard Armstrong and Jenny Slack asked me if I would coach some of the younger singers in Scottish Opera's new *Ring*, particularly the Rhinemaidens, Valkyries and Norns. It proved to be a very enjoyable and productive time, because in the course of my career I had sung no fewer than eleven roles in the *Ring* and I was able to pass on to the young what I had learned from experience: how to deal with the particularly tricky corners; the importance of clear enunciation of the text and the colouring of the voice; how to sustain a legato line; and, perhaps most crucial of all, the need to pay attention to the dynamics demanded by the composer. A lot of singers who have never sung Wagner before think you have to sing his music as loudly as possible all the time, but if you do that you won't have the stamina to get to the end of the opera – and the audience will feel as though it has been hit over the head with a sledgehammer.

DAME ANNE EVANS Soprano

The sets looked relatively simple but they weren't. The main elements were two curved walls. To move the walls required two men physically getting inside them and driving the hydraulic motors. A third man oversaw all the hydraulic and electric cables for it, and a fourth choreographed all the moves. Each section of wall had two and a half tons of counterweight on it to stop it tippling over. The people in the wall sections would be inside them for up to an hour and a half – they just had to stay there. In *Götterdämmerung* we had 50 crew on stage to do some of the scene changes.

PETER 'BEEF' ANDERSON Technical Stage Manager

The *Ring* cycle was an amazing experience for all of us in Wardrobe. We had so many costumes to deal with. The little Nibelung boys had glasses with small Maglite torches attached to them. We had to put in new batteries for every performance, just to make sure that they worked. What stands out most is that the backstage staff got to take a curtain call. Going out onto the stage was a terrifying but wonderful experience.

GLORIA DEL MONTE Wardrobe Mistress

And it was a triumph, actually – a real Company achievement. It was a big thing for the Company and it was a big thing for Scotland.

SIR BRIAN McMASTER Director, Edinburgh International Festival 1991–2006

Opposite: Mats Almgren as Hagen: *Götterdämmerung*, director Tim Albery, 2003.

Richard Holm as Loge, David Ward as Wotan: *Das Rheingold*, director Peter Ebert, 1967.

Victor Godfrey as Gunther, Helga Dernesch as Gutrune: *Götterdämmerung*, director Peter Ebert, 1968.

Leonore Kirschstein as Sieglinde, Charles Craig as Siegmund: *Der Ring des Nibelungen – Die Walküre*, director Peter Ebert, 1971.

Ticho Parly as Siegfried, Helga Dernesch as Brünnhilde: *Der Ring des Nibelungen – Götterdämmerung*, director Peter Ebert, 1971.

Der Ring des Nibelungen 1971

Who could forget that first *Ring* cycle? It was fraught with difficulties – it was not an easy time at all for Peter Hemmings and Alex Gibson – but to be there in the King's Theatre when the final curtain came down on *Götterdämmerung* was like being at a football match when the home team scores the winning goal – it was extraordinary.

JOHN DUFFUS Scottish Opera administration 1971–8

Helga Dernesch was a tremendous discovery. Alex was so impressed with her performance of Brünnhilde that he was keen to re-engage her in future roles for the Company. She went on to sing in *Der Rosenkavalier* and *Fidelio* with great success.

LADY GIBSON Wife of the founder of Scottish Opera

I was overwhelmed by what it did to me. I thought beforehand that it would be too tiring for me. But not a bit of it. It was magic. It took me back to kindergarten, where we used to be asked to choose music to be played at break times. I chose The Ride of the Valkyries. The teacher said, 'I don't think that's very suitable for sleeping.' I said, 'I don't want to sleep. I want to listen!' She asked me how I knew the music, and I replied, 'We have a record.'

MORAG MILLAR Wife of the late Ainslie Millar

Peter Hemmings found me at the side of the stage. I was there by myself. He said, 'You're here early. What are you doing?' I said, 'I've come to get my spear. I like to get the lightest one, you know.' He was so amused by that.

CATHERINE WILSON Soprano

Das Rheingold and Die Walküre

We started a *Ring* cycle in 1989 with John Mauceri and Richard Jones. Willard White was Wotan, Bonaventura Bottone was Loge. I must admit that I loved *Die Walküre* which we produced in 1991. It had loads of Richard's wit. The Valkyries, for instance, were on stilts and looked incredible in their long robes. It was pretty stunning to look at, in designs by Nigel Lowery.

JENNY SLACK Director of Planning 1986–2010

Above: Sir Willard White as
Wotan, Gerard Quinn
as Donner, Felicity Palmer
as Fricka, Justin Lavender as
Froh: *Das Rheingold*, director
Richard Jones, 1989.

Die Meistersinger von Nürnberg

When the Company presented *Die Meistersinger von Nürnberg* it was a marvellous achievement.
It was a brilliant, colourful production with that great musician Norman Bailey singing Hans Sachs.

ISABEL RODGER Wife of the late Ian Rodger

Above: Norman Bailey
(centre) as Hans Sachs,
with Elizabeth Harwood as
Eva and Allen Cathcart as
Walther: *Die Meistersinger
von Nürnberg*, director David
Pountney, 1976.

Tristan und Isolde

I almost made my Scottish Opera debut in 1968, when I was still a student at the Geneva Conservatoire. Alexander Gibson and Peter Hemmings auditioned me and offered me a Valkyrie and the cover of Gutrune in the Company's first *Ring* production. Unfortunately I couldn't accept, because I already had a contract to sing a Valkyrie in Geneva at exactly the same time. So my first appearance with Scottish Opera had to wait a further 26 years, when I sang Isolde, by which time Richard Armstrong was the Music Director. He and I had had a long working relationship in Wales and had sort of grown up musically together, so the Tristan was a natural progression for us. It was a big success and the Company took it to Lisbon, where the performances started so late that I didn't get to sing the Liebestod until long after midnight. I had to drink strong espressos to keep awake and then didn't sleep all night!

Of all the roles I sang I loved Isolde the most, and I think it was the one I performed best. The music just fitted my voice like a glove. Whenever I opened the score I discovered something new in it. The music always felt fresh.

DAME ANNE EVANS Soprano

It was the most simple, direct production – very honest. Beautifully lit and beautifully directed in a very understated way. And I had the huge pleasure of singing Brangäne with my great friends Anne Evans and Jeffrey Lawton. There was a great bond between us on stage, which was transmitted to the audience. It had a profound effect on the level of the performance.

KATHRYN HARRIES Soprano

Tristan und Isolde with Jeffrey Lawton and Anne Evans was the first Wagner that the Scottish Opera orchestra had played under Richard Armstrong. It was extraordinary because each performance you went to you heard the orchestra improve. We took the production to Lisbon and opened the new theatre there, along with *Peter Grimes*. It was a huge undertaking but a great success, and an extremely enjoyable tour. It was an action-packed summer because we then came back to Scotland and opened the Festival Theatre in Edinburgh with *Tristan und Isolde*. It was a big event.

RICHARD JARMAN Managing Director 1991–7

Tristan und Isolde with Richard Armstrong was an all-time high, a real highlight.

JANET BLOXWICH Principal Bassoon, The Orchestra of Scottish Opera

Opposite: Jeffrey Lawton as Tristan, Dame Anne Evans as Isolde: *Tristan und Isolde*, directors Yannis Kokkos and Peter Watson, 1994.
Overleaf: Elizabeth Byrne as Brünnhilde: *Götterdämmerung*, director Tim Albery, 2003.

50 Years of Memorable Moments

Of course, with a history spanning 50 years and hundreds of productions, it would be impossible to illustrate every Scottish Opera highlight. But certain productions did keep surfacing in contributors' memories. So here, in no particular order, is a selection of some of the most highly acclaimed or most visually arresting productions, featuring an array of operatic talent.

Some are Scottish premieres, some notable for unforgettable performances, and some have, quite simply, become our most distinguished productions. All have kindled marvellous memories across half a century.

Opposite: Edgaras Montvidas as Tom Rakewell: *The Rake's Progress*, director Sir David McVicar, 2012.

Der Rosenkavalier Richard Strauss

Scottish Opera has presented two productions of Richard Strauss' opera of 1911, and both have proved to be major landmarks in the Company's history. On 20 May 1971, Helga Dernesch, Dame Janet Baker and Elizabeth Harwood sang the roles of the Marschallin, Octavian and Sophie in Anthony Besch's production, designed by John Stoddart and conducted by Sir Alexander Gibson. Revivals followed in 1974 and 1978. Audiences then had to wait over 20 years for Sir David McVicar's new production, which debuted in 1999 with Joan Rodgers as the Marschallin. In subsequent revivals, Sarah Connolly has enjoyed notable success as Octavian.

It's a tremendous piece, a very difficult piece to put together. It was the first time I had sung Octavian. I think it was the first time Elizabeth Harwood had sung Sophie. Helga Dernesch was the Marschallin. We were good pals and worked very hard together. *Der Rosenkavalier* is not simple music. In the first scene, where Octavian and the Marschallin are in the bed, to try to settle into the show in order to do all the right actions and also follow the beat was a very difficult discipline because the music sort of meanders – you don't get any easy bars.

DAME JANET BAKER Mezzo-soprano

In 1971 I studied the Marschallin in English, as Peter Hemmings wanted to perform *Der Rosenkavalier* in English. I worked with Dame Janet Baker and Elizabeth Harwood – a great pleasure. In two of the performances we had a Baron Ochs as guest: Michael Langdon did the part all over the world but he had to learn it in English. When he arrived we discovered that he had only had time to study Acts I and II, but not Act III. This put me in the funny position – being Viennese – of singing to Mr Langdon – born in Wolverhampton, if I remember correctly – in English, while he replied in German!

HELGA DERNESCH Soprano

Helga Dernesch established an ongoing relationship with Scottish Opera. To hear her at the peak of her career, and to hear her sing the role of the Marschallin in English, was amazing. I remember the piano dress rehearsal going on and on, mainly due to technical difficulties. At about one o'clock in the morning, at the point where Helga Dernesch had to make her Act III entrance, Anthony Besch stopped the performance and complained about the way she was wearing her hat. I can think of some prima donnas who would have walked out, but she just took it!

JOHN DUFFUS Scottish Opera administration 1971–8

The highlight of my operatic memory is 12 June 1971, the last night of that season, at His Majesty's Theatre in Aberdeen – *Der Rosenkavalier*, with Alexander Gibson conducting. He had an amazing way of highlighting the waltz beat by introducing a momentary hesitation, which lifted the phrase out of the banal. The splendid production by Anthony Besch rolled on to the last Act, when the three leading ladies launched into the incomparable beauty of the trio. I was on the edge of my seat, with tears rolling down my cheeks, it was so compellingly beautiful.

THE HON JAMES BRUCE CBE 1927–2013
Scottish Opera Board member and Chairman of the Scottish Opera Endowment Trust

Opposite: Helga Dernesch as the Marschallin, Dame Janet Baker as Octavian: *Der Rosenkavalier*, director Anthony Besch, 1971.

This was a real challenge for me, at what was still quite an early stage in my career. There was the sheer scale of the opera to contend with, its dramatic complexity, the size of the cast, the lavish, romantic aura that audiences have come to expect; and all to be achieved on a budget that fell far short of what many houses would expect to spend on *Rosenkavalier*! I remember being quite feisty about the casting and other aspects of the production, which I designed myself. I wanted to get it right! Richard Armstrong and I are both strong personalities, but I think we worked well together. I was keen that Joan Rodgers should be the Marschallin and, happily, Richard was in complete agreement. Peter Rose was making his debut as Ochs and has since become one of the most celebrated singers of the role in the world. We explored the character for the first time together and tried to stay close to the authors' intentions, avoiding the traditional, boorish caricature. When he sang the role at the Metropolitan Opera, he had his Scottish Opera costumes flown over to New York! The show was taken up by other companies (English National Opera and Opera North) and we've now done it six times – to date. I've been able to direct every revival and the production has changed and grown with the years. I feel that it's in my blood now and I simply love coming back to it. We've been particularly fortunate in the casting of Octavian, with Stella Doufexis in the first years and Sarah Connolly in more recent revivals.

SIR DAVID McVICAR Director

One of the most beautiful productions I have seen in recent years was *Der Rosenkavalier.*

JAMES MacMILLAN Composer

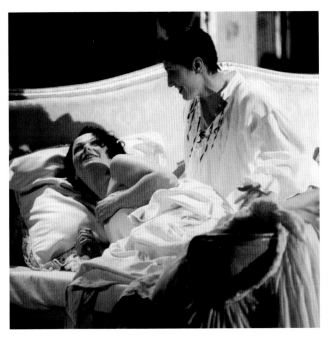

Joan Rodgers as the Marschallin, Stella Doufexis as Octavian: *Der Rosenkavalier*, 2002 revival of the 1999 Sir David McVicar production.

Sarah Connolly as Octavian, Daniel Sumegi as Baron Ochs: *Der Rosenkavalier*, 2006 revival of the 1999 Sir David McVicar production.

Sarah Connolly as Octavian, Lucy Crowe as Sophie: *Der Rosenkavalier*, 2006 revival.

Caitlin Hulcup as Annina: *Der Rosenkavalier*, 2006 revival.

Benjamin Britten Operas

With *Albert Herring* in 1967, Scottish Opera commenced a string of productions of Britten's chamber operas that proved a success with audiences at home and abroad. Throughout the 1970s and into the early 1980s, the Company toured the likes of *The Turn of the Screw* and *A Midsummer Night's Dream* across Europe, from Iceland to the former Yugoslavia, regularly conducted by Roderick Brydon, who had a great affinity with Britten's operas.

Albert Herring

Albert Herring was a great success from Day 1 and toured all over Europe. It was a calling card for the Company.

JANE HEMMINGS Wife of the late Peter Hemmings

The Turn of the Screw

I was having quite a bit of trouble with the design. I was staying with some friends in the country. I remember quite vividly looking out over the lawn one moonlit evening, with the trees beyond it, and thinking, 'That's the way it should look. All dappled leaves.' So I designed gauzy screens with a few set pieces which slid on and off, because we had to have very quick changes. They were beautifully lit by Charles Bristow, so everything looked filmy and dream-like. Anthony Besch did a very good production – you were never quite sure if everything was in the Governess' imagination or not.

JOHN STODDART Designer

Peter Grimes

Peter Hemmings asked me if I would like to sing with Scottish Opera in the 1966 Season. I knew Peter through Sadler's Wells productions but didn't know Scottish Opera's work. I said, 'Yes, please.' My first role was Nancy in *Albert Herring* in Perth. The theatre was small and intimate, but it was delightful and the appropriate size for the opera.

CATHERINE WILSON Soprano

A Midsummer Night's Dream

There was a mix-up with regard to hotel accommodation in Iceland. When we got to Reykjavik the children in the production had to be put into a different hotel. There were two problems. The first was that all the rooms had minibars which weren't locked. So within minutes the children were knocking back gin. The second was rather more serious, in that the floor below where the children were staying was a brothel for sailors. One boy realised what was going on and immediately started touting for business from his bedroom window!

EVELYN BRYSON Arts administrator

The Rape of Lucretia

Scottish Opera toured a lot with the Britten operas, and mainly to proper theatres. However, in Ljubljana there was just a large, outdoor courtyard with a high wall along one side and a street beyond. We had to be self-contained for this visit, which entailed taking all the required staging, building a proscenium arch, masking, gantries for the lighting, and even our own generator! The authorities closed the street for the duration of the performance. During the opera, Lucretia has to sing, 'How quiet it is tonight, even the street is silent.' Just at that moment someone, on a very squeaky bicycle, travelled the whole length of the wall – perfect timing but the ladies were less than happy!

JOHN LAWSON GRAHAM Scottish Opera 1963–2005

Gregory Dempsey as Albert Herring, Judith Pierce as Lady Billows:
Albert Herring, director Anthony Besch, 1967.

Catherine Wilson as the Governess, Timothy Oldham as Miles:
The Turn of the Screw, 1973 revival of the 1970 Anthony Besch
production.

Catherine Wilson as Ellen Orford: *Peter Grimes*, 1973 revival of the
1968 Colin Graham production.

John Robertson as Snout, Francis Egerton as Flute: *A Midsummer
Night's Dream*, 1979 revival of the 1972 Toby Robertson production.

Scottish Opera has continued to present Britten's operas up to the present day. *Death in Venice* was staged at the Edinburgh International Festival in 1983, Glasgow's Tramway provided a suitably atmospheric venue for a new production of *The Turn of the Screw* in 1994, and the same year the German Joachim Herz directed *Peter Grimes*. In 1987 there was a remarkable *Billy Budd*, directed by Graham Vick (see page 136). To mark the centenary of Britten's birth, the Company joined in early 2013 with the Royal Conservatoire of Scotland to present Olivia Fuchs' production of *A Midsummer Night's Dream*.

Opposite: Jeffrey Lawton as Peter Grimes, David Barrell as Captain Balstrode: *Peter Grimes*, 1997.

Craig Fraser as Tadzio, Anthony Rolfe Johnson as Aschenbach: *Death in Venice*, 1983.

Philip Salmon as Peter Quint, Duncan Russell as Miles: *The Turn of the Screw*, 1994.

Ariadne auf Naxos Richard Strauss

Part of my strategy when I was Director at the Edinburgh Festival was to profile the national companies in an international festival context. That meant doing festival projects – something that the Company might not normally do. *I due Foscari* was a comparatively rarely performed early Verdi opera of terrific quality and it came out really well. In the Festival's 50th anniversary year we did the original version of *Ariadne auf Naxos*, which had been given by Beecham and Glyndebourne at the Festival in 1950. When the production went back into the repertory, Scottish Opera staged it with the Prologue rather than the original play, which was clever, because it reflected in a meaningful way the history of the Festival but also gave the Company an opera that was different.

SIR BRIAN McMASTER Director, Edinburgh International Festival 1991–2006

With Martin Duncan's fine direction, Tim Hatley's witty sets and Richard Armstrong in the pit, Scottish Opera's production of *Ariadne auf Naxos* was the hit of the 1997 Edinburgh Festival, which had commissioned it. This was the rarely performed original version of Richard Strauss' work, which combines a shortened version of Molière's play *Le bourgeois gentilhomme* with the opera proper. The singers take part in the play, the very thought of which unnerved us, while the actors were unsure about working alongside the singers. Things went well in rehearsal, however, until we got into the large space of the Festival Theatre, where ironically it was discovered that the singers' spoken text could be heard more clearly than that of some of the actors, who were being very intimate, as though they were having private conversations. Everything got sorted out in the end and I have the happiest memories of the performances.

DAME ANNE EVANS Soprano

Opposite: Lisa Saffer as Zerbinetta, Dame Anne Evans as Ariadne, David Stephenson as Harlequin: *Ariadne auf Naxos*, director Martin Duncan, 1998.

The Bartered Bride Bedřich Smetana

When we did the circus scene at the end we had a tightrope artist. The rope was set up on the set — you wouldn't get away with that now! I remember being on stage in order to hold the anchor points down. It all had to be set up in about 2 minutes.

PETER 'BEEF' ANDERSON Technical Stage Manager

Opposite: Peter Bodenham as the Ring Master: *The Bartered Bride*, director David Pountney, 1978.

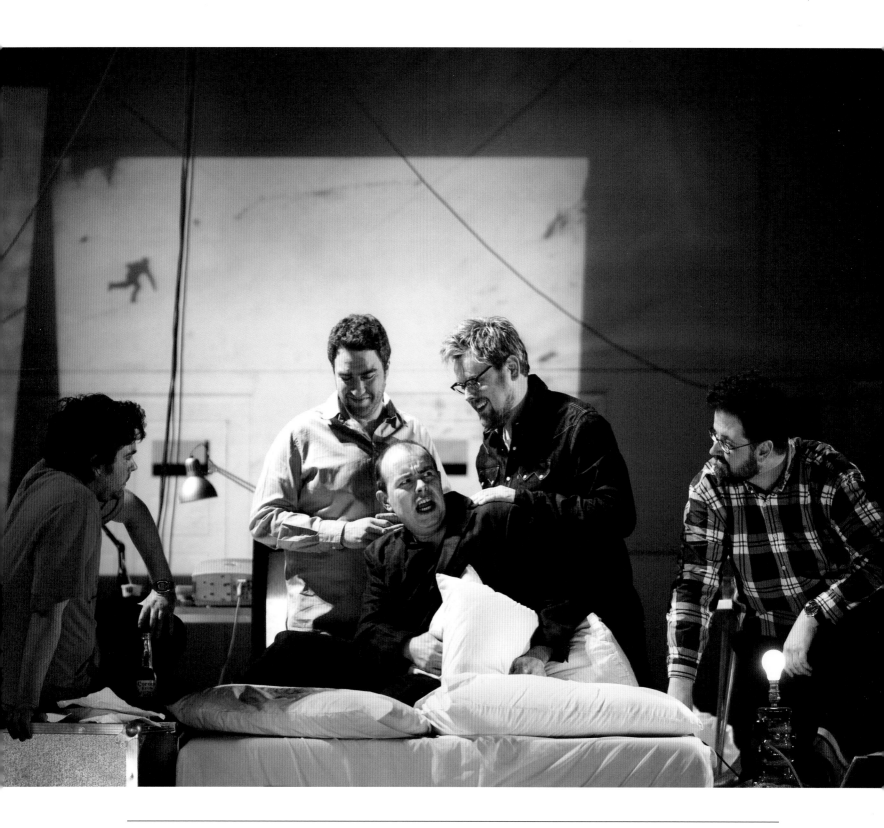

La bohème Giacomo Puccini

La bohème is one of the staples of the operatic repertoire, and Scottish Opera has been fortunate to have had three high-quality productions. Peter Ebert, the Company's Director of Productions from 1965 to 1975, first presented his much-revived traditional staging in 1967. Elijah Moshinsky's production of 1988 boasted, in the view of one reviewer, 'one of the great, breathtaking *Bohème* sets', designed by Michael Yeargan. By 2004, Rodolfo and Mimì had been brought firmly into the 21st century in Stewart Laing's contemporary take on Puccini's evergreen opera.

Opposite: Julian Hubbard as Schaunard, Avi Klemberg as Rodolfo, Adrian Powter as Benoit, Benjamin Bevan as Marcello, Christian Sist as Colline: *La bohème*, 2010 revival of the 2004 Stewart Laing production.

Luisa Bosabalian as Mimì, George Shirley as Rodolfo: *La bohème*, director Peter Ebert, 1967.

Jorge Pitta as Rodolfo, Jane Eaglen as Mimì: *La bohème*, director Elijah Moshinsky, 1988.

The Marriage of Figaro Wolfgang Amadeus Mozart

I can't thank Scottish Opera enough for the incredible start the Company gave to my career. I couldn't believe it when I got the offer of four major roles – it was like all my Christmases had come at once! I couldn't wait for *The Marriage of Figaro* and it proved to be such an exciting experience. To spend six weeks working with and learning from Sir Thomas Allen was priceless. Every day he gave me advice and direction that not only shaped what I did in that production but will continue to shape my performance in every show I do. To learn from someone so experienced in what I was trying to do was unbelievable.

NADINE LIVINGSTON Soprano

Francesco Facini as Dr Bartolo, Roderick Williams as Count Almaviva, Leah-Marian Jones as Marcellina, Harry Nicoll as Don Basilio, Nadine Livingston as Susanna, Thomas Oliemans as Figaro, Kate Valentine as Countess Almaviva: *The Marriage of Figaro*, director Sir Thomas Allen, 2010.

Kate Valentine as Countess Almaviva, Nadine Livingston as Susanna: *The Marriage of Figaro*, director Sir Thomas Allen, 2010.

Rise and Fall of the City of Mahagonny Kurt Weill

I had a most amazing first break. I had been studying in Russia and I came back to Manchester in the Autumn of 1985. In early 1986 that magic phone call came. Simon Rattle had had to withdraw from conducting *Mahagonny*. I was in a strange situation because I had never worked in a professional opera house before. My agent Howard Hartog put my name forward to Scottish Opera and they were willing to take a risk on me. I remember borrowing vocal scores and recordings from the Manchester University music department and trying to get a feel for Weill's music, and then there I was the next day in Glasgow and off we went! Everyone was incredibly warm and generous towards me.

SIAN EDWARDS Conductor

Opposite: Alexander Oliver as Fatty, Felicity Palmer as Leokadja Begbick: *Rise and Fall of the City of Mahagonny*, director David Alden, 1986.

Fidelio Ludwig van Beethoven

In 1970 Scottish Opera marked the bicentenary of Beethoven's birth with a production of his only opera, *Fidelio*. It stands out for Helga Dernesch's performance of Leonore, felt by many to be one of the best ever. A new production by Stephen Wadsworth was presented in 1991, with Tim Albery's stark, modern staging following in 1994.

I always enjoyed the beautiful opera houses in Edinburgh, Aberdeen, Newcastle and Leeds. In May 1970 I sang my first Leonore in *Fidelio*. Charles Craig was Florestan. Alexander Gibson was the conductor – a very nice man and a great conductor. Meanwhile I was Herbert von Karajan's Brünnhilde in *Siegfried* and *Götterdämmerung* at the Salzburg Easter Festival, and after Scottish Opera I was his Leonore too. I met my second husband, the Viennese tenor Werner Krenn, when we did *Fidelio* together in 1970. He was Jaquino. In 1975 I gave birth to my son, and in 1996 Peter Hemmings met him in Dallas, where I was singing Elektra. Peter said to him with a big smile, 'Without me, you wouldn't be here!

HELGA DERNESCH Soprano

We got the best out of Helga Dernesch, particularly in *Fidelio*. She was just astonishing, absolutely glorious.

JOHN CURRIE Chorus Master

The amount of goodwill that Bill McCue generated was enormous. People knew him for performing perhaps more popular music, but his warmth as a personality meant that people identified with him and would come to see him in opera. But it wasn't just his warmth of personality – he had a very, very good bass voice. He could have done roles such as Rocco in *Fidelio* anywhere.

DONALD MAXWELL Singer

William McCue as Rocco, Josephine McQueen as Marzelline, Helga Dernesch as Leonore: *Fidelio*, director Peter Ebert, 1970.

Josephine Barstow as Leonore: *Fidelio*, 1977 revival of the 1970 Peter Ebert production.

Kathryn Harries as Leonore, John Treleaven as Florestan: *Fidelio*, 1984 revival of the 1970 Peter Ebert production.

Elizabeth Anne Whitehouse as Leonore, Ai-Lan Zhu as Marzelline:
Fidelio, director Tim Albery, 1994.

I've had a pretty lucky time at Scottish Opera directing amazing pieces. *Fidelio* was the first time I had worked with Richard Armstrong. Leonora was Elizabeth Whitehouse, a wonderful Australian soprano. She was tall and really looked like a young man – like a tall, thinner kd lang. Matthew Best was also in it, and he went on to be Wotan in the *Ring* cycle. *Fidelio* is an impossible opera, but we latched onto one thing, and that was that it changes stylistically. It starts out as if it's a Mozart comedy, but then before you know it you are in Fidelio's hole of despair. We designed it to match that, with a chocolate-box opening, but as the evening went on it became darker and more monochrome. For me design is where things start. How do we tell a story through what it looks like? It was brilliantly designed by Stewart Laing.

TIM ALBERY Director

I think the best thing Scottish Opera did in my time there was *Fidelio*. It had the fantastic combination of Richard Armstrong conducting and Tim Albery directing. It was incredibly powerful.

RICHARD JARMAN Managing Director 1991–7

Opposite: Sarah Redgwick as Marzelline, Ulrich Dünnebach as Rocco, Elizabeth Byrne as Leonore: *Fidelio*, 2005 revival of the 1994 Tim Albery production.

Macbeth Giuseppe Verdi

It was a wonderful production. Luc Bondy at that time was doing major opera productions around the world, and had previously brought some of his theatre productions to Edinburgh, which had proved hugely successful. I was with Luc in Vienna one evening and found the opportunity to ask him about *Macbeth*, and he said he was interested. So Scottish Opera went ahead and developed the production.

SIR BRIAN McMASTER Director, Edinburgh International Festival 1991–2006

This was a great opportunity for Scottish Opera to get Luc Bondy working with the Company. It's quite clear we would not have had Luc Bondy working with the Company had it not been for the Edinburgh Festival. Luc loved the idea of doing *Macbeth* in Scotland and having the cachet of the Edinburgh Festival behind it. Luc knew of my work with Peter Stein on *Otello* and *Falstaff*, two other Shakespearean operas, at the Schaubühne in Berlin and was keen to work with me on *Macbeth*. Working with him was astounding. I've conducted lots of Verdi operas but I had avoided *Macbeth* because I thought it was pretty treacherous. It's not a fail-safe piece. But when Luc Bondy's name came up, I thought this had to be the moment to tackle the opera. He has a phenomenally fertile imagination.

SIR RICHARD ARMSTRONG Music Director 1993–2005

That was a marvellous production. It was expensive, yes, but it was quality. I saw it here in Scotland, but much more importantly I saw it in the Theater an der Wien in Vienna. I had to give a speech at the reception at the end of the performance. The culture minister drove me to tears with his praise of Scottish Opera. To go to Vienna and hear the culture minister praise our Company was utterly amazing. It typified how Scottish Opera is not just about a few venues in Scotland.

DUNCAN McGHIE Chairman 1999–2004

I was King Duncan. I played him in Vienna. I had to be dragged on stage covered in blood and placed on a bier. Kathleen Broderick as Lady Macbeth kept on nudging me and muttering, 'Move over!' I replied, 'I can't. I'm dead.'

JIM McJANNET Chorus Secretary and chorus member for 42 years

In the famous Luc Bondy production of *Macbeth*, I was one of the corpses in the pit. In the interlude before we went on, the stagehands had to remove all the paraphernalia of the witches and we all piled into the pit in a matter of seconds. We had to lie absolutely still for about 20 minutes. The pit was inches thick in shredded black plastic which got everywhere – it took at least two showers to get rid of it all!

LOUIS JONES Supporter of Scottish Opera since 1962

Opposite: Chorus of Scottish Opera: Act IV Scene 1, *Macbeth*, director Luc Bondy, 1999.

Gregory Dempsey as Steva: *Jenůfa*, director David Pountney, 1977.

Kerstin Meyer as Kabanicha, Josephine Barstow as Kátya: *Kátya Kabanová*, director David Pountney, 1979.

Curt Applegren as the Parson, Helen Field as the Vixen: *The Cunning Little Vixen*, director David Pountney, 1980.

Donald Maxwell as Shishkov, Alexander Morrison as Kedril: *From the House of the Dead*, director David Pountney, 1987.

Leoš Janáček Operas

When Scottish Opera staged Leoš Janáček's *Jenůfa* in 1977, in a co-production with Welsh National Opera, it came like a bolt from the blue for Scottish audiences. But over the next decade, the artistic triumvirate of conductor Sir Richard Armstrong, director David Pountney and designer Maria Björnson introduced *Kátya Kabanová*, *The Cunning Little Vixen*, *The Makropoulos Case* and *From the House of the Dead*, and the Czech composer's unique soundworld cast its spell.

In the 1970s I was the Music Director of Welsh National Opera, and one of my early plans was to put on a Janáček opera as soon as I could. *Jenůfa* seemed to be the right choice. I had previously prepared the opera with Rafael Kubelík during my time at the Royal Opera House, and that was a very special working relationship. I learned so much about the idiom from Kubelík who was a wonderful teacher and an extremely kind and generous man. I took the decision to invite a young director from Scottish Opera – David Pountney – whose production of *Kátya Kabanová* I had seen in Wexford, to direct *Jenůfa* in Wales. Peter Hemmings then approached WNO and said that it would be good to have Scottish Opera in on the deal because the Company hadn't ever performed a Janáček opera. As David had already been invited to direct it, it made a certain sense. *Jenůfa* was a big hit in Scotland. Following that, Peter Hemmings, Brian McMaster [WNO Managing Director] and I decided to embark on a cycle of the five major Janáček operas. *Kátya Kabanová* and *The Cunning Little Vixen* had their premieres in Scotland. All the productions were seen from Aberdeen in the north to Southampton in the south as a result of the collaboration between the two companies. It was that cycle of operas that really established Janáček in the UK.

SIR RICHARD ARMSTRONG Music Director 1993–2005

I said to Richard, 'Why don't we do all the major Janáček operas?' The initial problem was to attract an audience, but the best way is to approach that strategically and build that audience – and it worked. It was a major series, a major event.

SIR BRIAN McMASTER Director, Edinburgh International Festival 1991–2006

I had never heard Janáček before until I saw David Pountney's wonderful production of *Jenůfa*, which we did with Welsh National Opera. It was also the first visit of Richard Armstrong. There was a scene in which the chorus were scraping potatoes, which then ran down the sloping stage, which caused a certain amount of concern in the orchestra! But the combination of David Pountney, Richard Armstrong and the designer Maria Björnson in Janáček was simply fantastic.

LADY GIBSON Wife of the founder of Scottish Opera

I'm not sure that Janáček had been heard in Scotland before. It was a really exciting time to be introduced to this new repertoire. *Jenůfa* in particular was absolutely staggering, with such a clever design. I think people suddenly realised that Janáček was very singable.

JOHN LAWSON GRAHAM Scottish Opera 1963–2005

More recently there has been a further production of *Kátya Kabanová* and a wonderfully quirky staging by John Fulljames, in a co-production with Opera North, of *The Adventures of Mr Brouček*. Additionally, with small-scale touring productions over the years of *Jenůfa*, *The Makropoulos Case* and *Kátya Kabanová*, Janáček is no longer a stranger in the Scottish operatic landscape.

The Adventures of Mr Brouček sort of typifies Scottish Opera. The Company never went down the traditional route. There have always been quirky things – some of them have been to the audience's taste, others perhaps not. But there has always been a degree of innovation, and *Mr Brouček* is perhaps one that people will tick off their list and be grateful for seeing. Perhaps not great, though, to see Donald Maxwell taking his clothes off!

DONALD MAXWELL Singer

Opposite: Jeffrey Lloyd-Roberts as Starry Sky-Blue, John Graham-Hall as Mr Brouček: *The Adventures of Mr Brouček*, director John Fulljames, 2010.

Roderick Earle as Dikoy, Kathryn Harries as Kabanicha, Susan Chilcott as Kátya, Katija Dragojevic as Varvara: *Kátya Kabanová*, director Rennie Wright, 1999.

Carmen Georges Bizet

Carmen was a very beautiful show, very austere. The show was made with people on an empty floor. Just a revolving stage and a lot of chairs. It was about the journey of a body of people. The protagonist of that production was the chorus. It was a communal ritual. I remember it very fondly. It was a big step forward in my own work — it opened a door for a lot of work I've done since then.

GRAHAM VICK Director of Productions 1984–7

Opposite: Emily Golden as Carmen: *Carmen,* director Graham Vick, 1986.

Kathryn Harries as Judith: *Duke Bluebeard's Castle,* director Stefanos Lazaridis, 1990.

Catherine Malfitano as Constanze: *Seraglio,* director David Pountney, 1978.

Tosca Giacomo Puccini

For one of the Top 10 most-performed operas, it took quite a while for Scottish Opera to get round to staging Giacomo Puccini's *Tosca*. But when it did – in 1980 – the Company had an immediate success on its hands. By updating the action from Rome in the Napoleonic era to Mussolini's time during World War II, director Anthony Besch hit on a brilliant strategy of keeping the action relevant and gripping. Even after eight revivals of the original staging – and being hired out to opera companies around the world – this is a production that still has a life ahead of it.

Tosca is one of those operas that does what it says on the tin. It's a hugely enjoyable piece to work on because Puccini gives you all the information you need, so your work as a conductor is to bring to life what's in the score. The decisions have already been made by him because he was very particular about how he wanted the music to go. It just works, and that's what makes it so rewarding.

DEREK CLARK Head of Music

Opposite: Seppo Ruohonen as Cavaradossi, Marina Krilovici as Tosca: *Tosca*, director Anthony Besch, 1980.

I worked with director Anthony Besch on *Tosca*. I designed the sets. The first Tosca wasn't keen on throwing herself from the platform of Castel Sant' Angelo, which was about 15 feet above the stage floor. Anthony disdained the use of the usual mattresses to cushion her fall. He had heard of a system, successfully used at the Coliseum in London, of a pyramid of large cardboard boxes, set as a tower, each supposedly collapsing into the next on the impact of the falling body. Our Tosca looked at the cardboard boxes without enthusiasm. 'Look, it's quite safe,' said Anthony. 'I will demonstrate.' He went to the edge of the battlements and jumped. The boxes collapsed instantly like a pack of cards, and a shaken but unhurt Anthony crawled out from beneath the pile of cardboard. 'Get the mattresses,' he said.

PETER RICE Designer

The production was rehearsed in the Rankine Hall on the top floor of Elmbank Crescent. All the bases of the pillars in Act I had to be carried up the stairs. That was hard, hard work. And luckily, none of the beautiful stained-glass windows in the building was damaged.

PETER 'BEEF' ANDERSON Technical Stage Manager

I played Tosca with Matthew Best, who I got to know very well later on [as Wotan in the *Ring* cycle], as Scarpia. Anthony Besch was very particular and went into the minutest detail. He seemed to have a photographic memory. In the first duet with Scarpia, when he plants the seed in Tosca's mind about Cavaradossi's infidelity, I had to shed a tear. If we rehearsed that scene once, we must have done it 25 times! In the end Matthew and I couldn't do it for laughing. Anthony wanted the stabs in Act II to be very gruesome but also on a musical cue. That bit is very difficult musically and it makes it even more difficult to get your stabs timed correctly. We had a spring-loaded knife. I'd stabbed Scarpia twice when the dagger came apart in my hand. I still had nine more stabs to go! For the next performance we got a new knife from the Royal Shakespeare Company but that was very small. I went through quite a few knives during the run. I was quite into it – really committed to getting the stabs in time to the music!

ELIZABETH BYRNE Dramatic Soprano

It's a beautiful show, it just takes your breath away. It's great for the boys because they get to run around the church and annoy the Sacristan then get changed into their choristers' costumes for the Te Deum. And they really look forward to the end, with the guns and Tosca throwing herself off the battlements!

CATHIE ARBUCKLE Chaperone

Robert Poulton as Scarpia: *Tosca*, 2012 revival of the 1980 Anthony Besch production.

Elena Zelenskaya as Tosca: *Tosca*, 2004 revival.

Elizabeth Byrne as Tosca, Matthew Best as Scarpia: *Tosca*, 1997 revival.

Susannah Glanville as Tosca: *Tosca*, 2012 revival.

L'elisir d'amore Gaetano Donizetti

Right at the start of her career, Lisa Milne came from the Royal Scottish Academy of Music and Drama on contract to Scottish Opera. She was terrific and continues to have a flourishing career.

Simon Keenlyside auditioned for us in a small studio in Hamburg, and I thought, 'Blimey, this is fantastic.' Simon sang with us for, I think, five consecutive seasons. Since when he has more than made his mark worldwide!

JENNY SLACK Director of Planning 1986–2010

Opposite: Lisa Milne as Adina: *L'elisir d'amore,* 2000 revival of the 1994 Giles Havergal production.

Paul Charles Clarke as Nemorino, Cheryl Barker as Adina, Simon Keenlyside as Belcore: *L'elisir d'amore,* director Giles Havergal, 1994.

Dennis O'Neill as Nemorino, Federico Davia as Dulcamara: *L'elisir d'amore,* director Graham Vick, 1980.

Peter Glossop as Iago: *Otello*, director Anthony Besch, 1963.

Joan Carlyle as Desdemona: *Otello*, 1967 revival of the 1963 Anthony Besch production.

Kiri Te Kanawa as Desdemona, Charles Craig as Otello: *Otello*, 1972 revival of the 1963 Anthony Besch production.

Otello Giuseppe Verdi

Otello was a statement of intent at the start of Scottish Opera's second season. A production on a much larger scale than 1962's *Madama Butterfly* and *Pelléas et Mélisande*, it heralded the debut of the Company's amateur chorus, which made its mark immediately by its memorable entrance at the start of Verdi's 1887 opera. Between 1963 and 1977 the production showcased singers of the magnitude of Charles Craig, Peter Glossop, Luisa Bosabalian and Kiri Te Kanawa. It was the first opera (after the opening gala of *Die Fledermaus*) to be staged at Scottish Opera's permanent performing home, the Theatre Royal in Glasgow, in 1975.

The opening floor rehearsal for *Otello* was taken in a now-vanished Boys' Brigade hall in Anderston with pillars everywhere and a low ceiling. Anthony Besch, the director, sorted the 80-strong chorus into groups and then worked his way round the groups for about three-quarters of an hour. Then he said, 'Let's try that' and the first 45 seconds of the opening storm scene came out almost perfect. By the end of a three-hour rehearsal he not only had the first two or three minutes of the show licked, but he also knew just about everybody by name. Astonishing!

IAIN CAMPBELL Chorus Master 1962, Assistant to Chorus Master Leon Lovett 1963–5

Otello was simply fantastic. It was Charles Craig's first Otello. He had a lovely lady called Luisa Bosabalian as Desdemona. Peter Glossop was Iago. He had a very good dramatic baritone voice. I played Emilia. In the famous duet between Otello and Iago, standing backstage I could hardly hear Charles Craig. So I went as far away in the theatre as I could and listened. Charles' voice came through like a sword! I was greatly relieved. You didn't see any great effort, but out his voice went. On his first entry his voice was like a trumpet – not even Domingo could compete.

LAURA SARTI Singer

I think everyone will remember to their dying day the power of that production of *Otello* in the King's Theatre. There was such enthusiasm – everybody was doing their best because it was all new. It was something quite different from the first season the previous year. It was moving up a notch.

JANE HEMMINGS Wife of the late Peter Hemmings

My memories of *Otello* are very special, not only for the wonderful singing of Charles Craig and Peter Glossop, but because it marked the formation of the amateur chorus. As the curtain went up I was not prepared for the sound of the chorus as they emerged over the top of the set. I'd never seen anything like that before – it was one of the most exciting moments of my operatic life.

LADY GIBSON Wife of the founder of Scottish Opera

In the second season, *Otello* was a tremendous success. We had a huge volunteer chorus. When the curtain went up on that opening scene and the chorus burst onto the stage – that was what hooked me on opera for the rest of my life.

ISABEL RODGER Wife of the late Ian Rodger

When I remember those performances of *Otello*, it's all true what everybody says about those early years. I assisted on the *Otello* that opened the Theatre Royal, with Charles Craig, Peter Glossop, Sylvia Sass. I've done *Otello* myself in Berlin and at La Scala, and when I think back to how that *Otello* sounded in the Theatre Royal, it was amazing.

GRAHAM VICK Director of Productions 1984–7

L'Egisto Pier Francesco Cavalli

We took Cavalli's *L'Egisto* to Venice. It was quite extraordinary to take such a Venetian piece back to Italy and present it in a design that looked like the clockface from St Mark's, and find that the Venetians welcomed us with open arms.

DAFYDD BURNE-JONES Staff Director

It was a beautiful-looking production based on the zodiac. In order to get the set to La Fenice we of course had to load everything onto barges. John Fowler, the arts editor of *The Glasgow Herald*, was touring with us to do a piece in the paper. I invited him to take a lift on one of the barges. We sat on top of the scenery and sailed up the Grand Canal, lording it up. Everything had to be lifted from the canal directly into the theatre. Of course, the inevitable happened and a piece of the set fell into the water. Panic! It wasn't a problem for the bargee, though. He got a grappling hook and calmly got the piece back out again. Fortunately we could still use it, though it was a bit damp!

JOHN LAWSON GRAHAM Scottish Opera 1963–2005

Scottish Opera's performance of *L'Egisto* at London's Dominion Theatre coincided with the Great Transport Strike of 10 March 1982. The house lights dimmed at 7.15pm and two characters came out into the stage gloom and lay down in their appointed places. But now there were delays for latecomers from 7.15 to 7.30 and then for the delayed arrival of the programmes at 7.40. After 5 minutes of dull Prologue, a third of the orchestra lights went out! Frantic efforts to sort them out, and the performance began again at 7.55 – with dull Prologue! And those two poor characters (not required to sing immediately) were obliged to lay inert for some 40 minutes throughout all this – surely some sort of record!

PETER CROMBIE Audience Member

Opposite: Brian Bannatyne-Scott as Night: *L'Egisto*, 1984 revival of the 1982 John Cox production.

Dame Janet Baker (seated) as Dido, with Bernadette Greevy as Anna and Joseph Rouleau as Narbal: *The Trojans*, 1972 revival of the 1969 Peter Ebert production.

Katherine Ciesinski (right) as Cassandra: *The Trojans*, director Tim Albery, 1990.

The Trojans Hector Berlioz

Hector Berlioz's epic five-act opera *The Trojans*, composed between 1856 and 1858, has a distinguished performance history in Scotland. It was given its first British performance by the Glasgow Grand Opera Society in 1935. To mark the centenary of the composer's death in 1869, Scottish Opera staged the world's first complete performance of the opera, in English, in one evening. Directed by Peter Ebert and conducted by Sir Alexander Gibson, it starred Dame Janet Baker as Dido and Ronald Dowd as Aeneas. The production was revived in 1972.

In 1990, the Company mounted a new staging directed by Tim Albery and conducted by John Mauceri, this time in a co-production with Opera North and Welsh National Opera, as part of Glasgow's celebrations as European Capital of Culture. Along with the world premiere production of Judith Weir's *The Vanishing Bridegroom*, *The Trojans* enjoyed two complete performances at the Royal Opera House in December of the same year, the only time that Scottish Opera has visited Covent Garden.

It took us by storm because we had never seen anything like it on such a grand scale. Many people came up from London, including Daniel Barenboim and Jacqueline du Pré, as well as Colin Davis who was about to do it at Covent Garden. He was very amused by the horse, and made some interesting comments about it!

LADY GIBSON Wife of the founder of Scottish Opera

The Trojans took up a very large slice of my life. The show was produced with Opera North and Welsh National Opera, and Scottish Opera took the production to Covent Garden, which was a fantastic night in the theatre. For six or seven years, my life was very *Trojans*-heavy! It is one of the greatest operas ever written. It isn't the *Ring*, but it does have some of that scale and monumentality, and the music is breathtaking. As Cassandra we had Katherine Ciesinski, one of those fantastic singing actresses who could do anything and was pretty wild. She had a fantastic red dress with an enormous train on it. As Dido we had Kathryn Harries, who is one of the best British sopranos of her generation – she was intensely moving, and beautiful as well. Patricia Bardon was delightful as her sister – very still. Lucy Burge played Andromache, a silent, dance role. She was utterly astounding.

TIM ALBERY Director

Julius Caesar George Frideric Handel

When I became Managing Director, one of the productions I inherited was *Julius Caesar*, directed by Willy Decker. It was controversial musically in that it had various cuts that upset the purists, but it looked amazing and had a fantastic cast led by Michael Chance and Joan Rodgers – very powerful.

RICHARD JARMAN Managing Director 1991–7

It was directed by the wonderful Willy Decker. He did a lovely production with Joan Rodgers, three countertenors and all the sort of stuff I like! It was very striking – a yellow pyramid – and designed by John Macfarlane. It was Handel done on a big scale.

JENNY SLACK Director of Planning 1986–2010

Opposite: Joan Rodgers as Cleopatra: *Julius Caesar*, director Willy Decker, 1992.

Iolanthe Gilbert and Sullivan

In *Iolanthe*, starring Rikki Fulton as the Lord High Chancellor, the men's chorus were dressed for a shooting party, but some overly clever manoeuvres resulted in one of the less-than-nifty Peers dropping his gun, which promptly broke into three pieces. Rather than getting off stage, he proceeded to put the gun back together, much to the hilarity of the audience and the complete helplessness of his fellow Peers.

DAVID MORRISON Singer

Opposite: Rikki Fulton as Lord High Chancellor: *Iolanthe*, 1988 revival of the 1986 Keith Warner production.

Carol Rowlands as Mrs Eynesford Hill, Doreen Mantle as Mrs Higgins, Alan Oke as Freddy Eynesford Hill, Fiona Hendley as Eliza Doolittle: *My Fair Lady*, director Peter Lichtenfels, 1983.

Pelléas et Mélisande Claude Debussy

The 1973 Sadler's Wells performances were the only time in my opera-going experience that when the interval came I wanted to be left alone to be quiet with my thoughts. Particularly I remember George Shirley as the most ardent Pelléas, yet I don't really remember him from the earlier Boulez production at the Royal Opera House. It was completely overwhelming. It was then that Scottish Opera became imprinted on my consciousness.

RICHARD JARMAN Managing Director 1991–7

I did it first with George Shirley, an American tenor who was a great favourite at Scottish Opera, for three performances at Sadler's Wells. It was Colin Graham's production and it was beautiful. Jeannette Pilou had been the original Mélisande and I followed her. Many people said, 'Mélisande, that's not for you, you're a mezzo.' But it fitted me like a glove. I used to sleep with a copy of the score under my pillow – I just love Debussy and I love that opera.

ANNE HOWELLS Mezzo-soprano

I'd been a member of Welsh National Opera for two or three years, and while I was there we used to look at the headlines for other arts events going on elsewhere. At that time Scottish Opera was riding triumphantly over everything else. Alex Gibson and Peter Hemmings were taking the Company to great new heights – it was fantastic. I always wanted to go to Scottish Opera, and eventually I did. We performed at the Edinburgh Festival, with Alex conducting. It was lovely to be involved, and it fulfilled my ambition.

SIR THOMAS ALLEN Baritone and Director

Orion Pier Francesco Cavalli

We were doing *Orion* at the Edinburgh Festival and I remember Lillian Watson who sang Cupido had a curious little affair on her head which she said made her feel like a crown roast! She and I had to learn archery, and bet each other gin and tonics as to who could get the highest score. In rehearsal we got rather good at it. In my opening scene I had to sing 'Fire an arrow into the air', but I don't know what I did on the first night. I must have loaded my arrow incorrectly because it just flopped onto the floor. The audience broke up!

ANNE HOWELLS Mezzo-soprano

Orfeo ed Euridice Christoph Willibald Gluck

Janet Baker appeared in a production with choreography by Peter Darrell of Scottish Ballet. This was an example of how the different companies began to work with each other. It was quite controversial, but she gave such a focused, powerful performance. I can see her – the costume that she wore, the things that she did – even as I speak now.

GILES HAVERGAL Director, Citizens Theatre 1969–2003

George Shirley as Pelléas, John Shirley-Quirk as Golaud: *Pelléas et Mélisande*, 1973 revival of the 1972 Colin Graham production.

Anne Howells as Mélisande, Sir Thomas Allen as Pelléas: *Pelléas et Mélisande*, 1978 revival of the 1972 Colin Graham production.

Peter Jeffes as Apollo, Anne Howells as Diana: *Orion*, director Peter Wood, 1984.

Members of the Scottish Opera Ballet: *Orfeo ed Euridice*, director Peter Ebert, 1979.

The Golden Cockerel Nicholay Rimsky-Korsakov

It was an absolutely spectacular production. I haven't since been in a production as spectacular as that. It had to run like clockwork because all the scenery had to be flown in. The woman playing the Cockerel was a trapeze artist and she had to swing from the rafters above the stage doing fancy things like hanging by her ankles. It was very frightening because if she got it wrong there were going to be quite a lot of injuries! She always did her own rigging – she couldn't trust the technical boys to do it right. It was decided that King Dodon, played by Bill McCue, would be flown out at one point on a hammock. I was asked if I'd like to go in the hammock with him. I said I would not – it was far too risky! So I knelt under the hammock and did a few actions. But Bill was absolutely marvellous.

CLAIRE LIVINGSTONE Singer

My first trip to the opera was when I was about 14, to see *The Golden Cockerel* with my mother and uncle. The theatricality of the production is what sticks in my mind – it was visually stunning and I was bowled over. I went back to school the next day and told everyone about it!

KALLY LLOYD-JONES Director and choreographer

Opposite: William McCue as King Dodon, with John Robertson and Donald Maxwell as his sons Prince Guidon and Prince Afron: *The Golden Cockerel*, 1979 revival of the 1975 David Pountney production.

I remember working with Peter Capaldi on *The Golden Cockerel*. He was a dresser on that production. A lot of dressers came from the RSAMD for work experience.

GLORIA DEL MONTE Wardrobe Mistress

Idomeneo Wolfgang Amadeus Mozart

We were going to do a new *Idomeneo* but it was the one production in the season that impeded us from balancing the budget. I said that I was sorry but that we were going to have to cancel it. Richard Armstrong came to me and said that he had assembled a wonderful cast, including Thomas Randle, Lisa Milne and a very young Toby Spence, and that he really wanted to do the production. I said that we would do it, but only if it cost no more than £10,000. David McVicar had worked on some small shows at Opera North and was obviously a talent to be looked at. When we approached him, David said it was one of his favourite operas and agreed to do it, designing it himself. There was just a large coin for the set, we got M&S suits for the men and sheets for togas – and that was it. But it was fantastic. The hallmark of David's work is the way he directs people and he had a huge success.

RICHARD JARMAN Managing Director 1991–7

Scottish Opera was the first company to take on board David McVicar. He directed and designed *Idomeneo* on a very small budget indeed. I think everyone who saw it will remember it. It was incredibly beautiful to look at and very simple, with a small number of strong images. It was clear from the off that he knew exactly what he was doing.

DAFYDD BURNE-JONES Staff Director

Opposite: Toby Spence as Idamante, Thomas Randle as Idomeneo: *Idomeneo*, director Sir David McVicar, 1996.

Giles Tomkins as Don Basilio, Thomas Oliemans as Figaro, Adrian Dwyer as Count Almaviva, Karin Thyselius as Berta, Karen Cargill as Rosina, Nicholas Folwell as Dr Bartolo: *The Barber of Seville*, director Sir Thomas Allen, 2007.

Adrian Powter as Taddeo, and Beach Babes: *The Italian Girl in Algiers*, director Colin McColl, 2009.

Karen Cargill as Isabella: *The Italian Girl in Algiers*, director Colin McColl, 2009.

The Barber of Seville

Gioachino Rossini

I was introduced to Pat Hay at the Academy and loved working with her – she's done everything, including singing many times with Scottish Opera, and her passion for opera is so great. Meeting her changed my life.

I was invited to sing a duet from *The Barber of Seville* with Roland Wood at a fundraising event at Kate and Gavin Gemmell's house. Richard Armstrong was there. I'd never sung any Rossini – I wasn't sure it was for me – so it could all have gone wrong. Afterwards, I received a call from my agent asking if I would like to sing Rosina in a new Scottish Opera production. I phoned Pat to see what she thought. I think she screamed! For 18 months we worked on the role together. She was just fantastic. Her passion and enthusiasm for the piece rubbed off on me.

During the tour when we were in Inverness I felt quite unwell with my pregnancy. I warned my colleagues that if I opened one of the drawers in the desk I was going to be sick. My friend Karin Thyselius, who was playing Berta, offered to run towards me with a basket if she saw me running upstage!

KAREN CARGILL Mezzo-soprano

I like playing *The Barber of Seville* a lot. It's one of my favourite operas. I know all the words! I had to lead but I was completely relaxed – I love Italian opera. In Italy, audiences only really want Italian opera, so I am really happy that in Scotland I have the opportunity to play a variety of operas.

GIULIA BIZZI No.2 Second Violin, The Orchestra of Scottish Opera

The Italian Girl in Algiers

Gioachino Rossini

The day that I heard I would have to ride a Segway I was quite scared. Not only did I have to drive it while wearing four-inch stilettos, I had to sing fierce coloratura and top Bs. Before every show we had a 15-minute Segway call, so I could have a ride around the set before I went into Wigs. Ultimately I became quite addicted to it. I began on the Learner setting but had it changed to the Pro so that I could alter the speed to fit the drama of what I was singing. Poor Adrian Powter was scared I would run him down!

KAREN CARGILL Mezzo-soprano

Wozzeck Alban Berg

Peter Ebert had left Scottish Opera and a production was needed quickly for the Edinburgh Festival. John Drummond and I met with Alexander Gibson and David Pountney in a cafe in Regent Street in London and we decided to approach David Alden, who had already made waves in Scotland with a very controversial 'punk' *Rigoletto*, to direct a new production of Berg's *Wozzeck*. He agreed. It had a very simple design of lines of sheets across the stage, David Alden's great mastery of directing, a terrific Benjamin Luxon, and, above all, Alex in the pit. It was one of my Top Ten operatic moments – utterly riveting.

RICHARD JARMAN Managing Director 1991–7

Opposite: Francis Egerton as the Captain, Roderick Kennedy as the Doctor: *Wozzeck*, director David Alden, 1980.

The Merry Widow Franz Lehár

I remember Catherine Wilson singing many roles for Scottish Opera. She was the perfect Merry Widow and a humorous and delightful Rosalinde in *Die Fledermaus*. She also sang in many of the Britten operas. Catherine and her late husband Leonard Hancock, who was Head of Music, were very special people in the history of the Company.

LADY GIBSON Wife of the founder of Scottish Opera

Leonard Hancock was one of the mainstays of the Company as head of the music staff. Alex and Peter depended a great deal on Leonard. I don't know of anyone at that time who knew more about the voice then he did. Leonard also had a wonderful down-to-earth sense of humour.

JOHN DUFFUS Scottish Opera administration 1971–8

Leonard was very good at being dispassionate and having independent thoughts. It was always apparent that I was another singer, rather than his wife, when we were in rehearsals. We got married in Glasgow and had a reception at Peter and Jane Hemmings' house. I'd been to Harrods and bought a cake in the shape of a ship. We were pushing the boat out!

CATHERINE WILSON Soprano

I copied the line of Catherine Wilson's costume for *The Merry Widow* from what was called The Gibson Girl line – heavily corseted and a forward figure! It was made in London by Bonn & Mackenzie. When I saw the dress at the fitting it was breathtaking.

JOHN STODDART Designer

Opposite: Catherine Wilson as Hanna Glawari, Marco Bakker as Danilo: *The Merry Widow*, director Anthony Besch, 1973.

Billy Budd Benjamin Britten

One of the best things Scottish Opera has done was Graham Vick's production of *Billy Budd*. The opera is very much about the enclosed world of the ship and Chris Dyer's design brilliantly suggested both the physical ship and a Blakean moral universe with heaven and hell. Philip Langridge, a wonderful singing actor, was terrific as Vere opposite John Tomlinson's disturbingly seductive Claggart. Mark Tinkler was a great Billy. One of the things that is so hard to cast in *Billy Budd* is a young, strikingly handsome man in the title role. Mark Tinkler had previously sung the role at the Royal Northern College of Music and had had a great personal success, and he was perfect as the golden boy.

PAUL MALONEY Staff Director 1986–8

You have to have a real knowledge about the structure of society to pull off this opera. Graham Vick captured it perfectly. And we had a great cast, including, at the revival, Simon Keenlyside, in virtually his UK debut, Philip Langridge and John Tomlinson – it was pretty glamorous. The atmosphere on stage was electric from beginning to end. I think it encapsulated everything that Benjamin Britten had wanted. It was certainly one of the high-points of my time at Scottish Opera.

RICHARD MANTLE Managing Director 1985–91

I had the great good fortune to work under the baton of Richard Armstrong for my first *Billy Budd*. He was in firm control and yet still able to give me all the latitude that a singer could wish for. That was great good luck. However, I always tended to fill the chasm in my own head between what I wanted to do with my voice and what I was able to do with physicality – not always a good idea. One of my colleagues in the chorus once said, just loud enough for me to hear, 'Somebody tell Simon it's *Billy Budd*, not bloody Billy Smart!' How we laughed.

SIMON KEENLYSIDE Baritone

People used to come into the library if they wanted a bit of peace or to listen to the singers rehearsing next door in the Rankine Hall. I remember Simon Keenlyside came in when he was playing Billy Budd, at the break in the floor run. I think he wanted to hide out of the way, and to try to keep in character for the second half.

HELEN LAMBERT Music Librarian 1977–2002

Opposite: Philip Langridge (top left above cannon) as Captain Vere, Mark Tinkler (bottom right) as Billy Budd: *Billy Budd*, director Graham Vick, 1987.

Nicholas Ransley as Normanno: *Lucia di Lammermoor*, director John Doyle, 2007.

Bülent Bezdüz as Edgardo, Andrew Schroeder (back to camera) as Enrico, Alan Fairs (with bible) as Raimondo, Sarah Pring as Alisa, Sally Silver as Lucia, Adriano Graziani as Arturo, Nicholas Ransley as Normanno: *Lucia di Lammermoor*, director John Doyle, 2007.

Lucia di Lammermoor Gaetano Donizetti

Taking John Doyle's production of *Lucia di Lammermoor* to St Petersburg in 2008 and working with some astonishing singers, including Anna Netrebko, and having Valery Gergiev prowling around was an exceptional experience. There was a 20-minute ovation on the first night. I felt hugely proud to have our work from here in Scotland being seen in front of an international audience in such a famous theatre as the Mariinsky.

DAFYDD BURNE-JONES Staff Director

Lulu Alban Berg

As a teenager in Aberdeen I was given tickets by my aunt and uncle to see Scottish Opera perform at His Majesty's Theatre. The first production I saw was *Lulu*. That performance changed my life, as it was the moment I decided that I wanted to be an opera singer. Little did I know then how big a part Scottish Opera would play in helping me to achieve my dream. When I was still a student the Royal Scottish Academy of Music and Drama, I entered the John Noble bursary competition, which was run by Scottish Opera. I won the bursary prize and this led to me being offered an audition with the Company. I was offered a three-year principal contract. The Company helped me to grow in confidence, and I gradually made the transition from student to professional. Every time I have worked at Scottish Opera, it has felt like coming home.

LISA MILNE Soprano

Stafford Dean as La Roche, Margaret Marshall as Countess
Madeleine: *Capriccio*, director John Cox, 1985.

Beverly Morgan as Lulu, Justin Lavender as the Painter, Ian McKinven
as the Professor of Medicine: *Lulu*, director John Cox, 1987.

Diana Montague as Cherubino, Margaret Marshall as Countess
Almaviva: *The Marriage of Figaro*, director John Cox, 1986.

Carmen Giannattasio as Violetta, Federico Lepre as Alfredo:
La traviata, director Sir David McVicar, 2008.

Carmen Giannattasio as Violetta, Richard Zeller as Giorgio Germont:
La traviata, director Sir David McVicar, 2008.

Carmen Giannattasio as Violetta, Alan Fairs as Dr Grenvil, Federico
Lepre as Alfredo, Katherine Allen as Flora: *La traviata*, director Sir
David McVicar, 2008.

Federico Lepre as Alfredo, Carmen Giannattasio as Violetta:
La traviata, director Sir David McVicar, 2008.

La traviata Giuseppe Verdi

The David McVicar production of *La traviata* is one that I feel will stand out in the memory of most people, for its richness and complexity, the scale of the set, the attention to detail and the quality of the music-making. I was greatly taken by it.

COLIN McCLATCHIE Chairman 2008–

I had worked with Carmen Giannattasio in Berlin and had instantly fallen in love; I thought she possessed such an extraordinary talent. So, when *La traviata* was proposed, I was determined to cast her as Violetta. Everything about the show was created with her in mind. Even the slight period shift of a few decades was done to better suit her petite but voluptuous figure to the fashions of the Belle Epoque, rather than the full, somewhat dumpy crinolines of the 1850s. In Act III, as Violetta dies of tuberculosis, Carmen was prepared to play complete loss of dignity with heart-breaking conviction. She was damp with sweat, retching blood and never really rose from her death-bed. One of the most truthful and touching moments was when Violetta finally tries to get up and dress for church. There was no big pantomime in our version; she dragged herself to her feet and then simply fell to the floor. From that moment, she wasn't going anywhere and she died in this same position, gently cradled in Alfredo's arms. In the intimate space of the Theatre Royal, we could scale down a piece that can often be overblown, visually speaking. *Traviata* happens in drawing rooms and bedrooms, not palaces! The idea for Violetta's tombstone to be the floor of the set came from a visit to the grave of the real-life Lady of the Camellias, Marie Duplessis, in Paris. The epitaph that is carved across the front of her tomb became the giant lettering that ran across our set.

SIR DAVID McVICAR Director

I really enjoyed David McVicar's *La traviata*. I think he's a wonderful director, and I would follow him across the world to see his productions.

LADY GIBSON Wife of the founder of Scottish Opera

La belle Hélène Jacques Offenbach

I met Patrice Caurier and Moshe Leiser in Long Beach to discuss *La belle Hélène*, which was the greatest fun – all the business of the Eurotunnel with the train crashing onto the stage. John Wells was wonderful to work with too and he did a very witty translation. When I knew I was leaving Scottish Opera I said to Moshe and Patrice that if I worked at another opera company they would be the first directors I invited. When I went to the Royal Opera House, I brought them in for *La Cenerentola*. Mark Elder, the conductor of that production, still says it was the most inspired decision!

RICHARD JARMAN Managing Director 1991–7

It was a party from start to finish. I adore Caurier and Leiser, they are so clever. It was a lovely cast and we had so many laughs. John Wells wrote the English translation. One line was, 'But I'll take some lipstick for my fabled lips', which was followed by a line which wasn't anything special. So I changed the second line to, 'Should the need arise to launch a thousand ships.' John rang up and said, 'Oh, clever girl!' In the Act I finale I changed a line to 'Just go my old duck, no one gives a ... damn.' John rang up again and said, 'We don't do that – terribly vulgar!' But I did it every night! It was a ball. I had the greatest time of my life in that show.

ANNE HOWELLS Mezzo-soprano

Opposite: Anne Howells
as Helen: *La belle Hélène*,
directors Patrice Caurier and
Moshe Leiser, 1995.

The Rake's Progress Igor Stravinsky

This was my reward for *Traviata*! Alex Reedjik asked me to choose a title for my next production with Scottish (something which actually doesn't happen often; the theatre will normally suggest a piece to a director). It was a long-held ambition of mine to do *The Rake's Progress* – over 20 years in fact! What we got onto the stage turned out to be the show I'd had in the back of my mind all that time. It gave the chorus a chance to shine and they truly did. The commitment with which they played the lunatics in the final Bedlam scene was something quite out of the ordinary. The rapport I've developed with the chorus over the years has been fantastic and we share a real sense of enjoyment in each other. I met the designer John MacFarlane when he designed *Julius Caesar* for Scottish Opera in 1992. I introduced myself at drinks after the show and asked for his contact details. I was quite young at the time and he wasn't all that keen! I had to say, 'But, I really *am* a director!'

We've since worked together often and I've done some of my best productions with him. I knew he would be my *Rake's Progress* designer if I ever got the chance. It needed a painter's eye and I wanted the show to depend on old-fashioned, low-tech approaches like painted flats and drops. I'd always imagined the extreme, hypertheatrical costumes and wigs but John took them to a different level. I adored working with Sian Edwards on the show. She's a very fine conductor and simply one of the nicest collaborators I've ever had. I couldn't have been happier than when I made this production.

SIR DAVID McVICAR Director

Opposite: Karen Murray as Mother Goose, Edgaras Montvidas (back to camera) as Tom Rakewell: *The Rake's Progress*, director Sir David McVicar, 2012.

Terence Sharpe as Dr Bartolo, Ludmilla Andrew as Berta: *The Barber of Seville*, 1987 revival of the 1985 Robert David MacDonald production.

The arrival of the 'Middle Eastern dictator' at the Theatre Royal, Glasgow: *Oberon*, director Graham Vick, 1985.

Patricia Hay as Karolina with well-behaved beagle: *The Two Widows*, director David Pountney, 1979.

The Barber of Seville
Gioachino Rossini

Robert David MacDonald, my colleague at the Citizens Theatre, did a really, really funny production of *The Barber of Seville* in his own very brilliant translation. I later used that translation for my production of *The Barber of Seville* at Welsh National Opera.

GILES HAVERGAL Director, Citizens Theatre 1969–2003

Robert David MacDonald's production of *The Barber of Seville* was a wonderful 1950s confection. It was designed to be as entertaining as it could be. He was determined to put every possible gag into that show. The audience loved it. Ludmilla Andrew, an incredibly famous soprano, who sang Turandot for us at one point, played Berta the maid in slacks, a sweater, horn-rimmed specs and a beret over a bob-wig dyed purple. Milla was quite an artist and Berta is a tiny role, but she stole the entire show opening bottles of beer with her teeth and singing with a lit cigarette hanging out of the corner of her mouth. She was an extraordinarily funny woman.

DAFYDD BURNE-JONES Staff Director

Oberon Carl Maria von Weber

I set that in an abandoned cinema in the middle of the desert. The show was originally a pantomime opera. Part of the nature of the piece demands visual fantasy. Its weakness is the libretto, so John Cox got Anthony Burgess to write a new one, which was a great idea. It was an unbelievably energetic show, spectacularly theatrical. On the first night we had searchlights outside the theatre, 'demonstrators' on the pavement and a 'Middle Eastern dictator' in the royal box. It was completely crazy! On that evening the audience howled and cheered. It was a wild success. La Fenice immediately bought the production for Venice. I thought it was a big breakthrough moment. Then came the reviews, which were across-the-board dreadful, and the show never recovered.

GRAHAM VICK Director of Productions 1984–7

The Two Widows Bedřich Smetana

When we toured *The Two Widows* to Newcastle, we were given a different dog from the beagle we had had in Glasgow. Each time I started to sing, the labrador began to howl so I indicated to Bill McCue to remove it from the stage as quickly as possible. Bill took the dog across stage to the wings. In the opera there is at that point a planned gunshot. Unfortunately from the audience point of view, it seemed as if the dog had been taken offstage and shot!

PATRICIA HAY Lyric Soprano

Falstaff Giuseppe Verdi

Scottish Opera has presented three productions of Verdi's final opera. The first premiered in 1966 with Sir Geraint Evans giving a definitive performance as the scheming knight; it was revived in 1976 and 1977. A new production by Ian Judge followed in 1991, with a third, by Dominic Hill, in 2008.

Unfortunately, ten days before the opening night of *Falstaff* the Costume Department found themselves without a Costume Supervisor. The costumes for *Falstaff* were in an elaborate Tudor style, but were all in pieces and unfinished. The 50 or so chorus costumes common to both *Falstaff* and *Faust* (a clever economy!) were also not nearly ready. Fortunately, one of the outside costume-makers, an Australian of indefatigable spirit named Shirley Reid, came speeding up from Windsor and took everything in hand. By the dress rehearsal, miraculously, all the chorus costumes and most of the principals' costumes had been completed. As senior cutter, Shirley was entrusted with Sir Geraint Evans' costume as Falstaff himself. Ironically, after working day and all night for over a week his was the only costume she had not quite finished. On the opening night Geraint had to be sewn into his doublet before going on stage! Like the great artist he was, he was completely relaxed and understanding.

PETER RICE Designer

In the paint shop at Stobcross Hall there was Pauline Whitehouse, her assistant Philip Bradshaw, Tom McDonald, a well-known artist, and me. In props we had Rodney Ford. I always remember Rodney and his ornamental trees for *Falstaff*. Peter Rice, the designer, needed the trees in quantity. To make them, Rodney made a basic shape with fabric and wire, then liberally applied glue to keep the foliage in place and hung the trees upside down to dry. Rodney used to appear at teabreaks dripping with glue, but quite unfazed!

PETER CROMBIE Scenic Artist

Ian Wallace as Pistol, Francis Egerton as Bardolph, Sir Geraint Evans as Falstaff: *Falstaff*, director Peter Ebert, 1966.

Sarah Walker as Mistress Quickly, Maria Prosperi as Alice Ford, Fiona Kimm as Meg Page, Gordon Sandison (in laundry basket) as Falstaff: *Falstaff*, director Ian Judge, 1991.

Patricia Hay as Nannetta, Claire Livingstone as Meg Page, Elizabeth Bainbridge as Mistress Quickly, Catherine Wilson as Alice Ford: *Falstaff*, 1976 revival of the 1966 Peter Ebert production.

Manon Jules Massenet

Manon was one of the highlights of my conducting career. I wanted to do *Manon* because I could see that the French repertoire had been neglected, apart from *Carmen*. In *Manon*, you have everything – big choruses, ballet, wonderful music – and I liked the production very much. The Orchestra and I felt very at ease doing this new repertoire. Massenet's music is more like a scent than a sound, something almost intangible. The Orchestra sounded very French.

FRANCESCO CORTI Music Director 2008–13

Opposite: Act III Scene 1, *Manon*, director Renaud Doucet, 2009.

Commissions and Premieres

New and less well-known operas have always been at the forefront of Scottish Opera's activities. In the very first season, the Company made its intentions clear with a production of Debussy's *Pelléas et Mélisande* – not exactly an obvious repertoire choice – and in 1963 presented Dallapiccola's *Volo di notte*. As recently as 2005 Scottish Opera gave the UK stage premiere of John Adams' controversial 1991 opera *The Death of Klinghoffer* at the Edinburgh International Festival.

The Company's first world premiere came in 1968 with *Full Circle* by Robin Orr, which was revived at the following year's EIF alongside the Company's second commission, *The Undertaker* by John Purser.

Through the 1970s there were notable premieres of operas by Iain Hamilton, Robin Orr, Thomas Wilson and Thea Musgrave, and the commitment to Scottish composers continued with Edward Harper's reworking of Ibsen's *Hedda Gabler* in 1985, James MacMillan's *Inés de Castro* at the 1996 EIF, David Horne's *Friend of the People* in 1999 and Sally Beamish's *Monster* in 2002. Scottish Opera marked Glasgow's year as European Capital of Culture in 1990 with the world premiere of Judith Weir's *The Vanishing Bridegroom*.

Since 2008 the innovative *Five:15 Operas Made in Scotland* project has brought together Scottish and Scottish-based composers and writers – often working in the art form for the first time – to create some of the most exciting and thought-provoking stage works of recent years, culminating in one Scottish and three world premieres at the EIF in 2012, a sure sign that new opera has played – and will continue to play – a central role at Scottish Opera.

Opposite: Winton Thomson as Eldest Son, William Peel as Bad Robber, Virginia Kerr as the Bride, Gordon Wilson as Youngest Son, Tom McVeigh as Bad Robber, Iain Paton as Middle Son: *The Vanishing Bridegroom*, director Ian Spink, 1990.

Inés de Castro James MacMillan, 1996

It took ten years from first conversation to first night. Operas have a long gestation period and that was certainly the case with *Inés de Castro*. It was in the mid-1980s when Richard Mantle and others at Scottish Opera asked about a new piece. However, I think I probably started to write it in 1993 and had it ready for 1995, for production in 1996.

I saw a stage work of John Clifford's play *Inés de Castro* at the Traverse in the late 1980s and it just seemed very operatic. It made an immediate impact on me. There was a dark, brooding, threatening atmosphere to the stage work which needed to be carried over into the opera. When I read the text of the play I noticed that the author had mentioned that there should be a sense of ritual about how the work should be staged, and of course what is opera if it is not a ritualistic form? There is a sort of background religious aura to the Inés de Castro story, and there were certain liturgical chants that kept on coming and going throughout the piece. The first piece of the text is a sort of hymn to the Virgin, so I took the Stabat Mater musical theme from plainsong and worked that into the background of the drama. Anything of a devotional character, therefore, had Mary, this suffering woman, at the heart of it, and of course *Inés de Castro* is about a woman who suffers.

It was a very exciting journey for me. I had always loved opera – Beethoven's *Fidelio* was a big influence on me when I was a youngster. It was Scottish Opera productions like *Götterdämmerung* in the early 1970s that had such an impact. I never thought then that I would write my own opera for Scottish Opera. In fact, *Inés de Castro* is dedicated to the memory of Sir Alexander Gibson, as it was his productions that I had seen as a teenager in Glasgow.

We had a very interesting and beautiful production from Jonathan Moore, which went over to Porto. It was a little bit scary taking what was basically Portugal's national story back to the country it came from. It was like a Portuguese opera company coming to Scotland with an opera about William Wallace or Robert the Bruce!

JAMES MacMILLAN Composer

Opposite: Helen Field as Inés de Castro, Amy Riach as Little Girl: *Inés de Castro*, 1999 revival of the 1996 Jonathan Moore production.

When James MacMillan was 30 or something, I asked him if he would be interested in doing a retrospective of his work as I thought it would be interesting to assess where he had got to as a composer up that point. You can do that in a festival context and I think the international audience found it interesting. So when he came to write his first major opera, I was keen, he was keen and Scottish Opera were keen to stage it at the Festival.

SIR BRIAN McMASTER Director, Edinburgh International Festival 1991–2006

I knew James MacMillan through the John Currie Singers, with whom my wife was involved, and he was writing very interesting choral music. I persuaded him to write his first opera, but the gestation took quite a while! The premiere eventually happened at the Edinburgh Festival after I had left Scottish Opera. I also worked very closely with Judith Weir on *The Vanishing Bridegroom*, which was a piece that I think was much under-rated. It was based a lot on Scottish fiddle music, was an engaging story and we had a good production. It felt like a great Scottish opera.

RICHARD MANTLE Managing Director 1985–91

I was so pleased that an emerging composer, as James MacMillan then was, had already been commissioned to compose a new opera when I became Music Director of Scottish Opera. What was exciting was watching the ideas develop, showing the right kind of encouragement and support but not getting in the way, and checking on the practicalities of staging a new work.

SIR RICHARD ARMSTRONG Music Director 1993–2005

I think *Inés de Castro* turned out to be one of the most remarkable operas to be composed over the past 30 or 40 years. James MacMillan was a very accomplished opera composer from the word Go. It was a big prize to have it premiered at the Edinburgh Festival.

RICHARD JARMAN Managing Director 1991–7

I was Bianca, Pedro's poor maligned wife. It was terrifying creating a new role – especially with James MacMillan being the local lad – but I really enjoyed it. It was a hard sing because the role was written at the extremes of my voice, but it was an exciting project.

ELIZABETH BYRNE Dramatic Soprano

This was the first new commission that I had worked on as a freelance production manager. It really opened my eyes to the power of new work in a Scottish context. I had already worked on *Visitatio Sepulchri* with Jimmy but this was the first time Scottish Opera had really embraced him. While critics had their mixed views, audiences loved his visceral offering. I loved the moment when the burnt body arrived in rehearsals and the parcel was opened. Boy, it looked real!

ALEX REEDIJK General Director 2006–

Approaches to Porto had been made before my time by John Lawson Graham and Jenny Slack. A big new venue was under construction but was not ready for tour. We performed in a huge 3,000-seat barn-like hall with a stage at one end. I remember the Scottish Opera lorries squeezing through Porto's tiny streets expertly manipulated by the Company's drivers with great aplomb!

CHRISTOPHER BARRON Chief Executive 2000–5

Opposite: Jon Garrison as Pedro: *Inés de Castro*, 1999 revival of the 1996 Jonathan Moore production.

Full Circle Robin Orr, 1968

I was heavily involved in the stage management for *Full Circle*. I helped Michael Geliot with the lantern slides and trying to get them into sync. Very ambitiously, it was decided that we would use three projectors. The slides were of scenes of Glasgow tenements and served as a backdrop for the set, which at that time was a very exciting way of visualising the production. But it was also a huge headache because, without today's technology, the stagehands just had to rely on a small cue light to tell them when to change the slides. Sometimes in rehearsal they would be upside down or out of sequence. We had to do it time and time again to get it right, but by first night it was perfect.

SARAH CHESTER née Chapman-Mortimer, Stage Management 1968–73

Alex Gibson and Bill McCue were great together. You could just sit back and let them entertain you. Bill was very proud of the fact he appeared in every season of Scottish Opera. He really was something.

ISABEL RODGER Wife of the late Ian Rodger

Bill McCue was hysterically funny, whether he was on stage or at a dinner party at Alexander Gibson's house. Bill was one of the instigators of fun. He could also break an atmosphere, which was fantastic on occasions. And he had a lovely, warm, proper bass voice. He said to me, 'Pat, I've been your father, I've been your uncle, I've been your guardian – but I've never been your lover!'

PATRICIA HAY Lyric Soprano

Opposite: Bill McCue (left)
as the Barman: *Full Circle*,
director Michael Geliot,
1968.

Candide Leonard Bernstein

Leonard Bernstein's *Candide* opened as a musical on Broadway on 1 December 1956, but flopped. Following a London production in 1959 and revivals in the US by Hal Prince, Bernstein produced a two-act version for opera companies in 1982, premiered by New York City Opera.

By 1988 Bernstein was working with John Mauceri, Scottish Opera's Music Director, on a version that would convey his final wishes. With the writers of the original book, Lillian Hellman and Hugh Wheeler, both dead, John Wells was commissioned to write a new one. Bernstein attended rehearsals in Glasgow, and the production of what has come to be known as the 'Scottish Opera Version' opened on 19 May 1988. Following its Scottish Opera run, the show transferred to the Old Vic in London, with Patricia Routledge as the Old Lady, and won two Olivier Awards.

Candide is a wonderful piece but it is fraught with problems. It never seems to work with the public. It's a crazy story which needed sorting out, really. It's a minefield of rights and negotiations. John Mauceri wanted to create a new book – not lyrics, they were sacrosanct – so we asked John Wells to write it, and Jonathan Miller to direct. It was pretty blue-chip. John wrote the book and we were summoned to the USA to read it to Leonard Bernstein. John read the book to me on the plane over, doing all the voices, and I was in tears of laughter. When we arrived we were driven up to Connecticut and read it through to Bernstein in his house. Two things I remember: the piece has two so-called Syphilis Songs. When he'd heard them, Bernstein rushed over to his piano stool and got out some music. It was a third Syphilis Song that he wanted to be included. After dinner and much drink he began to read to us the Psalms of David. Extraordinary! Then he came to Glasgow for rehearsals. We had a glamorous opening night and transferred to the Old Vic in London. It was great to be involved with those people.

RICHARD MANTLE Managing Director 1985–91

It's hard to know how to describe it. In some ways it was an absolute nightmare for me, but it was also hugely memorable. I think Bernstein had been disappointed when *Candide* was first produced on Broadway in 1956. He had a vision of how the piece should be, but lots of the music was cut and never performed. John Mauceri was a friend of Bernstein and they took the opportunity to restore as much as possible of Bernstein's music in the Scottish Opera production. However, it seemed that a lot of the decisions were being made during rehearsals, so I was constantly running to catch up! I was in daily contact with Bernstein's archivist asking for heaps of 'trunk' [cut] music to be sent over by FedEx from New York. On one occasion, Nickolas Grace, who was playing Pangloss, put his head round the door and handed me and Myra Mackay, who was assisting me, a pack of sandwiches to keep us going! The cast got the almost-final version of the vocal score on the day of the dress rehearsal.

HELEN LAMBERT Music Librarian 1977–2002

Opposite: Ann Howard as Old Lady, Marilyn Hill Smith as Cunégonde, Bonaventura Bottone as the Governor: *Candide*, directors Sir Jonathan Miller and John Wells, 1988.

Mary Queen of Scots Thea Musgrave, 1977

In Act III, Mary is a wanted person and has a baby, the future James VI. It wasn't an easy scene. I had to pick up the doll of the baby but it felt so heavy. I made a bit of a fuss and said it wasn't the right weight for a new-born baby. The maker said it was the weight I had previously asked for, but I didn't agree. We decided to have a backstage sweepstake to guess the weight of the baby. I lost!

CATHERINE WILSON Soprano

My first solo role at the Theatre Royal was in *Mary Queen of Scots* by Thea Musgrave, which I thought was rather a good piece. It had a lot of strong drama and a marvellous performance from Catherine Wilson as Mary. My first line was 'The Earl of Bothwell' — not the most sensational way to make your debut with Scottish Opera!

DONALD MAXWELL Singer

Opposite: David Hillman as Darnley, Catherine Wilson as Mary: *Mary Queen of Scots*, director Colin Graham, 1977.

Life with an Idiot Alfred Schnittke, 1992

Scottish Opera and English National Opera co-produced the UK premiere of *Life with an Idiot*. The production opened in London on 1 April 1995 and at the Theatre Royal, Glasgow on 11 May.

I was guest conducting in Holland and I read that the premiere of *Life with an Idiot* was going to take place in Amsterdam. I went along to see it and found it compelling. I was looking for contemporary pieces not known to British audiences, so I proposed that Scottish Opera secure the rights for the British premiere. It turned out that someone at English National Opera had had the same idea! So we decided to get together. The production wasn't particularly well received in London. We followed on quite soon after but didn't have the technical gremlins ENO had suffered. It is a most extraordinary piece and we did play it up for all it was worth. There was a lot of controversy about the ideas and the language. But it was wacky, very funny and very political. It was an absolute wow! We invited audience members to an after-show symposium to hear their comments and ask questions. About 400 people turned up. At the end I asked if it was right for Scottish Opera to stage this kind of show, and the response was overwhelmingly supportive.

SIR RICHARD ARMSTRONG Music Director 1993–2005

Opposite: Alasdair Elliott as Vova: *Life with an Idiot*, director Jonathan Moore, 1995.

Catherine Gayer as Christina, Lenus Carlson as Archie Weir: *Hermiston* by Robin Orr, director Toby Robertson, 1975.

Gail Pearson as Mary Wollstonecraft Godwin, Stephen Rooke as Percy Bysshe Shelley, Arlene Rolph as Jane Clairmont: *Monster* by Sally Beamish, director Michael McCarthy, 2002.

William Neill as Eilert Loevborg, Kathryn Harries as Hedda: *Hedda Gabler*, director Graham Vick, 1985.

Hedda Gabler Edward Harper, 1985

Hedda Gabler was a beautiful piece. I'd already done *Fanny Robin* and had got to know Eddie. It was a wonderful experience. I had just done *The Rape of Lucretia* at English National Opera with Kathryn Harries, and I knew she was ideal for Hedda Gabler. I got Kathryn to meet Eddie, and he wrote it for her voice. She was a remarkable and perfect actress for Hedda.

GRAHAM VICK Director of Productions 1984–7

John Shirley-Quirk as Gil-Martin, Philip Langridge as the Sinner: *The Confessions of a Justified Sinner* by Thomas Wilson, director Michael Geliot, 1976.

The Knot Garden Sir Michael Tippett

The Knot Garden, Sir Michael Tippett's third opera, premiered at the Royal Opera House in 1970. Scottish Opera presented the first UK production of the opera outside London in 2005 to mark the centenary of the composer's birth.

In many ways I have to thank Scottish Opera because they gave me my first chance to design my first big opera [*Orlando* by Handel] and my first chance to direct [*Samson and Delilah* by Saint-Saëns]. They took a risk but they were incredibly supportive and helped me a lot. I think I have an affinity with Tippett. I designed *The Midsummer Marriage* for Scottish Opera. And I loved *The Knot Garden*. It suited me because it's so crazy. You have to make your own kind of logic out of it, and it was exciting to do that.

ANTONY McDONALD Director and Designer

It was a wonderful piece of theatre, a daring and dangerous thing to do. I was very proud of it. Sometimes you have to put your neck on the line.

Opposite: Andrew Shore as Faber, Hilton Marlton as Dov: *The Knot Garden*, director Antony McDonald, 2005.

CHRISTOPHER BARRON Chief Executive 2000–5

I proudly listen to the first complete opera recordings made by the Company, *Regina* and *Street Scene*, and working with Decca's great engineers and producers who have preserved some of the magic of that time we were together. Our Josephine Barstow album brings me renewed pleasure every time I hear it. What sounds we made in Govan Town Hall. How the orchestra played! The chorus was impeccable.

JOHN MAUCERI Music Director 1987–93

John Mauceri left an interesting legacy. He conducted repertoire the Company would never have tackled if he hadn't been Music Director and persuaded people to invest in it.

JENNY SLACK Director of Planning 1986–2010

Opposite: Rebecca de Pont Davies as An Actor, Toby Stafford-Allen as Chao Sun, Jane Harrington as Little Moon: *A Night at the Chinese Opera* by Judith Weir, director Lee Blakeley, 2008.

Fiona Kimm as Olga Olsen, Elaine MacKillop as Greta Fiorentino, Meriel Dickinson as Emma Jones: *Street Scene* by Kurt Weill, director David Pountney, 1989.

Theresa Merritt as Addie, Otis Munyangiri as Chinky-Pin, Susan Roberts as Alexandra Giddens: *Regina* by Marc Blitzstein, director Robert Carsen, 1991.

Five:15 Operas Made in Scotland 2008–10

I bumped into Craig Armstrong at a performance in 2006, who looked most bemused when I suggested he was late with his new work – that was the moment that sparked *Five:15* and led to the real discussions about building 'opera muscles' here in Scotland. Then I met David MacLennan at a party and he suggested Òran Mór as the perfect venue for the inaugural season. I brought together Michael McCarthy as dramaturg and Derek Clark, our Head of Music, as conductor, and with their input began to believe that we might just pull this off – and we did! We tapped into the creative juices of so many Scottish writers and composers who suddenly realised that their aspirations to ascend the summit of composition might just be realised – great people like Craig, Sandy McCall Smith, Ian Rankin, Nigel Osborne and Suhayl Saadi, and of course, later on, the discovery of and growth of our relationship with Stuart MacRae and Louise Welsh that led to winning the South Bank Sky Arts Award and a nomination for an Olivier.

ALEX REEDIJK General Director 2006–

I've premiered 15 new 15-minute operas. It's very exciting when something new lands on your desk and you don't know what it's going to be like. You open it – and then you panic! But the principals of The Orchestra of Scottish Opera have become very adept at playing these pieces and in a sense we discovered them together. It was challenging, but the whole project for me was definitely one of the highlights of my time so far at Scottish Opera.

DEREK CLARK Head of Music and Five:15 Conductor

The Company has to be innovative. We can't just produce the same pot-boilers all the time. One of the recent ways of how to innovate was the *Five:15* journey. It allowed the Company to innovate in a relatively risk-free manner and showcase talent in a way that wouldn't have been possible in a main opera production. It also brought Scottish Opera in contact with composers and authors who wouldn't normally be associated with the art form. I couldn't help but be impressed by the international interest that the *Five:15* project attracted. *Five:15* has given Scottish Opera an international dimension and an international reputation, and resulted in international collaborations.

COLIN McCLATCHIE Chairman 2008–

Sometimes there is a feeling that the Company does hard new work in difficult times. But if national companies don't take the lead, it is much less likely that there will be any new work. The involvement of Scottish writers has been a big draw. I think the new formula that Alex Reedijk devised has worked very well. People are copying it everywhere!

JENNY SLACK Director of Planning 1986–2010

Top row: Kate Valentine with Ashley Neilson: *The King's Conjecture*, 2008; Elizabeth McCormack and Wajahat Khan: *The Queens of Govan*, 2008; Alexander Grove and Lise Christensen: *Dream Angus*, 2008.
Second row: Paul Keohone and Lise Christensen: *The Perfect Woman*, 2008; Kate Valentine and Alexander Grove: *Gesualdo*, 2008; Richard Rowe: *The Lightning-Rod Man*, 2009.
Third row: Phil Gault and Lise Christensen: *Happy Story*, 2009; Mary O'Sullivan and Arlene Rolph: *White*, 2009; Lise Christensen, Richard Rowe and Arlene Rolph: *Death of a Scientist*, 2009.
Fourth row: Mary O'Sullivan: *Remembrance Day*, 2009; Miranda Sinani and Dean Robinson: *Zen Story*, 2010; Lee Bissett and Kally Lloyd-Jones: *Sublimation*, 2010.
Fifth row: Alexander Grove and Martin Lamb: *The Money Man*, 2010; Jeremy Huw Williams: *74° North*, 2010; Lee Bissett: *The Letter*, 2010.

Touring
the Nation

In September 1966 twelve singers from Scottish Opera began a 76-date, three-production tour of Scotland and the North of England as part of the Arts Council-promoted Opera for All venture — an undertaking that would become a first template for the Company's touring throughout Scotland in subsequent years.

From the early days of Scottish Opera Go Round in the late 1970s, through productions of such unlikely operas as *Jenůfa* and *Don Carlos* in the 1980s, to hugely popular recent productions of *Cinderella* and *The Merry Widow* and the ongoing four-singers-and-a-pianist *Essential Scottish Opera/Opera Highlights* tours, opera has been — and continues to be — a regular artistic staple in Scotland, welcomed by perennially enthusiastic audiences in village halls, community centres, theatres and concert halls right across the country.

Every Autumn and Spring, vans and minibuses are packed with sets, costumes, lighting, a piano — and of course the singers and pianist — in a bid to take opera to the furthest parts of the country, from Shetland to the Borders and from the Outer Hebrides to Galloway. Indeed, for the past 40 years and more, nationwide touring has been in Scottish Opera's DNA.

Opposite: Omar Ebrahim as Macbeth, David Marsh as Banquo: *Macbeth*, Scottish Opera Go Round, director Richard Jones, 1987.

I sang solos with the Glasgow Grand, and indeed with Edinburgh Grand, which Richard Telfer, one of the original founders of Scottish Opera, had set up. So I was already known. From 1966 I gave up my job and became a singer with Opera for All. For the next few years I worked 35 weeks a year for Scottish Opera – major roles in Opera for All and supporting roles with the main company. We had seven weeks' rehearsal for the three Opera for All shows. We were very fortunate in the first season because Geoffrey Gilbertson, a stage manager from Glyndebourne, produced the *Cinderella* himself and rehearsed Peter Ebert's *Madam Butterfly* and Anthony Besch's *Così fan tutte*. I got many elements of stagecraft from them.

JOHN ROBERTSON Singer

Opera for All was a commando course. We travelled miles and miles over Scotland and England in all weathers in the Winter. The chaps had to put up the set and lighting with the help of two technical staff and the girls had to do ironing if there weren't volunteer people there to do it. We also had to dress the wigs and get everything else organised. You had to have good health and an iron constitution.

ANN BAIRD Singer, and Manager Opera for Youth and Opera Go Round

The singers would load and unload the van. We became very adept at loading the van quickly but carefully after shows in order to get out for last orders. There were three tours each year, each of thirteen weeks all over the UK. We shared out the driving of the minibus, and the wagon with the sets was driven either by the Company Manager or the Chief Technician. It was a great learning experience.

JOHN LAWSON GRAHAM Scottish Opera 1963–2005

Opposite: The cast and crew of the 1985 Scottish Opera Go Round production of *Carmen* show off their means of transport. Opera for All casts travelled in a similar fashion.

Peter Hemmings was a hard taskmaster, but as Jane, his wife, said, 'He doesn't work anyone harder than he does himself.' He was very supportive, coming out to see what was going on. He would come to visit us on Opera for All tours – I've seen Peter helping to load up the van. I remember one evening of *The Barber of Seville*, I sang my little heart out for him as Rosina and at the end of the performance he said, 'Yes, very good, but your petticoat was hanging down!'

ANN BAIRD Singer, and Manager Opera for Youth and Opera Go Round

I played Madam Butterfly in the Opera for All production directed by Peter Ebert. In rehearsal, the emotion of the piece started to get to me. Peter stopped the rehearsal and said, 'Pat, your job is not to get upset. Your job is to convey the emotion, felt by the character, to the audience and still be detached enough to read the time on the clock at the back of the hall.' It was the best advice!

PATRICIA HAY Lyric Soprano

I'm ever impressed by the level of affection and ownership shown to the Company throughout Scotland and don't know of anywhere else where this is so methodically and enthusiastically achieved in any art form.

CHRISTOPHER BARRON Chief Executive 2000–5

The great thing about Scottish Opera Go Round is that all the productions are conceived specifically for that scale of performance with complete integrity. Very early on you forget that the accompaniment is just a piano – the pianists are usually brilliant at evoking the orchestral colours of the score – and you are invariably in a small, very intimate auditorium with a really good cast of singing actors: it's completely compelling. Some of the most exciting performances I've seen have been under those circumstances.

It's interesting to see the calibre of people who directed and designed for Opera Go Round and went on to wider success elsewhere: Keith Warner directed *Tosca* and *Carmen* for Opera Go Round, Richard Jones did a fantastic *Macbeth*, designed by Nigel Lowery, and Matthew Richardson, Antony McDonald and Ian Spink all directed brilliant, often quite radical, productions. Mark Tinkler, who played Billy Budd on the main stage, later directed *The Grand Duchess of Gerolstein* for Opera Go Round.

PAUL MALONEY Staff Director 1986–8

The pianists are some of the most talented people in the Company, because they have to have the skills to play the piano, be able to coach in other languages, the ability to hear what the singers are doing, the knowledge to be able to coach properly and sing in other parts, and the sensitivity to know how best to do that. They are the most brilliant all-rounders.

Mark Dorrell played the piano for the Opera Go Round tour of *Don Carlos* – absolutely staggering! For the first couple of performances he was a complete wreck. But by the end of the tour his endurance was so great that he stayed out with the audience during the interval and had a cup of tea brought to him.

LORNA MURRAY General Manager, Scottish Opera Go Round 1988–99

I really loved doing *Essential Scottish Opera*. There's no doubt you learn what your tolerances are when you're in a minibus with five other people touring around Scotland for seven weeks. The tour taught me so much about coping vocally and how to look after yourself. It was a great endurance test!

KAREN CARGILL Mezzo-soprano

John Hall as Philip II, Adrian Clarke as Rodrigo, Anne Williams-King as Elizabeth de Valois: *Don Carlos*, Scottish Opera Go Round, director David Walsh, 1988.

Colin McKerracher as Beppe, Sylvia Mitton as Nedda: *I Pagliacci*, Scottish Opera Go Round, director Mike Ashman, 1989.

René Linnenbank as Osmin, Iain Paton as Pedrillo: *Seraglio*, Scottish Opera Go Round, director Nick Broadhurst, 1992.

Huw Rhys-Evans as Fritz, Carol Rowlands as the Grand Duchess: *The Grand Duchess of Gerolstein*, Scottish Opera Go Round, director Mark Tinkler, 1994.

Regina Haley as Emilia Marty, Tom McVeigh as Baron Jaroslav Prus: *The Makropoulos Case*, Scottish Opera Go Round, director Antony McDonald, 1998.

Felicity Hammond as Gretel: *Hansel and Gretel*, Scottish Opera Go Round, director Gordon Anderson, 2000.

Nicholas Ransley as Ramiro, Caryl Hughes as Angelina: *Cinderella*, director Harry Fehr, 2008.

Stephanie Corley as Hanna Glawari, with admirers: *The Merry Widow*, director Clare Whistler, 2009.

Peter Quilliam-Cain gave me two bits of excellent advice. The first: Always say that the radio in the Company van is broken. This stopped everyone arguing over the music choice. The second: Something will always turn up. And even when we needed to get a piano up the steps into the Aros Hall in Tobermory, something did turn up — a passing rugby team!

LORNA MURRAY General Manager, Scottish Opera Go Round 1988–99

I remember many miserable B&B rooms on tour with coin-in-the-slot machines for heat and hot water which frequently failed in the bitterest weather; my tiny apartment in Queen's Park with its ridiculous Baby Belling; and nine holes of golf early each morning in Helensburgh with stunning views of the Clyde on one side and Loch Lomond on the other, followed by a hasty dash by train to Elmbank Crescent for a 10.30 call. The Scottish train journeys were always a delight, especially those in the Highlands and the first train south with a piping hot breakfast as we trundled over Beattock summit.

GRAHAM CLARK Tenor

Matthew Richardson produced a superb *Jenůfa* for Opera Go Round. It toured for a year and got deservedly stunning reviews, then it was revived for the Brighton Festival where it won awards. It was an extremely powerful show because, being piano-accompanied and so close, all became deeply involved in the drama. Brenda Hurley was the repetiteur – simply an outstanding pianist coupled with an outstanding cast. A show that lived with me for many years.

PETER QUILLIAM-CAIN Stage Manager

I started working on Opera Go Round in 1988. I always wanted that job as I thought it was the best job in the world – and it turned out that it was. Later on I bought the Opera Go Round piano and it's still in my house – it had done seven tours and 35,000 miles! The top is reinforced, I think because someone in the cast had to stand on top of it in *Jenůfa*.

LORNA MURRAY General Manager, Scottish Opera Go Round 1988–99

Opposite: Virginia Kerr as Jenůfa: *Jenůfa*, Scottish Opera Go Round, director Matthew Richardson, 1986.

Pioneering Education and Outreach

Of Scottish Opera's four core activities – main-stage productions, smaller-scale touring, new commissions, education and outreach – it is perhaps the latter that is least visible to regular audiences. Yet every year the work of the Scottish Opera Education Department provides thousands of schoolchildren, young people and those who may not be able to access the Arts by conventional means – of whatever age – with the opportunity to create, perform and explore this most all-encompassing of the art forms in ways that are relevant to them.

But this isn't a new development. Since the early 1970s Scottish Opera has been taking opera into schools, workplaces and community centres, with the emphasis on participation and collaboration with professional performers and creative teams, often in ambitious touring productions.

Today the department has broadened its work, from the enchanting *BabyO* for the Under 18 Months, through *SensoryO* for toddlers, via the ever-popular Primary Schools tour to *AerialO*, the Company's innovative ongoing project in which able-bodied and disabled schoolchildren 'buddy up' to perform in midair.

The acclaimed Connect Company has developed over recent years as a stimulating introduction to performing opera – both as singers and musicians – for those aged 14 to 21.

Scottish Opera continues its annual collaboration with the Royal Conservatoire of Scotland (formerly the RSAMD) on a main-stage production, and auditions a handful of graduates each year to join its Emerging Artists programme, providing an all-important bridge between the academic and professional worlds.

Opposite: Pupils from Hutchesons' Grammar School, Glasgow, perform *The Legend of Slim McBride and the Lost Tribe*: Primary Schools tour, 2013.

Ainslie Millar felt very strongly that something ought to be done at an education and outreach level. He wanted opera to go out to schools and there had been occasional performances, but I think it was felt that something a bit more permanent was required. An advertisement appeared for somebody to set up an educational unit for Scottish Opera. That person should have academic qualifications and theatrical experience. I got the job. I believed that if you want to get young people interested, you have to get them involved, so I went the workshop route. I was awarded seed money from the Carnegie Trust and the workshops were bought in by outside organisations, Education departments, community centres and, in England, Regional Arts Associations, particularly in Newcastle and the Northern Arts area. My first real ally was Kirsty Adam, the head of Arts in Fife, and Strathclyde Region was very supportive and allowed us to visit all six divisions. At the end of every workshop, the children were given a badge saying, 'Scottish Opera. I am an opera singer', of which they were inordinately proud.

I contacted Peter Naylor, teacher of harmony and counterpoint at the RSAMD, who was also a composer. I described what I wanted. A workshop that had to be very simple, very melodic and be able to be learned very quickly. It had to include simple fugues and rounds, so that the children could make a big ensemble sound. For the libretto I asked Cliff Hanley, the writer and broadcaster, who I knew through the light music side of Radio Scotland, who got quite excited about it all. I gave him the structure and he came back with *The Mountain People* – the Picts, the Scots and the Romans. Each group of approximately 30 children had their own bit to perform. The climax was an exciting, energetic mock battle!

We premiered in Elmbank Crescent with a hundred children, with me conducting like a demented windmill. When I looked round, Alex Gibson had a grin on his face from ear to ear. He was so supportive. In addition to the piano accompaniment, played by Peter himself, we had two tables with percussion instruments ranging from triangles to tubes with macaroni inside and strings of foil bottle tops. The teachers tended to put the four rowdiest children on percussion as they felt that it would be a control and they wouldn't be able to run around and create havoc. Peter was never conscious of this. He didn't know that he had the unruly kids. He'd say, 'Excuse me, would you mind awfully, when I nod my head would you bang that drum?', which got the reply, 'Aye, all right.' He treated them so beautifully that they all worked for him perfectly.

We then went on to commission *London's Burning*. I worked on that with Ann Sandison [now actress Ann Louise Ross], Gordon Hunter and composer Frank Spedding, also of the RSAMD.

ANN BAIRD Singer, and Manager Opera for Youth and Opera Go Round

Opposite: *London's Burning*, 1974.

We got a grant from the Manpower Commission to employ 11 people for a year. The idea of the Company was to go across the board, touring the Highlands and Islands with piano-accompanied performances and to go into factories. It was a huge success. They were heady days — we were absolutely flying. We were taking real, bold work out around the whole of Scotland — powerful, modern productions. We had a success in village halls with the types of productions that had caused a furore in the Theatre Royal with *Don Giovanni*! Audiences came across the country to have an experience.

GRAHAM VICK Director of Productions 1984–7

We would go out to places like IBM, with a tiny, one-foot-high platform, two lights, three girls, a tenor, a pianist and two technicians, and put on a show. I suppose it was a bit like Wilfred Pickles' show during the '40s and '50s, *Workers' Playtime*. We would perform to between 100 and 200 people in canteens during the cacophony of lunchtime.

PETER QUILLIAM-CAIN Stage Manager

In 1984 I was a 23-year-old graduate Secondary/Primary teacher in English Literature and Theatre Studies. I saw an ad for what was the first Scottish Opera post of Education Officer. It was set up with part funding from what was then Strathclyde Regional Council. At that time the Director of Productions was an almost-as-young Graham Vick. At my interview he asked me if I had any ideas for getting opera out to new audiences. I suggested getting a flat-bed lorry and taking performances into communities, and I think that might have clinched it for me!

I felt we should broaden out beyond the Primary Schools tour to work with adults, young people and children, so we did a whole series of community partnerships. We worked with Highland Regional Council and did a couple of large site-specific pieces. We worked with the Northern Ireland Arts Council, who wanted us to go and work in areas that had virtually no tradition of what is sometimes perceived as the 'high arts' — such as opera. We gained Peace and Reconciliation funding as well as support from The Peter Moores Foundation, and worked with communities on both sides of the border. The shows were developed in partnership with the local communities and were about things that had local relevance. In one of the Irish shows we looked into the strong tradition — for much of the 20th century — of the dance halls, which was how people, especially in rural communities, met up and socialised. We based our piece on William Trevor's wonderful short story *The Ballroom of Romance* — it had as much relevance to teenagers as it did to folks in their seventies. In Ballymena we cast a teenage girl who had the most amazing untrained voice — so amazing that we wrote a piece for her.

JANE DAVIDSON Director of Outreach & Education

Opposite: *Belfast Life*, 2000.

The Elephant Angel

In 1982, Carl Davis and John Wells wrote *Peace*, which was based on Greek myth. It needed five principal singers and a chorus of secondary school students, and toured round schools. Over 30 years later, *The Elephant Angel*, by Scottish Opera's Composer in Residence Gareth Williams, is an almost direct descendant of *Peace*, in that it has principal singers, plus a chorus of primary school children that changes with each new venue, though this time it has been performed in small theatres and the children have promoted their own performance to their local community.

JANE DAVIDSON Director of Outreach & Education

Opposite: Scottish Opera Emerging Artist 2011/12 Marie Claire Breen and pupils from East Renfrewshire Junior Choir perform *The Elephant Angel*, director Lissa Lorenzo, 2012.

Auntie Janet Saves the Planet

Auntie Janet Saves the Planet was the first in a series of three interactive 'eco' operas for Under 5s! Auntie Janet, a lonely chicken and her new-found friends Sergeant George the brown hare, Mavis the song thrush and Madame Pipistrelle the soprano bat went on a quest to stop the bulldozers destroying their part of the forest. This production enabled us to plug into government priorities for early years learning, such as numeracy and literacy, as well as citizenship and biodiversity issues. It was a good example of producing work to a very high artistic standard which also subtly addressed various social issues.

JANE DAVIDSON Director of Outreach & Education

Opposite: Frances Morrison Allen as Madame Pipistrelle, Katie Punter as Mavis and Steven Struthers as Sergeant George: *Auntie Janet Saves the Planet*, 2009.

We became aware that there was very little performance work for infants and wanted to create a piece using classically trained voices that would enable parents to introduce their babies, and later on toddlers, to sound and song. Since 2009, *BabyO* has become a phenomenon, in demand at international arts festivals in Hong Kong, Abu Dhabi, Australia and New Zealand, as well as the UK. It's become our best export!

ALEX REEDIJK General Director 2006–

In 2002 the Minister of Culture made a speech announcing that the Scottish Executive was looking for exciting initiatives to reintroduce the work of Robert Burns to Scottish children. Working with North Ayrshire and East Ayrshire councils, we commissioned Karen McIver and Ross Stenhouse to create a version of *Tam o' Shanter*. We did it four times in different parts of Scotland and children from the USA, Norway, Finland and Germany came to learn and perform it alongside Scottish children. It already felt quite international in that sense, and then it went to the 2010 Commonwealth Games in Delhi and was performed there for the First Minister. The following year we heard that the First Minister was going to China, so we took it there too. We discovered in China that when you press the button at pedestrian crossings you hear 'Coming through the rye'. So subliminally the Chinese have been getting Robert Burns all their lives! *Tale o' Tam* has done an amazing ambassadorial job for Scottish Opera.

JANE DAVIDSON Director of Outreach & Education

Karen McIver conducts Nadine Livingston and Iain Paton as they perform *Tale o' Tam* with No.4 School, Beijing, China, 2011.

Adam Miller and members of Scottish Opera's Connect Company perform *Dr Ferret's Bad Medicine Roadshow* at the Citizens Theatre, Glasgow, 2011.

I think the orchestra gets a lot out of its relationship with the Royal Conservatoire of Scotland. It's good to work with young people and I think the ongoing collaboration between Scottish Opera and the Conservatoire is much more hands-on and inclusive than partnerships elsewhere. You get to know the students very well across a whole run of performances in major theatres.

ANTHONY MOFFAT Leader, The Orchestra of Scottish Opera

During my third year studying at the Royal Scottish Academy of Music and Drama I was chosen to play alongside The Orchestra of Scottish Opera during the production of *Cinderella*. You learn fast and become most skilled from being in contact with seasoned professionals.

EMMA STEVENSON Viola, The Orchestra of Scottish Opera

Opposite: Natalie Montakhab as the Vixen, Elin Pritchard as the Fox: RSAMD and Scottish Opera co-production, *The Cunning Little Vixen*, 2011.

James Birchall (left of main group) as Dolokhov, Andrew McTaggart (2nd left), The Robertson Trust Scottish Opera Emerging Artist 2012/14, as Matveyev, Vahagn Margaryan (centre) as Tikhon Shcherbaty, Benjamin Vale (2nd right) as Prince Andrei's Orderly, Nicholas Morris (right) as Lt Colonel Vassily Denisov: RSAMD and Scottish Opera co-production, *War and Peace*, 2010. This production marked the world premiere of the original version of Prokofiev's *War and Peace*, edited by Rita McAllister.

In running wardrobe, a very rewarding part of our work is the Touch Tours. On *Manon* some of the costumes were hired and some were made by Scottish Opera. One blind lady could tell the difference in quality between the two, and pointed out a problem with one of the hired costumes!

GLORIA DEL MONTE Wardrobe Mistress

Opposite: Rhys Jenkins as Rigoletto with Head of Music Derek Clark and The Orchestra of Scottish Opera, *Rigoletto* Unwrapped, Festival Theatre, Edinburgh, 2011.

Behind the Scenes

To stage opera requires a team – a huge team – of administrators and planners; costume, wigs, set, props and lighting technicians; music rehearsal and stage management staff; marketers, publicists and fundraisers; and of course the director, designer and conductor.

This section takes a peek behind the façades of Scottish Opera's present premises in Glasgow, at Elmbank Crescent and Edington Street, as well as Stobcross Hall, which played such an important role in the Company's early years. There are also some famous visitors, a couple of high-profile publicity stunts, a glimpse into the artists' dressing rooms and quite literally the 'inside story' on the infamous Trojan Horse.

And this is where you can see a little of what goes on in the rehearsal room, with a number of directors at work, as well as see the Company's three Music Director successors to Sir Alexander Gibson, and The Orchestra of Scottish Opera through the years.

Opposite: Inside the costume store at Scottish Opera's Production Studios, Edington Street, Glasgow.

John Wells and Richard Ingrams hunched over my tiny press office typewriter, giggling like schoolboys as they compose the next instalment of Dear Bill letters for *Private Eye*. Wells, who has written the hilarious libretto for Scottish Opera's *La vie Parisienne*, is living in Glasgow for the six-week rehearsal period; Ingrams has flown in from London to remind him he also has magazine deadlines to meet. A cerebral Jonathan Miller gliding about elegantly, mostly with his jaw artfully cupped in his hands as he examines the stage for imperfections in his new *The Magic Flute*. Accompanying a defiant Graham Vick to be interviewed by Kirsty Wark for the BBC Scotland current affairs programme *Seven Days,* to justify putting a toilet on stage for his production of *Don Giovanni*. A wan Margaret Marshall standing mid-stage in an exquisite peach organza gown to deliver her heart-rending 'Porgi, amor' as the Countess in the John Byrne-designed production of *The Marriage of Figaro*. And my most enduring memory is Sir Alexander Gibson at the podium, arms aloft and facial expression inscrutable as he conducts his final *Madama Butterfly*; the light from the pit casts the shadow of his hands upwards across the darkened auditorium in a perfectly magical moment.

CATE DEVINE Press Officer 1984–8

I worked as Company Manager in pre-technological times, the mid-'80s. Thursdays were a nightmare because I had to do the schedule on the typewriter – every mistake had to be sorted out with TippEx and we were co-ordinating wardrobe calls, coaching sessions and rehearsals for three productions at a time. When a director wanted to change a rehearsal call, I had to phone everybody, and this was before answering machines were widespread and well before mobiles! When the Company was on tour, I couldn't leave the company office because that was the only place people could reach me. Luckily, there was a steady stream of people coming and going, including Hazel Hunter and Helen McLeod, the Wigs ladies, so it was never dull.

LORNA MURRAY Company Manager 1986–8

Opposite: 39 Elmbank Crescent, Glasgow, built in 1907 for the Institution of Engineers and Shipbuilders in Scotland, has been Scottish Opera's administrative headquarters since 1968.

May and Davie McKinnon ruled Elmbank Crescent with a rod of iron. They provided coffee in the morning and tea in the afternoon. John Shirley-Quirk was once foolish enough to ask if there was a choice in the afternoon. The response was, 'Aye, you can take it or leave it!'

CLAIRE LIVINGSTONE Singer

May and Davie come straight to mind when I remember Scottish Opera. At big parties there would be Scottish country dancing and May would be handed from one partner to another to stop her falling on the floor. She was magnificent!

GRAHAM VICK Director of Productions 1984–7

We had a number of dinners at Elmbank Crescent for chief executives of companies who we thought would be interested in donating to the Theatre Royal refurbishment funds. For these, we brought in outside caterers. Getting agreement for the caterers to use May's kitchen took longer than contract negotiations with some singers!

JOHN DUFFUS Scottish Opera administration 1971–8

When I started I had two assistants – Rita and Betty. They were not in any way sympathetic to the Company and were scandalised by everything that happened in it. I would get them to write the cheques, and would hand over a list of singers and roles, and the appropriate amounts. They would write a fee slip for each cheque, I would take the cheques to the theatre, and one of the Company directors would sign the cheques at the interval. We had one occasion where a cheque was made out to Don Basilio! When I later pointed this out to Betty, she said, 'Well, if you can have Don Garrard singing Pimen in *Boris Godunov*, why can't you have Don Basilio singing Bill McCue?' How do you answer that?

RENTON THOMSON Company Accountant 1966–74

Building sets for *Albert Herring* at Stobcross Hall, Glasgow, with Willie Corr (far right), 1966.

Arthur More, Head of Wardrobe, supervising the making of costumes at Stobcross Hall, 1966.

Bruce Millar, son of Ainslie and Morag Millar, sewing at Stobcross Hall.

Technical directors are very often large personalities. Scottish Opera's special variety in the '70s was a slender, wiry Irishman who was the only person I have ever actually seen being flown up into the air holding on to the curtain during the applause. Pip Flood-Murphy was at least as eccentric as his name suggests, and coped with a mixture of blarney, charm, desperation, pure physical muscle and subtle behind-the-scenes manoeuvring with the monstrous demands of touring the *Ring*, or doing a repertoire such as I remember one week in Liverpool: 'Das Turn of La Magic Herring' – *Das Rheingold*, *The Turn of the Screw*, *La traviata*, *The Magic Flute* and *Albert Herring*!

DAVID POUNTNEY Director of Productions 1975–80

I came to Scottish Opera in 1975. My first job was making a giant teabag out of muslin so that the caterers could put it in their urn!

GLORIA DEL MONTE Wardrobe Mistress

We had been working very long hours at our workshop in Cowlairs in order to get a set finished, and we were all very tired. Roddy Fraser, our head of department, was looking at some design drawings by holding them up to his face as if reading a newspaper. Unfortunately he also had a cigarette in his mouth and then presumably nodded off, because all of a sudden there was a burnt hole in the middle of the drawings. We all stood around whistling the theme from the TV show *Bonanza*, which opens in similar fashion. Roddy woke up, put out the flames and eventually saw the funny side of things.

BRIAN THOMPSON Carpenter

Stobcross Hall had at least three floors: a ground floor suitable as a scenery shop with good height and enough space to allow a set to be erected and for painters to operate; a basement refurbished with a painting floor and I think room for a bit of modest scene painting round the edges; and an upstairs area used for music rehearsals. It must have been here that the segments of ramp for *Die Walküre* were assembled for I remember one evening (and probably into the following early morning) texturing them with some strange grey goo whose nature I have long forgotten.

Albert Herring was designed by Adam Pollock, a Swinging Sixties interior designer and Anthony Besch protégé. I had to paint the standing set upright and it was no fun doing lettering on the gauze of the windows while standing on steps. Learner though I still was, it struck me that this was a mighty heavy set to take on tour. It had been built by master carpenter Willie Corr, who was quite a character. I am sure Willie had checked what would load onto a pantechnicon but had not paid enough attention to the doors of Stobcross Hall. Unfortunately, the shop sets for *Albert Herring* wouldn't go through them. So Willie cut the set in two. Not vertically – horizontally!

PETER CROMBIE Scenic Artist

I have been privileged to sing with Scottish Opera since 1983. I have many memories of great successes but there have also been hilarious incidents. The chorus are sometimes offstage for long periods, particularly in Mozart operas, and it can be easy to miss calls to the stage. On one occasion the chorus was assembled in the Green Room but the chatter completely blocked out the call. The set had a double door which when opened should have revealed the chorus but instead opened on just one tenor who then decided to go on and give a solo rendition of the tenor line!

DAVID MORRISON Singer

Inside the Costume Department at Scottish Opera's Production Studios, Edington Street, Glasgow, which were purpose-built in 1997 with the help of National Lottery funding.

Costume Department, Production Studios.

Inside the workshop at Scottish Opera's Production Studios, Edington Street, Glasgow.

Paul Goodwin rehearses The Orchestra of Scottish Opera for *Orlando* at Edington Street, Glasgow, 2011.

We had at least 60 pairs of stockings for *The Rake's Progress* that had to be washed and couldn't be tumble-dried, so they had to be dried overnight and then all paired up. Everything has to be marked with the singer's initials – on stockings, we mark the toes.

GLORIA DEL MONTE Wardrobe Mistress

I was tempted out of retirement, having sung in opera choruses for well over 50 years, to take part in *Aida*. As priests we wore long black cassocks, but underneath we wore black plastic trousers that seemed to be made out of bin bags, inside which we sweated greatly. In response to our complaints, the Wardrobe Department simply cut the trousers at the crotch, an action that brought advice – too late – from out front that we should wear black underpants for all performances!

IAIN McGLASHAN Extra Chorus member 1978–2012

What makes me proudest of Scottish Opera, now that many of the industries such as shipbuilding have gone, is that through our workshops we still have a company that makes things using traditional crafts. I think that is something that doesn't get sung about enough!

JOHN DUNCAN Stage Manager

Her Majesty The Queen was with us in 1990, the year Glasgow was Europe's City of Culture. Our short concert included excerpts from *Carmen* (Prince Philip said of my conducting style, 'You gave a new meaning to 'Lords a-leaping') as well as the opportunity to perform Walton's *Orb and Sceptre*, which had been composed for Her Majesty's coronation. A brief cocktail party one week later with Prime Minister Thatcher proved to be an object lesson in how a great politician is really a great artist, improvising on everything each of us said to her and using it in her speech back to us.

JOHN MAUCERI Music Director 1987–93

Opposite: Her Royal Highness The Duchess of Gloucester, Patron of Scottish Opera, inspects props for *Manon* with General Director Alex Reedijk and Technical & Operations Director Steve Green at the Company's Production Studios, 2009.

Her Majesty The Queen, attended by Peter Ebert (extreme left), meets dignitaries including Theatre Manager David Jackson (right) after a performance of *Fiddler on the Roof* at the Theatre Royal, Glasgow on 1 November 1980.

Amoco were sponsoring *The Marriage of Figaro* in Aberdeen and Thomson Smillie had persuaded us all to visit a North Sea oil rig. I don't like flying but Thomson said it was only a hop and a skip. It was an hour – with your life jacket on and no alcohol allowed!

CLAIRE LIVINGSTONE Singer

I was a student and I had been working as a stagehand at the King's Theatre on the Calum Kennedy summer show. When that show finished, Scottish Opera came into the theatre. I was on the stage crew of three productions: Anthony Besch's *Der Rosenkavalier*, David Pountney's *The Magic Flute* and *Elegy for Young Lovers*, which was designed by Ralph Koltai. You changed the scenery overnight, lit the show during the day, did the show, then started all over again. I didn't leave the theatre for two weeks. I used to sleep on a pile of black curtains in the back dock! The Koltai set for *Elegy for Young Lovers* was enormous and made out of scaffolding and large Perspex blocks. You had to climb the scaffolding and lock the blocks onto it, to create a large pyramid. It looked incredible but it was very dangerous. The *Rosenkavalier* set was much more traditional with theatre flats that you cleated together with ropes – there was skill involved in that which it took me a while to learn. From the wings I got to hear and learn three very different operas. It was a splendid apprenticeship, carried out with a hammer and a screwdriver.

DAFYDD BURNE-JONES Staff Director

I was 21 and I had come to Glasgow for the first time. It was quite scary in the evenings on Stobcross Street. It was down by the river and if you had to go down there alone in the dark it was quite a challenge.

SARAH CHESTER née Chapman-Mortimer, Stage Management 1968–73

Claire Livingstone (left) with Cynthia Buchan and Malcolm Donnelly during their flying visit to an Amoco oil rig in the North Sea, 1987.

The stage crew build the set of *Elegy for Young Lovers*, 1970.

Preparing two sculptures for the set of *The Pearl Fishers*, 1981.

Sir Alexander Gibson conducts the Scottish National Orchestra at the sitzprobe for *Otello* at the Dalintober Hall, Glasgow, 1970s.

John Mauceri conducts the Scottish Opera Orchestra in a rehearsal for *Die Walküre* at Woodside Halls, Glasgow, 1991.

Initially filling a gap in its Spring schedule, the Scottish National Orchestra, of which Sir Alexander Gibson was Principal Conductor from 1959 to 1984, played for most of Scottish Opera's early productions. By the late 1960s the BBC Scottish Symphony Orchestra was playing for some productions, and from the mid-1970s the Scottish Chamber Orchestra was also engaged. The mostly freelance Scottish Philharmonia was in the pit on a number of occasions in the late 1970s.

The performance of *The Bartered Bride* at Newcastle's Theatre Royal on 7 February 1980 marked the debut of Scottish Opera's own dedicated orchestra, the Scottish Opera Orchestra, which changed its name to The Orchestra of Scottish Opera in 1992 and plays for all the Company's main-stage and medium-scale orchestra-accompanied productions.

The Orchestra of Scottish Opera.

The deepest well of laughter was undoubtedly Thomson Smillie, the Head of Press and Marketing, whose infectious humour rippled throughout the Company. Thomson was born to communicate – at any rate he could certainly never stop talking – and if he didn't have a story to tell he would invent one, except there were plenty of stories. The *Ring* with David Ward and Helga Dernesch, *The Trojans* with Janet Baker and Ronald Dowd, *Otello* with Kiri Te Kanawa and Charles Craig. These were big stories, and Thomson told them with flair and humour.

DAVID POUNTNEY Director of Productions 1975–80

Opposite: A publicity stunt in Elmbank Crescent, Glasgow, for *Die Fledermaus*, 1978. Catherine Wilson, who played Rosalinde, offers some coppers to 'down-and-out' Billy Connolly, who took the speaking part of Frosch the jailer.

Peter Ebert and Dame Janet Baker during a break in rehearsals for *Orfeo ed Euridice*, 1979.

Alan Cumming and Forbes Masson as Barry and Victor at the post-performance reception for *Lulu*, 1987.

My first day with Scottish Opera in 1975 buzzed with trepidation and excitement. A happy, gabby, mostly unintelligible Glaswegian taxi driver whisked me to Elmbank Crescent and I entered to a welcome as warm and as generous as I could ever have wished. Peter Hemmings greeted me with a huge handshake, several future colleagues were there – Malcolm Donnelly, Gordon Sandison, Norman White – and all my anxiety disappeared in a flash.

GRAHAM CLARK Tenor

I was deeply happy in Scotland. Wales is my home, and always has been, but the west of Britain, the mountains and wild coasts, has nourished me every bit as much as the music I have committed to memory. Most Spring and Summer days, after work at Elmbank Crescent, I would get in my VW Beetle and escape to the sublime beauty of the Trossachs to mess about in the long evenings until it got dark.

SIMON KEENLYSIDE Baritone

Nelly Miricioiu in her dressing room at the Theatre Royal, Glasgow with director John Cox: *Manon Lescaut*, 1982.

Sir Alexander Gibson backstage at the King's Theatre, Glasgow.

Helga Dernesch as Cassandra: *The Trojans*, 1969, backstage at the King's Theatre, Glasgow.

Peter van der Bilt as Count Almaviva: *The Marriage of Figaro*, 1968, backstage at the King's Theatre, Glasgow.

Anita Valkki as Brünnhilde: *Die Walküre*, 1966, backstage at the King's Theatre, Glasgow.

As a schoolboy and student I appeared as an extra with Scottish Opera between 1965 and 1974. These were fun times which helped to cultivate my passion for opera. Of all the events that occurred during those years *The Trojans* in 1969 provided the most interesting incident, one remembered even now by those still around – that of the Trojan Horse.

The production was largely traditionally costumed using the minimalist style of set that Scottish Opera pioneered. The visual conception of the Horse was of a large siege engine modified into the shape of a horse, on four large wheels. It had a capacious body in which six of us, as Greeks, were placed to climb down ropes at the end of Act I.

During one of the stage rehearsals at Glasgow's King's Theatre, there was violent shaking as the Horse was wheeled on. As it came to a halt, 'us inside' were alarmed to note that the body was not level. We were exhorted in true stage crew parlance to vacate as quickly as possible! As we descended on our ropes we saw that one of the wheels – about one metre in diameter from memory – was buried in the stage up to its axle. The rehearsal programme was quickly rescheduled and the future contents of the horse cut from six to a symbolic two. At the next rehearsal, and indeed for some time thereafter, the hole was covered by planking, a source of personal amusement. I can now lay claim to having broken the King's stage!

DALE BILSLAND Scottish Opera extra 1965–74

Opposite: A crowd of interested onlookers gathers to watch the notorious Trojan Horse being winched into the King's Theatre, Edinburgh, 1972.

Bernstein's *Candide* in Glasgow was extraordinary. Bernstein visited and ran everyone off their feet. He was enormously energetic and a hugely powerful figure. After its Scottish performances we took the production to the Old Vic where it was nominated for three Olivier Awards, and won two including Musical of the Year— quite a triumph.

DAFYDD BURNE-JONES Staff Director

Opposite: Managing Director Richard Mantle, director Sir Jonathan Miller, composer Leonard Bernstein and conductor Justin Brown at rehearsals for *Candide* in the Theatre Royal, Glasgow, 1988.

A BBC TV camera crew recording a rehearsal of *L'Egisto* at the Theatre Royal, Glasgow, 1982.

There were friends in the orchestra and chorus who helped assuage the loneliness of being away from my family. Before the internet, cable television and cellular phones, one still had to depend on airmail and long-distance (and expensive) phone calls to keep in touch. But piccolo player Ewan Robertson taught me that the best way to poach a salmon is to put the fish in the dishwasher! And chorister Scott Cooper created the funniest name for the offices on Elmbank Crescent, which he invariably called Mel Blanc Crescent. And the Grahams and the Mantles kindly had me to their homes on those Sundays when I would otherwise get in the car and drive to Loch Lomond, just to see it again. Congratulations to all of you who have been a part of the 'curious story' and the brilliant things you have done! And thank you, again, for letting me be a small part of your great country and its magnificent history.

JOHN MAUCERI Music Director 1987–93

Opposite: Francesco Corti (Music Director 2008–13), conducting *The Flying Dutchman*, 2013.

John Mauceri (Music Director 1987–93), conducting *Carmen*, 1986.

Sir Richard Armstrong (Music Director 1993–2005), at the Theatre Royal, Glasgow during rehearsals for *Die Walküre*, 2001.

Peter Hemmings was a sober character, with the manner and appearance of a civil servant and a certain touch of the cherubic schoolboy, but an absolute burning passion for the art form carefully zipped up under the suited exterior, and he knew how to recognise and foster imagination in others. Peter had a formidable grasp of detail and knew exactly what was going on – he opened everyone's mail for one thing! He was loyal and utterly trustworthy. He had only one fault: he turned out to be irreplaceable.

Leonard Hancock was the back-room boy of the trio, but knew more than the others put together. He was a superlative coach, a vastly experienced judge of singers – I learnt everything I know by sitting through hours of auditions with him – and someone with an organic understanding of how music works. He was very well educated in that now old-fashioned sense – knew his Latin, his Greek, could do German grammar correctly, had all the mythological significances at his fingertips – but wore this knowledge lightly, with an impish sense of humour, and a sense of proportion about the opera business that belonged to a man who had been a navigator in a Lancaster through the war. You couldn't bullshit Leonard.

By far the most talented of all of us and the most difficult to read was Alex Gibson, an instinctive and passionate artist who was at the same time cannier than he seemed. Alex was a really good conductor who had, I think, deliberately thrown away whatever he might have once had as so-called 'conducting technique' in order not to have any 'method' which got in the way of direct contact with the music. This could of course be frustrating because, in contrast to most of his colleagues, his was not a method suited to preparation, but ultimately exclusively focused on performance. But the performances could transcend all of his better-organised colleagues with ease.

I looked on and learnt, and was privileged beyond measure to be close to these people, starting and inspiring a new, young company.

DAVID POUNTNEY Director of Productions 1975–80

Director Anthony Besch (centre) with Elizabeth Harwood: *Der Rosenkavalier*, 1971.

Director Peter Ebert with the men's chorus: *Fidelio*, 1970.

Director David Pountney (right) with choreographer Peter Darrell: *The Bartered Bride*, 1978.

Director Graham Vick (left) with Music Director John Mauceri: *Carmen*, 1986.

Director Tim Albery: *The Trojans*, 1990.

Director Nuria Espert (right) with Yoko Watanabe: *Madama Butterfly*, 1987.

Savitri was my first experience of anything big, ever. I worked with Janet Baker, Philip Langridge and John Shirley-Quirk. I was just 24, but all three of them were so generous, respectful and interested. It was an object lesson in how to go about one's life. So I had to step up to the mark. I will never forget the first day of rehearsals. I had a flat in Finnieston and I can remember trying to choose what to wear. Would I wear my favourite pullover? No, it's got a hole in it, and I'm working with Janet Baker. How about a suit? Or is that trying too hard? It was just awful! In the end I put on a blue-grey corduroy suit and a sleeveless Fair Isle jumper. I felt comfortable in that jumper. I went into the rehearsal and everyone was so open that I realised I could do it. I remember seeing what great artists could be. All three of them were completely transparent. They brought all their intellect, their musicianship and their humanity into the rehearsal room, but only as a vehicle for the work. It was extraordinary. There was an incredible chemistry on that show, and it was a complete confirmation that this was the direction my life was going to take.

GRAHAM VICK Director of Productions 1984–7

When I think of Scotland and Scottish Opera, my mind is flooded with images and a smile comes to my face. Betty, my wife, and I first came to Scotland in 1977, when I was guest conductor for four performances of *Otello*, in a revival directed by Graham Vick. We stayed at the White House on Great Western Road. Since there was a big gap between performances two and three, we rented a small car and headed off to the islands of Lewis and Harris, spent a night in Stornoway, then were hosted by Lady Aberdeen at Haddo House and fell in love with the land and its people. I suspect we were as foreign as people could be. There was total incredulity at my slicing bananas onto my cornflakes at the breakfast at Haddo: 'What an amazing concoction' was one comment.

JOHN MAUCERI Music Director 1987–93

I did my placement from college with Scottish Opera, during the season they were doing *From the House of the Dead* and *The Flying Dutchman*. Maria Björnson, the designer of *House of the Dead*, got me painting hundreds and hundreds of plastic sausages. I came back as Stage Manager in 2006 for *Der Rosenkavalier* with David McVicar. It was a big show to start off on, but from then on I was hooked. I'm a huge David McVicar fan. When he's here everyone knows the Headmaster is in! It's exciting to work with someone like that because they know what they want. For me the attraction is the scale of the shows, something that you don't really get in commercial theatre. It's a real pleasure to work on them.

JOHN DUNCAN Stage Manager

Opposite: Director Sir David McVicar (centre) with Natalia Dercho and Ian Storey: *Madama Butterfly*, 2000.

Director Jonathan Moore (left) with Music Director Sir Richard Armstrong and composer James MacMillan: *Inés de Castro*, 1996.

Director Sir Thomas Allen: *The Barber of Seville*, 2011.

Theatre Royal Glasgow

One way or another, the Theatre Royal in Hope Street has been at the heart of Glasgow entertainment for almost 150 years. Designed by Charles Phipps in 1867, the theatre hosted everyone from Sarah Bernhardt to Stanley Baxter before being converted into the STV studios in 1957. When the broadcaster moved out in 1974, Scottish Opera bought the theatre with public support, creating Scotland's first national opera house and gaining its own permanent performing home the following year.

For the past nearly four decades, Glasgow audiences have been able to enjoy opera, as well as dance, drama, musicals and comedy, in the beautifully restored A listed auditorium, complete with its ornate ceiling and gilded plasterwork – a wonderful example of the very best of Victorian architecture.

As Scottish Opera's 50th Anniversary Season ends, the Theatre Royal is beginning its next exciting chapter. Work is underway to improve the theatre's public spaces, providing enlarged foyers and access for everyone to all levels, as well as a roof terrace and space for education activities – a dramatic new landmark designed by Glasgow architects Page\Park and due to be completed as the city hosts the 2014 Commonwealth Games.

Opposite: The auditorium of the Theatre Royal Glasgow, 2011.

Peter went to the King's Theatre to arrange to put on the *Ring* cycle but they said they were full and couldn't accommodate Scottish Opera. I think that was the catalyst to start talking to other people about performing elsewhere. Bill Brown of STV said that the Theatre Royal would soon not be needed and then everybody realised that of course it had previously been used as an opera house.

JANE HEMMINGS Wife of the late Peter Hemmings

The Theatre Royal had opened with a special perfomance of *Die Fledermaus* but work was still going on when *Otello*, the first opera in the new season, was in rehearsal on stage. I was Emilia. There were still workmen there, putting the final touches to the theatre. Alexander Gibson was conducting and Anthony Besch was sitting in the stalls with a colleague. Some of the workmen listened but some carried on talking to their friends. Eventually Alex turned round and said, 'I can't continue with this chattering going on. Please would you all shut up.' There was a deathly hush. Anthony Besch muttered something. A big hand came out of the darkness and grabbed him by the scruff of the neck. A broad Glaswegian voice said, 'Did you no' hear what the big man said?' Anthony was absolutely floored!

CLAIRE LIVINGSTONE Singer

The first season at the Theatre Royal was sold by subscription and opened with *Otello*. But where to put the VIPs and donors to the Theatre Royal fund? We couldn't turf the subscribers out of their seats. So it was decided to do a gala performance of *Die Fledermaus* on the previous evening, with a cabaret in Act II. STV broadcast Act II 'live' to the ITV national network but the cabaret was taking longer than expected. The network controllers were increasingly concerned they might have to pull the plug on the TV relay if there was any chance it would overrun, as *News at Ten* had absolute priority. Thankfully, the curtain came down literally seconds beforehand.

JOHN DUFFUS Scottish Opera administration 1971–8

We turned the Theatre Royal into a ballroom twice to celebrate the Company's 21st and 25th anniversaries, having dinner in a marquee set up in a car park that was then beside the theatre. The idea was conceived by my wife Sara who raised all the sponsorship and organised both events. They created good PR, as well as enabling contact to be made with many of Scotland's leading companies and people. They raised £75,000 and £140,000 respectively after all expenses, equivalent today to some £500,000.

SIR RAYMOND JOHNSTONE Chairman 1983–6

The 1987 Butterfly Ball, held at the Theatre Royal to mark Scottish Opera's 25th anniversary.

Opposite: The auditorium of the Theatre Royal Glasgow, from the upper circle, on the theatre's reopening as the performing home of Scottish Opera, 1975.

Director of Productions Peter Ebert and Music Director Sir Alexander Gibson outside the newly reopened Theare Royal, 1975.

Tenor Charles Craig onstage with Peter Ebert at the gala opening of the Theatre Royal, 14 October 1975.

Sir Alexander Gibson with Chorus Master John Currie and General Administrator Peter Hemmings in the Theatre Royal, 1975.

When property developments around the Theatre Royal meant that a small piece of land right next door became available, I just thought, 'It's a once-in-a-century chance – we've got to do it.' In a way I see it as our duty, as owners, to make sure that the theatre caters to the needs of a modern audience and, when access is an issue and audiences can't get to the loo or get an interval drink on a busy night, you know something needs to change. The new foyers will solve all this, and give us a new education suite to help encourage new audiences, so that the theatre can continue to be used and loved by generations to come.

ALEX REEDIJK General Director 2006–

Alex Reedijk, David Page of Page\Park Architects and Cabinet Secretary for Culture and External Affairs Fiona Hyslop on site at the Theatre Royal, 13 March 2013.

The distinctive curve of the new building begins to take shape, March 2013.

The 50th Anniversary Season

Quality, variety, innovation and entertainment have been the watchwords throughout Scottish Opera's 50th Anniversary Season.

Every production has been new to the Company, from Sir Thomas Allen's Steampunk-inspired *The Magic Flute* to the Pythonesque production of Gilbert and Sullivan's *The Pirates of Penzance* in partnership with The D'Oyly Carte Opera Company. The three operas gaining their world premieres at the 2012 Edinburgh International Festival have gone on to win and be nominated for major arts awards, and the Company has emphasised its commitment to touring in Scotland with performances of *La traviata* and *Opera Highlights* in 50 far-flung but welcoming venues.

The Company's Emerging Artists programme continues to go from strength to strength, with this year's singers appearing throughout the season, and Composer in Residence Gareth Williams producing *The Elephant Angel* with writer Bernard MacLaverty for performance by Scottish Opera's Connect Company of young people alongside schoolchildren from across Scotland and Northern Ireland. And of course there has been the latest collaboration with the Royal Conservatoire of Scotland, this year on Britten's *A Midsummer Night's Dream*.

We hope that Sir Alexander Gibson and his fellow founders would be proud of this anniversary season and of what Scottish Opera has achieved since 1962. We hope that you have enjoyed and been stimulated by your visits over the years to Scottish Opera, no matter where in Scotland or abroad they may have been. And we hope that you will continue to journey together with us for many years to come.

Opposite: Richard Burkhard as Papageno: *The Magic Flute*, director Sir Thomas Allen, 2012.

New Opera Made in Scotland

The Lady from the Sea

Craig Armstrong and Zoë Strachan, 2012

Winner of a Herald Angel Award at the
2012 Edinburgh International Festival

Above: Claire Booth as Ellida:
director Harry Fehr.

New Opera Made in Scotland

Clemency

James MacMillan and Michael Symmons Roberts, 2011

Above: Adam Green, Eamonn Mulhall and Andrew Tortise as the Triplets, Grant Doyle as Abraham, Janis Kelly as Sarah: Linbury Studio, Royal Opera House, director Katie Mitchell, 2011.

New Opera Made in Scotland

In the Locked Room

Huw Watkins and David Harsent, 2012

Nominated with *Ghost Patrol* in the Outstanding Achievement in Opera category at The Olivier Awards, 2013

Above: Louise Winter as Susan, Håkan Vramsmo as Pascoe: director Michael McCarthy.

Ghost Patrol

Stuart MacRae and Louise Welsh, 2012

Winner in the Opera category at the South Bank Sky Arts Awards, 2013
Nominated with *In the Locked Room* in the Outstanding Achievement in
Opera category at The Olivier Awards, 2013

Above: Nicholas Sharratt
as Sam, James McOran-
Campbell as Alasdair:
director Matthew
Richardson.

The Magic Flute

Wolfgang Amadeus Mozart

Nominated in the Best Costume Designer category
at the International Opera Awards, 2013

Opposite: Laura Mitchell as Pamina, Nicky Spence as Tamino in the
2012 production directed by Sir Thomas Allen.

Mari Moriya as The Queen of the Night.

Cameron Nixon, Daniel Doolan and Andrew Halliday as The Three Boys.

Werther

Jules Massenet

Opposite: Jonathan Boyd as Werther in the 2013 production directed by Pia Furtado.

Viktoria Vizin as Charlotte.

Roland Wood as Albert, Jonathan Boyd as Werther.

The Flying Dutchman

Richard Wagner

Opposite: The Flying Dutchman's crew in the 2013 production directed by Harry Fehr.

Rachel Nicholls as Senta.

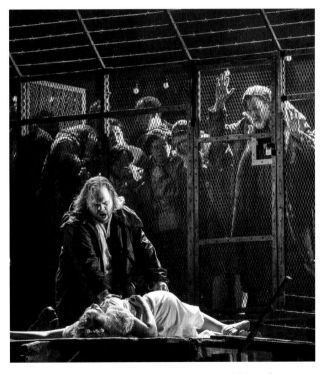

Peteris Eglitis as The Dutchman, Rachel Nicholls as Senta, Scott Wilde as Donald.

The Pirates of Penzance

Gilbert and Sullivan

Opposite: Steven Page as The Pirate King with his pirate crew in the 2013 production directed by Martin Lloyd-Evans.

Sam Furness as Frederic, Ellie Laugharne as Mabel.

Richard Suart as Major-General Stanley with his many daughters.

La traviata

Giuseppe Verdi

A Midsummer Night's Dream

Benjamin Britten

Opera Highlights

Opposite: Elin Pritchard as Violetta, Robyn Lyn Evans as Alfredo: *La traviata*, director Annilese Miskimmon, 2012.

Elinor Rolfe Johnson as Tytania: *A Midsummer Night's Dream*, director Olivia Fuchs, 2013.

Eleanor Dennis and Nicky Spence: *Opera Highlights*, director Adrian Osmond, 2013.

Scottish Opera First Nights

The number of performances indicates the total number for the run across all theatres.

Names are listed in the order: conductor, director (and revival director, if different), designer, lighting designer.

Costume designers, choreographers, movement directors and video designers are indicated as such as appropriate.

* indicates production revival.

EIF indicates Edinburgh International Festival.

1962

5 June   ***Madama Butterfly*** Puccini
3 performances
King's Theatre, Glasgow

Alexander Gibson & James Lockhart/
Dennis Arundell/Mark King/Charles Bristow

6 June   ***Pelléas et Mélisande*** Debussy
3 performances
King's Theatre, Glasgow

Alexander Gibson/Dennis Arundell/
Mark King/Charles Bristow

1963

27 May   ***Otello*** Verdi
4 performances
King's Theatre, Glasgow

Alexander Gibson/Anthony Besch/
Ralph Koltai/Charles Bristow

28 May   ***Die Entführung aus dem Serail*** Mozart
5 performances
King's Theatre, Glasgow

Leon Lovett/Peter Ebert/Peter Rice/
Charles Bristow

29 May   **Double Bill**
4 performances
King's Theatre, Glasgow

Volo di notte Dallapiccola
Alexander Gibson/Peter Ebert/
Ralph Koltai/Charles Bristow

L'heure espagnole Ravel
Brian Priestman/Anthony Besch/
Peter Rice/Charles Bristow

1964

14 May   ***Faust*** Gounod
5 performances
King's Theatre, Glasgow
King's Theatre, Edinburgh

Alexander Gibson & Roderick Brydon/
Anthony Besch/Peter Rice/Charles Bristow

16 May   ***Don Giovanni*** Mozart
6 performances
King's Theatre, Glasgow
King's Theatre, Edinburgh

Leon Lovett/Peter Ebert/
Ralph Koltai/Charles Bristow

19 May   * ***Otello*** Verdi
5 performances
King's Theatre, Glasgow
King's Theatre, Edinburgh

Alexander Gibson/Anthony Besch/
Ralph Koltai/Charles Bristow

1965

14 May   ***Boris Godunov*** Mussorgsky
6 performances
King's Theatre, Glasgow
His Majesty's Theatre, Aberdeen
King's Theatre, Edinburgh

Alexander Gibson/Michael Geliot/
Ralph Koltai/Charles Bristow

15 May   ***Madama Butterfly*** Puccini
8 performances
King's Theatre, Glasgow
His Majesty's Theatre, Aberdeen
King's Theatre, Edinburgh

Norman del Mar & Roderick Brydon/
Peter Ebert/David Wilby/Charles Bristow

20 May   * ***Don Giovanni*** Mozart
5 performances
King's Theatre, Glasgow
His Majesty's Theatre, Aberdeen
King's Theatre, Edinburgh

Alexander Gibson/Peter Ebert/
Ralph Koltai/Charles Bristow

1966

11 April   ***Albert Herring*** Britten
9 performances
Perth Theatre
King's Theatre, Glasgow
King's Theatre, Edinburgh
His Majesty's Theatre, Aberdeen

Roderick Brydon/Anthony Besch/
Adam Pollock/Charles Bristow

6 May   ***Falstaff*** Verdi
7 performances
King's Theatre, Glasgow
King's Theatre, Edinburgh
His Majesty's Theatre, Aberdeen

Alexander Gibson/Peter Ebert/
Peter Rice/Charles Bristow/
Shelah Wells (choreographer)

13 May   ***Die Walküre*** Wagner
8 performances
King's Theatre, Glasgow
King's Theatre, Edinburgh
His Majesty's Theatre, Aberdeen

Alexander Gibson/Peter Ebert/
Michael Knight/Charles Bristow

18 May   * ***Faust*** Gounod
5 performances
King's Theatre, Glasgow
King's Theatre, Edinburgh
His Majesty's Theatre, Aberdeen

Roderick Brydon/Anthony Besch/
Peter Rice/Charles Bristow

1967

12 April   ***Così fan tutte*** Mozart
9 performances
Perth Theatre
King's Theatre, Glasgow
His Majesty's Theatre, Aberdeen
King's Theatre, Edinburgh

Alexander Gibson/Anthony Besch/
John Stoddart/Charles Bristow

14 April   * ***Albert Herring*** Britten
4 performances
Perth Theatre
King's Theatre, Glasgow
His Majesty's Theatre, Aberdeen
King's Theatre, Edinburgh

Roderick Brydon/Anthony Besch/
Adam Pollock/Charles Bristow

6 May   ***Das Rheingold*** Wagner
5 performances
King's Theatre, Glasgow
His Majesty's Theatre, Aberdeen
King's Theatre, Edinburgh

Alexander Gibson/Peter Ebert/
Michael Knight/Charles Bristow

11 May   ***La bohème*** Puccini
7 performances
King's Theatre, Glasgow
His Majesty's Theatre, Aberdeen
King's Theatre, Edinburgh

Roderick Brydon/Peter Ebert/
Peter Rice/Charles Bristow

17 May * *Otello* Verdi
5 performances
King's Theatre, Glasgow
His Majesty's Theatre, Aberdeen
King's Theatre, Edinburgh

Alexander Gibson/Anthony Besch/
Ralph Koltai/Charles Bristow

22 Aug *The Rake's Progress* Stravinsky
4 performances
King's Theatre, Edinburgh (EIF)

Alexander Gibson/Peter Ebert/
Ralph Koltai/Charles Bristow

4 Sep *The Soldier's Tale* Stravinsky
6 performances
Assembly Hall, Edinburgh (EIF)

Alexander Gibson/Wendy Toye/
Carl Toms/Charles Bristow

1968

9 April *The Marriage of Figaro* Mozart
13 performances
Perth Theatre
King's Theatre, Glasgow
His Majesty's Theatre, Aberdeen
King's Theatre, Edinburgh
Theatre Royal, Newcastle

Alexander Gibson & Leonard Hancock/
Anthony Besch/John Stoddart/
Charles Bristow

10 April **Double Bill**
3 performances
Perth Theatre

Full Circle Orr (World Premiere)
Alexander Gibson/Michael Geliot/
Neil Parkinson/Charles Bristow

* *The Soldier's Tale* Stravinsky
Alexander Gibson/Wendy Toye/
Carl Toms/Charles Bristow

3 May * *Boris Godunov* Mussorgsky
6 performances
King's Theatre, Glasgow
His Majesty's Theatre, Aberdeen
King's Theatre, Edinburgh

David Lloyd-Jones/Michael Geliot/
Ralph Koltai/Charles Bristow

11 May * *Madama Butterfly* Puccini
6 performances
King's Theatre, Glasgow
His Majesty's Theatre, Aberdeen
King's Theatre, Edinburgh

Alexander Gibson/Peter Ebert/
David Wilby/Charles Bristow

15 May *Götterdämmerung* Wagner
5 performances
King's Theatre, Glasgow
His Majesty's Theatre, Aberdeen
King's Theatre, Edinburgh

Alexander Gibson/Peter Ebert/
Michael Knight/Charles Bristow

19 June * *Albert Herring* Britten
2 performances
Teatro della Pergola, Florence

Roderick Brydon/Anthony Besch/
Adam Pollock/Charles Bristow

19 Aug *Peter Grimes* Britten
6 performances
King's Theatre, Edinburgh (EIF)
Theatre Royal, Newcastle

Alexander Gibson/Colin Graham/
Alix Stone/Charles Bristow

26 Aug *Il ballo delle ingrate* Monteverdi
5 performances
George Hotel, Edinburgh (EIF)

Roderick Brydon/Peter Ebert/
Jack Notman/Alexander Bennett

12 Dec *The Gondoliers* Gilbert and Sullivan
6 performances
King's Theatre, Edinburgh

James Loughran/Joan Cross/Jack
Notman/Clover Roope (choreographer)

16 Dec **Double Bill**
2 performances
King's Theatre, Edinburgh

Full Circle Orr
Alexander Gibson/Ian Watt-Smith/
Bernard Culshaw

* *The Soldier's Tale* Stravinsky
Alexander Gibson/Wendy Toye/
Carl Toms/Charles Bristow

1969

5 April * *Così fan tutte* Mozart
11 performances
Perth Theatre
King's Theatre, Glasgow
King's Theatre, Edinburgh
His Majesty's Theatre, Aberdeen

Alexander Gibson & Leonard Hancock/
Anthony Besch/John Stoddart/
Charles Bristow

9 April * *Full Circle* Orr
7 performances
Perth Theatre
King's Theatre, Glasgow
King's Theatre, Edinburgh

Alexander Gibson & Leonard Hancock/
Ian Watt-Smith/Bernard Culshaw

Note: *Full Circle* played as part of a double bill with Scottish
Ballet Theatre's *La ventana* in Perth, and as part of a triple bill
with *La ventana* and *Breakaway* in Glasgow and Edinburgh.

11 April * *Albert Herring* Britten
8 performances
Perth Theatre
King's Theatre, Glasgow
Opernhaus, Hanover
Opernhaus, Dortmund
Theater Augsburg
His Majesty's Theatre, Aberdeen
King's Theatre, Edinburgh

Roderick Brydon/Anthony Besch/
Adam Pollock/Charles Bristow

3 May *The Trojans* Berlioz
5 performances
King's Theatre, Glasgow
King's Theatre, Edinburgh

Alexander Gibson/Peter Ebert/
Hans Ulrich Schmückle/Sylta Busse
Schmückle (costumes)/Charles
Bristow/Laverne Meyer (choreographer)

15 May * *The Gondoliers* Gilbert and Sullivan
8 performances
King's Theatre, Glasgow
King's Theatre, Edinburgh
His Majesty's Theatre, Aberdeen

James Loughran/Joan Cross/Jack
Notman/Clover Roope (choreographer)

Note: The performance on 22 May at the King's Theatre,
Edinburgh was attended by Her Majesty The Queen,
HRH The Duke of Edinburgh and HRH The Princess Anne.

1 Sep **Double Bill**
10 performances
The Gateway, Edinburgh (EIF)

* *Full Circle* Orr
Alexander Gibson/Ian Watt-Smith/
Bernard Culshaw

The Undertaker Purser (World Premiere)
Alexander Gibson/Ian Watt-Smith/
Ken Wheatley/Alex Reid (costumes)

5 Dec *Cinderella* Rossini
4 performances
King's Theatre, Edinburgh

Bryden Thomson/Colin Graham/
Emanuele Luzzati/Colin Graham

1970

26 Mar *The Turn of the Screw* Britten
12 performances
His Majesty's Theatre, Aberdeen
Theatre Royal, Newcastle (2 visits)
Perth Theatre
King's Theatre, Glasgow
King's Theatre, Edinburgh
Pjodleikhusid, Reykjavik

Roderick Brydon/Anthony Besch/
John Stoddart/Charles Bristow

28 Mar * *Cinderella* Rossini
13 performances
His Majesty's Theatre, Aberdeen
Theatre Royal, Newcastle
Perth Theatre
King's Theatre, Glasgow
King's Theatre, Edinburgh

Bryden Thomson/Colin Graham/
Emanuele Luzzati/Colin Graham

2 April * *Don Giovanni* Mozart
10 performances
His Majesty's Theatre, Aberdeen
Theatre Royal, Newcastle
King's Theatre, Glasgow
King's Theatre, Edinburgh

Alexander Gibson & Leonard Hancock/
Peter Ebert/Ralph Koltai/Nadine Baylis
(costumes)/Charles Bristow/Marjorie
Middleton (choreographer)

1 May **Fidelio** Beethoven
12 performances
King's Theatre, Glasgow (2 visits)
King's Theatre, Edinburgh
His Majesty's Theatre, Aberdeen

Alexander Gibson/Peter Ebert/
Hans Ulrich Schmückle/Sylta Busse
Schmückle (costumes)/Charles Bristow

20 July **The Magic Flute** Mozart
16 performances
Royal Lyceum Theatre, Edinburgh (2 visits)
King's Theatre, Glasgow
His Majesty's Theatre, Aberdeen
Theatre Royal, Newcastle

Alexander Gibson & Christopher
Seaman/Peter Ebert/Geoffrey Scott/
Alex Reid (costumes)/André Tammes

Note: This production opened to coincide with the Commonwealth Games in Edinburgh.

25 Aug **Elegy for Young Lovers** Henze
5 performances
King's Theatre, Edinburgh (EIF)
King's Theatre, Glasgow
His Majesty's Theatre, Aberdeen

Alexander Gibson/Hans Werner Henze/
Ralph Koltai/Fausti Moroni (costumes)/
Charles Bristow

1 Oct * **Albert Herring** Britten
4 performances
Pjodleikhusid, Reykjavik
Theatre Royal, Newcastle

Roderick Brydon/Anthony Besch/
Adam Pollock/Charles Bristow

12 Dec **La traviata** Verdi
3 performances
Royal Lyceum Theatre, Edinburgh

James Loughran/Ian Watt-Smith/
Bernard Culshaw/Alex Reid (costumes)/
Charles Bristow

1971

11 Mar * **Albert Herring** Britten
4 performances
Perth Theatre
His Majesty's Theatre, Aberdeen
Theatre Royal, Newcastle
Royal Court Theatre, Liverpool

Roderick Brydon & Leonard Hancock/
Anthony Besch/Adam Pollock/
Charles Bristow

13 Mar * **The Turn of the Screw** Britten
4 performances
Perth Theatre
Royal Court Theatre, Liverpool
King's Theatre, Edinburgh
His Majesty's Theatre, Aberdeen

Roderick Brydon/Anthony Besch/
John Stoddart/Charles Bristow

16 Mar * **La traviata** Verdi
15 performances
Perth Theatre
His Majesty's Theatre, Aberdeen (2 visits)
Theatre Royal, Newcastle
Royal Court Theatre, Liverpool
King's Theatre, Glasgow
King's Theatre, Edinburgh

James Loughran/Ian Watt-Smith/
Bernard Culshaw/Alex Reid (costumes)/
Charles Bristow

18 Mar * **The Magic Flute** Mozart
8 performances
Perth Theatre
His Majesty's Theatre, Aberdeen
Royal Court Theatre, Liverpool
King's Theatre, Glasgow

Christopher Seaman/Peter Ebert/
Geoffrey Scott/Alex Reid (costumes)/
André Tammes

30 Mar * **Das Rheingold** Wagner
9 performances
His Majesty's Theatre, Aberdeen
Theatre Royal, Newcastle
Royal Court Theatre, Liverpool
King's Theatre, Glasgow
King's Theatre, Edinburgh

Alexander Gibson/Peter Ebert/
Michael Knight/Charles Bristow

8 May **Siegfried** Wagner
5 performances
King's Theatre, Glasgow
King's Theatre, Edinburgh
His Majesty's Theatre, Aberdeen

Alexander Gibson/Peter Ebert/
Michael Knight/Charles Bristow

Note: Alexander Gibson conducted the Scottish National Orchestra in Acts I and III of Siegfried at the BBC Proms on 10 August.

20 May **Der Rosenkavalier** R Strauss
7 performances
King's Theatre, Glasgow
King's Theatre, Edinburgh
His Majesty's Theatre, Aberdeen

Alexander Gibson/Anthony Besch/
John Stoddart/Charles Bristow

26 July **The Barber of Seville** Rossini
15 performances
Royal Lyceum Theatre, Edinburgh
MacRobert Centre, Stirling
Theatre Royal, Newcastle
King's Theatre, Edinburgh
King's Theatre, Glasgow

Gary Bertini & Roderick Brydon/
Ian Watt-Smith/Bernard Culshaw/
Alex Reid (costumes)/Roger Jackson

26 Aug * **Die Walküre** Wagner
3 performances
King's Theatre, Edinburgh (EIF)

Alexander Gibson/Peter Ebert/
Michael Knight/Charles Bristow

27 Sep **The Rake's Progress** Stravinsky
6 performances
MacRobert Centre, Stirling
Theatre Royal, Newcastle
King's Theatre, Edinburgh
King's Theatre, Glasgow

Alexander Gibson & Roderick Brydon/
David Pountney/Ralph Koltai/
Roger Jackson

Note: The first performance of this new production was also the inaugural performance at the MacRobert Centre.

7 Oct * **Don Giovanni** Mozart
8 performances
MacRobert Centre, Stirling
Theatre Royal, Newcastle
King's Theatre, Edinburgh
King's Theatre, Glasgow

Bryden Thomson/Peter Ebert – Ian
Watt-Smith (revival)/Ralph Koltai/
Nadine Baylis (costumes)/
Charles Bristow

11 Dec * **Götterdämmerung** Wagner
1 performance
King's Theatre, Glasgow

Alexander Gibson/Peter Ebert/
Michael Knight/Charles Bristow

13–18 Dec **Der Ring des Nibelungen** Wagner
1 complete cycle
King's Theatre, Glasgow

Alexander Gibson/Peter Ebert/
Michael Knight/Charles Bristow

1972

14 Mar * **Così fan tutte** Mozart
16 performances
MacRobert Centre, Stirling
Royal Court Theatre, Liverpool
Theatre Royal, Newcastle
Perth Theatre
King's Theatre, Glasgow
His Majesty's Theatre, Aberdeen
King's Theatre, Edinburgh

Alexander Gibson/Anthony Besch/
John Stoddart/Charles Bristow

24 Mar **A Midsummer Night's Dream** Britten
18 performances
MacRobert Centre, Stirling
Grand Theatre, Leeds
Royal Court Theatre, Liverpool
Theatre Royal, Newcastle
Perth Theatre
King's Theatre, Glasgow
His Majesty's Theatre, Aberdeen (2 visits)
King's Theatre, Edinburgh (2 visits)
National Theatre, Reykjavik

Roderick Brydon/Toby Robertson/
Robin Archer/Michael Outhwaite/
Eleanor Fazan (choreographer)

28 Mar * ***The Barber of Seville*** Rossini
14 performances
Grand Theatre, Leeds
Royal Court Theatre, Liverpool
Theatre Royal, Newcastle
King's Theatre, Glasgow
His Majesty's Theatre, Aberdeen
King's Theatre, Edinburgh
Royal Lyceum Theatre, Edinburgh

Roderick Brydon, Neil Dodd & Gary
Bertini/Ian Watt-Smith/Bernard Culshaw/
Alex Reid (costumes)/Roger Jackson

1 April * ***Die Walküre*** Wagner
3 performances
Grand Theatre, Leeds
Royal Court Theatre, Liverpool
Theatre Royal, Newcastle

Alexander Gibson/Peter Ebert/
Michael Knight/Charles Bristow

5 May * ***Otello*** Verdi
7 performances
King's Theatre, Glasgow
His Majesty's Theatre, Aberdeen
King's Theatre, Edinburgh

Alberto Erede/Anthony Besch/
Ralph Koltai/Alex Reid (costumes)/
Charles Bristow

18 May ***Pelléas et Mélisande*** Debussy
5 performances
King's Theatre, Glasgow
King's Theatre, Edinburgh

Alexander Gibson/Colin Graham/
John Fraser/Charles Bristow

24 July * ***The Marriage of Figaro*** Mozart
16 performances
Royal Lyceum Theatre, Edinburgh
King's Theatre, Glasgow
Grand Theatre, Leeds
Theatre Royal, Newcastle
MacRobert Centre, Stirling
His Majesty's Theatre, Aberdeen
King's Theatre, Edinburgh

Gary Bertini & Roderick Brydon/Anthony
Besch/John Stoddart/Charles Bristow/
Jeremy Sutcliffe (choreographer)

24 Aug * ***The Trojans*** Berlioz
6 performances
King's Theatre, Edinburgh (EIF)
King's Theatre, Glasgow
Grand Theatre, Leeds
Theatre Royal, Newcastle

Alexander Gibson/Peter Ebert/
Hans Ulrich Schmückle/Sylta Busse
Schmückle (costumes)/Charles Bristow

12 Sep ***Don Pasquale*** Donizetti
12 performances
King's Theatre, Glasgow
Grand Theatre, Leeds
Theatre Royal, Newcastle
MacRobert Centre, Stirling
His Majesty's Theatre, Aberdeen
King's Theatre, Edinburgh

Alexander Gibson & David Frame/Peter
Ebert/Peter Rice/Charles Bristow

Note: The performance on 9 Oct at His Majesty's Theatre,
Aberdeen was attended by Her Majesty Queen Elizabeth
The Queen Mother.

1973

12 Jan * ***The Turn of the Screw*** Britten
8 performances
MacRobert Centre, Stirling
Teatro Nacional de São Carlos, Lisbon
Rivoli Theatre, Porto
Empire Theatre, Sunderland
Royal Court Theatre, Liverpool

Roderick Brydon/Anthony Besch/
John Stoddart/Charles Bristow

12 Mar ***The Coronation of Poppea*** Monteverdi
11 performances
MacRobert Centre, Stirling
Royal Court Theatre, Liverpool
King's Theatre, Glasgow
Theatre Royal, Newcastle
King's Theatre, Edinburgh
His Majesty's Theatre, Aberdeen

Raymond Leppard & Roderick Brydon/
Anthony Besch/Roger Butlin/Joyce
Conwy Evans (costumes)/Howard Eldridge

15 Mar * ***Don Pasquale*** Donizetti
14 performances
MacRobert Centre, Stirling
Empire Theatre, Sunderland
Royal Court Theatre, Liverpool
Perth Theatre
King's Theatre, Glasgow
Theatre Royal, Newcastle
King's Theatre, Edinburgh

Alexander Gibson & David Frame/
Peter Ebert/Peter Rice/Charles Bristow

22 Mar * ***The Marriage of Figaro*** Mozart
13 performances
MacRobert Centre, Stirling
Empire Theatre, Sunderland
Royal Court Theatre, Liverpool
Perth Theatre
King's Theatre, Glasgow
King's Theatre, Edinburgh

His Majesty's Theatre, Aberdeen
Roderick Brydon & Gary Bertini/
Anthony Besch/John Stoddart/Charles
Bristow/Jeremy Sutcliffe (choreographer)

28 April ***Tristan und Isolde*** Wagner
14 performances
King's Theatre, Glasgow
Theatre Royal, Newcastle
King's Theatre, Edinburgh
His Majesty's Theatre, Aberdeen
Sadler's Wells, London
Grand Theatre, Leeds

Alexander Gibson/Michael Geliot/
Ralph Koltai/Maria Björnson
(costumes)/Robert Ornbo

10 May * ***Peter Grimes*** Britten
6 performances
King's Theatre, Glasgow
Theatre Royal, Newcastle
King's Theatre, Edinburgh
His Majesty's Theatre, Aberdeen

Roderick Brydon/Colin Graham –
Ian Watt-Smith (revival)/
Alix Stone/Charles Bristow

19 June ***The Merry Widow*** Lehár
28 performances
King's Theatre, Glasgow (2 visits)
Royal Lyceum Theatre, Edinburgh (2 visits)
MacRobert Centre, Stirling
Theatre Royal, Newcastle
Grand Theatre, Leeds
His Majesty's Theatre, Aberdeen
Grand Theatre, Wolverhampton

Bryden Thomson, Neil Dodd &
Alexander Gibson/Anthony Besch/
John Stoddart/Charles Bristow/
Virginia Mason (choreographer)

30 Aug * ***Pelléas et Mélisande*** Debussy
6 performances
Sadler's Wells, London
King's Theatre, Glasgow
Theatre Royal, Newcastle
Grand Theatre, Leeds
His Majesty's Theatre, Aberdeen

Alexander Gibson/Colin Graham –
David Pountney (revival)/
John Fraser/Charles Bristow

11 Sep * ***Madama Butterfly*** Puccini
9 performances
King's Theatre, Glasgow
Theatre Royal, Newcastle
Grand Theatre, Leeds
His Majesty's Theatre, Aberdeen
Grand Theatre, Wolverhampton

Alexander Gibson & David Frame/
Peter Ebert – David Pountney (revival)/
David Wilby/Charles Bristow

Note: The performance on 25 Sep at the Theatre Royal,
Newcastle was attended by Princess Alexandra.

20 Sep   *The Donkey* Oliver (World Premiere)
5 performances
MacRobert Centre, Stirling
Theatre Royal, Newcastle
Grand Theatre, Leeds
His Majesty's Theatre, Aberdeen
Grand Theatre, Wolverhampton

David Frame/David Pountney/
Joyce Fieldsend (piano)

Note: This Opera for Schools production toured alongside Scottish Opera's main-stage productions.

8 Dec   * *La traviata* Verdi
3 performances
Royal Lyceum Theatre, Edinburgh

James Loughran/Ian Watt-Smith/Bernard Culshaw/Alex Reid (costumes)/Charles Bristow/Jim Hastie (choreographer)

12 Dec   * *A Midsummer Night's Dream* Britten
3 performances
Royal Lyceum Theatre, Edinburgh
MacRobert Centre, Stirling

Roderick Brydon/Toby Robertson/
Robin Archer/Michael Outhwaite/
Eleanor Fazan (choreographer)

1974

10 Jan   * *A Midsummer Night's Dream* Britten
6 performances
Forum, Leverkusen
Gärtnerplatz, Munich
Staatstheater, Stuttgart
Jahrhunderthalle, Höchst
Theater der Stadt, Schweinfurt

Roderick Brydon/Toby Robertson/
Robin Archer/Michael Outhwaite/
Eleanor Fazan (choreographer)

8 Feb   *The Magic Flute* Mozart
37 performances
King's Theatre, Glasgow (2 visits)
Perth Theatre
MacRobert Centre, Stirling
King's Theatre, Edinburgh
His Majesty's Theatre, Aberdeen
Plus venues in Dundee, Elgin, Oban,
Whitehaven, Darlington, Kelso, Sheffield,
York, Sunderland, Oxford.

Christopher Seaman, Lawrence Foster
& Leonard Hancock/David Pountney/
David Fielding/Maria Björnson
(costumes)/Victor Lockwood

16 Mar   *The Catiline Conspiracy* Hamilton
(World Premiere)
10 performances
MacRobert Centre, Stirling
Theatre Royal, York
Empire Theatre, Sunderland
New Theatre, Oxford
King's Theatre, Glasgow
Theatre Royal, Newcastle
King's Theatre, Edinburgh
His Majesty's Theatre, Aberdeen

Alexander Gibson & Leonard Hancock/
Anthony Besch/Luciana Arrighi/
Charles Bristow

19 Mar   * *The Merry Widow* Lehár
10 performances
Theatre Royal, York
Empire Theatre, Sunderland
New Theatre, Oxford
King's Theatre, Glasgow
King's Theatre, Edinburgh

David Frame & Alexander Gibson/
Anthony Besch/John Stoddart/Charles
Bristow/Virginia Mason (choreographer)

Note: The performance at the King's Theatre in Glasgow on 7 May was attended by Her Majesty The Queen and HRH The Duke of Edinburgh.

25 Mar   * *La traviata* Verdi
10 performances
Empire Theatre, Sunderland
New Theatre, Oxford
King's Theatre, Glasgow
Theatre Royal, Newcastle
King's Theatre, Edinburgh
His Majesty's Theatre, Aberdeen

James Loughran/Ian Watt-Smith/
Bernard Culshaw/Alex Reid (costumes)/
Charles Bristow/Jim Hastie (choreographer)

27 April   * *Fidelio* Beethoven
10 performances
King's Theatre, Glasgow
Theatre Royal, Newcastle
King's Theatre, Edinburgh
His Majesty's Theatre, Aberdeen

Alexander Gibson/Peter Ebert/
Hans Ulrich Schmückle/Sylta Busse
Schmückle (costumes)/Charles Bristow

9 May   * *Boris Godunov* Mussorgsky
7 performances
King's Theatre, Glasgow
King's Theatre, Edinburgh
His Majesty's Theatre, Aberdeen

Gary Bertini/Michael Geliot –
David Pountney (revival)/Ralph
Koltai/Elizabeth Friendship (costumes)/
Charles Bristow

19 July   * *Elegy for Young Lovers* Henze
7 performances
MacRobert Centre, Stirling
Royal Lyceum Theatre, Edinburgh
King's Theatre, Glasgow
Grand Theatre, Leeds
Theatre Royal, Newcastle

Roderick Brydon/Hans Werne Henze –
David Pountney (revival)/Ralph Koltai/
Fausto Moroni (costumes)/Charles Bristow

19 Aug   *Alceste* Gluck
6 performances
King's Theatre, Edinburgh (EIF)
The Maltings, Snape, Aldeburgh

Alexander Gibson/Anthony Besch/
John Stoddart/Charles Bristow/
Peter Darrell (choreographer)

10 Sep   * *Der Rosenkavalier* R Strauss
9 performances
King's Theatre, Glasgow
Grand Theatre, Leeds
Theatre Royal, Newcastle
His Majesty's Theatre, Aberdeen
King's Theatre, Edinburgh

Alexander Gibson/Anthony Besch –
David Pountney (revival)/
John Stoddart/Charles Bristow

26 Sep   *The Lion, The Witch and The Wardrobe*
McCabe (World Premiere)
3 performances
Theatre Royal, Newcastle
His Majesty's Theatre, Aberdeen
MacRobert Centre, Stirling

David Frame/Jeremy Sutcliffe/
David Burrows/Joyce Fieldsend (piano)

Note: This Opera for Youth production toured alongside Scottish Opera's main-stage productions.

27 Sep   *Lucia di Lammermoor* Donizetti
8 performances
Theatre Royal, Newcastle
His Majesty's Theatre, Aberdeen
King's Theatre, Edinburgh

Roderick Brydon/John Copley/Henry
Bardon/Alix Stone (costumes)/Charles
Bristow/Jim Hastie (choreographer)

17 Oct   * *The Barber of Seville* Rossini
7 performances
MacRobert Centre, Stirling
Gaiety Theatre, Ayr

David Frame/Ian Watt-Smith – Brenda
Stanley (revival)/Bernard Culshaw/
Alex Reid (costumes)/Roger Jackson

7 Dec   * *La bohème* Puccini
3 performances
King's Theatre, Edinburgh

Charles Groves/Peter Ebert/Peter Rice/
Charles Bristow

1975

3 Jan   * *The Turn of the Screw* Britten
5 performances
MacRobert Centre, Stirling
Erholungshaus Theater, Leverkusen
Staatstheater, Stuttgart
Stadtheater, Fürth

Roderick Brydon/Anthony Besch/
John Stoddart/Charles Bristow

10 Jan   * *Elegy for Young Lovers* Henze
7 performances
Teatro Nacional de São Carlos, Lisbon
Erholungshaus Theater, Leverkusen
Staatstheater, Stuttgart
Stadtheater, Fürth

Alexander Gibson/Hans Werner Henze –
David Pountney (revival)/Ralph Koltai/
Fausto Moroni (costumes)/
Charles Bristow

31 Jan   * ***The Barber of Seville*** Rossini
32 performances
Venues in Kirkcaldy, Kelso, Elgin, Oban,
Greenock, Dundee, St Andrews, Barrow,
Darlington, Sheffield, Sunderland,
Liverpool, York, Perth, Edinburgh

Neil Dodd, David Frame & John Currie/
Ian Watt-Smith – Brenda Stanley (revival)/
Bernard Culshaw/Alex Reid (costumes)/
Victor Lockwood

13 Mar   * ***Lucia di Lammermoor*** Donizetti
16 performances
MacRobert Centre, Stirling
Empire Theatre, Sunderland
Royal Court Theatre, Liverpool
Theatre Royal, York
King's Theatre, Glasgow
His Majesty's Theatre, Aberdeen
King's Theatre, Edinburgh
Theatre Royal, Newcastle

Roderick Brydon/John Copley/Henry
Bardon/Alix Stone (costumes)/Charles
Bristow/Jim Hastie (choreographer)

19 Mar   * ***La bohème*** Puccini
16 performances
Empire Theatre, Sunderland
Royal Court Theatre, Liverpool
Theatre Royal, York
King's Theatre, Glasgow
His Majesty's Theatre, Aberdeen
King's Theatre, Edinburgh
Theatre Royal, Newcastle

Roderick Brydon/Peter Ebert/
Peter Rice/Charles Bristow

25 April   ***Un ballo in maschera*** Verdi
10 performances
King's Theatre, Glasgow
His Majesty's Theatre, Aberdeen
King's Theatre, Edinburgh
Theatre Royal, Newcastle

Alexander Gibson/John Copley/Carl Toms/
Charles Bristow/Jim Hastie (choreographer)

8 May   * ***Pelléas et Mélisande*** Debussy
6 performances
King's Theatre, Glasgow
His Majesty's Theatre, Aberdeen
King's Theatre, Edinburgh
Theatre Royal, Newcastle

Alexander Gibson/Colin Graham –
David Pountney (revival)/
John Fraser/Charles Bristow

14 June   ***Die Fledermaus*** J Strauss
16 performances
King's Theatre, Edinburgh
Theatre Royal, Newcastle
His Majesty's Theatre, Aberdeen
Grand Theatre, Leeds
Theatre Royal, Glasgow

David Frame & Alexander Gibson/
David Pountney/David Fielding/
Alex Reid (costumes)/Charles Bristow/
Jim Hastie (choreographer)

Note: The performance on 14 Oct heralded the opening of the
Theatre Royal in Glasgow. The occasion was marked by a *Fanfare
for the Theatre Royal* by Robin Orr, and an Act II cabaret.

27 Aug   ***Hermiston*** Orr (World Premiere)
10 performances
King's Theatre, Edinburgh (EIF)
The Maltings, Snape, Aldeburgh
Theatre Royal, Newcastle
His Majesty's Theatre, Aberdeen
Grand Theatre, Leeds
Theatre Royal, Glasgow

Alexander Gibson & Roderick Brydon/
Toby Robertson/Robin Archer/
Robin Ornbo

4 Sep   * ***Don Giovanni*** Mozart
8 performances
The Maltings, Snape, Aldeburgh
Theatre Royal, Newcastle
His Majesty's Theatre, Aberdeen
Grand Theatre, Leeds

Lawrence Foster, Alexander Gibson &
Roderick Brydon/Peter Ebert –
David Pountney (revival)/Ralph Koltai/
Nadine Baylis (costumes)/Charles
Bristow/Jim Hastie (choreographer)

15 Oct   * ***Otello*** Verdi
4 performances
Theatre Royal, Glasgow

Alexander Gibson/Anthony Besch/
Ralph Koltai/Alex Reid (costumes)/
Charles Bristow

27 Oct   ***Don Giovanni*** Mozart
5 performances
Gaiety Theatre, Ayr
Arts Guild, Greenock
MacRobert Centre, Stirling

David Frame/Jeremy Sutcliffe/
Ralph Koltai/Victor Lockwood

12 Nov   ***Ariadne auf Naxos*** R Strauss
4 performances
Theatre Royal, Glasgow

Norman del Mar/Anthony Besch/
Peter Rice/John B Read/
Jim Hastie (choreographer)

26 Nov   * ***Così fan tutte*** Mozart
4 performances
Theatre Royal, Glasgow

Gary Bertini/Anthony Besch/
John Stoddart/Charles Bristow

10 Dec   ***The Golden Cockerel*** Rimsky-Korsakov
5 performances
Theatre Royal, Glasgow

Alexander Gibson/David Pountney/Sue
Blane/Maria Björnson (costumes)/Charles
Bristow/Jim Hastie (choreographer)

18 Dec   * ***A Midsummer Night's Dream*** Britten
2 performances
MacRobert Centre, Stirling

Roderick Brydon/Toby Robertson/
Robin Archer/Victor Lockwood/
Eleanor Fazan (choreographer)

1976

1 Jan   * ***Die Fledermaus*** J Strauss
8 performances
Theatre Royal, Glasgow
Royal Court Theatre, Liverpool
Empire Theatre, Sunderland
King's Theatre, Edinburgh

David Frame/David Pountney/David
Fielding/Alex Reid (costumes)/Charles
Bristow/Jim Hastie (choreographer)

7 Jan   * ***A Midsummer Night's Dream*** Britten
11 performances
Theatre Royal, Glasgow
Royal Court Theatre, Liverpool
Empire Theatre, Sunderland
King's Theatre, Edinburgh
Walhalla Theater, Wiesbaden
Theatre Royal, York

Roderick Brydon/Toby Robertson/
Robin Archer/Victor Lockwood/
Eleanor Fazan (choreographer)

21 Jan   * ***Don Giovanni*** Mozart
11 performances
Theatre Royal, Glasgow
Royal Court Theatre, Liverpool
Empire Theatre, Sunderland
King's Theatre, Edinburgh
His Majesty's Theatre, Aberdeen

Lawrence Foster & Roderick Brydon/
Peter Ebert – David Pountney (revival)/
Ralph Koltai/Alex Reid/Charles
Bristow/Jim Hastie (choreographer)

4 Feb   * ***Madama Butterfly*** Puccini
5 performances
Theatre Royal, Glasgow

David Frame/Peter Ebert/David Wilby/
Victor Lockwood

18 Feb   * ***Falstaff*** Verdi
11 performances
Theatre Royal, Glasgow
King's Theatre, Edinburgh
Theatre Royal, Newcastle
His Majesty's Theatre, Aberdeen

Alexander Gibson & Leonard Hancock/
Peter Ebert/Peter Rice/Charles
Bristow/Jim Hastie (choreographer)

1 Mar   * ***Don Giovanni*** Mozart
18 performances
Tait Hall, Kelso
Town Hall, Elgin
Corran Halls, Oban
Civic Hall, Barrow
Civic Theatre, Darlington
Crewe Civic Centre
Gaumont, Doncaster
Whitehall Theatre, Dundee
Adam Smith Theatre, Kirkcaldy

John Currie/Jeremy Sutcliffe/
Ralph Koltai/Victor Lockwood

6 April   * ***Ariadne auf Naxos*** R Strauss
7 performances
Empire Theatre, Sunderland
MacRobert Centre, Stirling
King's Theatre, Edinburgh
His Majesty's Theatre, Aberdeen
Theatre Royal, York

Norman del Mar/Anthony Besch/
Peter Rice/John B Read/
Jim Hastie (choreographer)

16 April   ***The Rape of Lucretia*** Britten
7 performances
MacRobert Centre, Stirling
Perth Theatre
King's Theatre, Edinburgh
Walhalla Theater, Wiesbaden
Staatstheater, Stuttgart

Roderick Brydon/Anthony Besch/
John Stoddart/Victor Lockwood

27 April   * ***The Golden Cockerel*** Rimsky-Korsakov
4 performances
King's Theatre, Edinburgh
Theatre Royal, Newcastle

Bryden Thomson/David Pountney/
Sue Blane/Maria Björnson (costumes)/
Charles Bristow/Jim Hastie
(choreographer)

12 May   * ***Otello*** Verdi
4 performances
King's Theatre, Edinburgh
Theatre Royal, Newcastle
His Majesty's Theatre, Aberdeen

John Mauceri/Anthony Besch/Ralph
Koltai/Alex Reid (costumes)/Charles Bristow

15 June   ***The Confessions of a Justified Sinner***
Wilson (World Premiere)
13 performances
Theatre Royal, York
Eden Court, Inverness
King's Theatre, Edinburgh
Grand Theatre, Leeds
His Majesty's Theatre, Aberdeen
Theatre Royal, Newcastle
Theatre Royal, Glasgow

Norman del Mar & John Currie/
Michael Geliot/Alexander McPherson/
Victor Lockwood/John Broome
(movement & fight arranger)

29 June   * ***The Merry Widow*** Lehár
20 performances
Eden Court, Inverness
King's Theatre, Edinburgh
Grand Theatre, Leeds
His Majesty's Theatre, Aberdeen
Theatre Royal, Newcastle
Theatre Royal, Glasgow

Neil Dodd, Peter Stanger, Alexander
Gibson & David Frame/Anthony Besch –
Jeremy Sutcliffe (revival)/John Stoddart/
Charles Bristow/Virginia Mason
(choreographer)

Note: A performance at the Theatre Royal, Glasgow on 22 Nov
was filmed by STV before an invited audience.

23 Aug   ***Macbeth*** Verdi
10 performances
King's Theatre, Edinburgh (EIF)
Grand Theatre, Leeds
His Majesty's Theatre, Aberdeen
Theatre Royal, Newcastle

Alexander Gibson & James Conlon/
David Pountney/Ralph Koltai/
Nick Chelton

Note: A special dress rehearsal was held on 20 Aug at the
Theatre Royal, Glasgow attended by the American Ambassador
Anne Armstrong, and British and American Friends of Scottish
Opera.
Note: A minute's silence was observed at the beginning of the
performance on 4 Dec at the Theatre Royal, Glasgow to mark
the death of Benjamin Britten.

3 Sep   * ***The Magic Flute*** Mozart
13 performances
Theatre Royal, Glasgow (2 visits)
Grand Theatre, Leeds
His Majesty's Theatre. Aberdeen
Theatre Royal, Newcastle
MacRobert Centre, Stirling

Gary Bertini & David Frame/David
Pountney/David Fielding/Maria
Björnson (costumes)/Victor Lockwood

6 Oct   * ***La bohème*** Puccini
5 performances
Theatre Royal, Glasgow

Alexander Gibson/Peter Ebert/
Peter Rice/Charles Bristow

17 Nov   * ***Don Pasquale*** Donizetti
5 performances
Theatre Royal, Glasgow

David Frame/Peter Ebert/Peter Rice/
Charles Bristow

15 Dec   ***Die Meistersinger von Nürnberg*** Wagner
4 performances
Theatre Royal, Glasgow

Alexander Gibson/David Pountney/
Maria Björnson/Charles Bristow & Victor
Lockwood/Jim Hastie (choreographer)

28 Dec   ***Hansel and Gretel*** Humperdinck
4 performances
Theatre Royal, Glasgow

Note: This Opera for Youth production was given using glove
puppets and staged in the afternoon.

1977

1 Jan   * ***The Merry Widow*** Lehár
14 performances
Theatre Royal, Glasgow
Empire Theatre, Sunderland
Opera House, Manchester
Empire Theatre, Liverpool
King's Theatre, Edinburgh

David Frame/Anthony Besch –
Jeremy Sutcliffe (revival)/
John Stoddart/Charles Bristow/
Virginia Mason (choreographer)

3 Jan   ***Hansel and Gretel*** Humperdinck
5 performances
Theatre Royal, Glasgow

Note: This Opera for Youth production was given using glove
puppets and staged in the afternoon.

19 Jan   * ***Fidelio*** Beethoven
17 performances
Theatre Royal, Glasgow (3 visits)
King's Theatre, Edinburgh
Theatre Royal, Newcastle
Grand Theatre, Wolverhampton

Lawrence Foster, Alexander Gibson &
Walter Weller/Peter Ebert/Hans Ulrich
Schmückle/Sylta Busse Schmückle
(costumes)/Charles Bristow

Note: The performance on 26 April at the King's Theatre,
Edinburgh marked the 25th anniversary of Alexander Gibson's
operatic conducting debut at Sadler's Wells.

2 Feb   * ***The Rape of Lucretia*** Britten
8 performances
Theatre Royal, Glasgow
Teatr Wielki, Lodz
Palace of Culture, Warsaw

Roderick Brydon/Anthony Besch/
John Stoddart/Victor Lockwood

16 Feb   ***Jenůfa*** Janáček
9 performances
Theatre Royal, Glasgow
King's Theatre, Edinburgh
His Majesty's Theatre, Aberdeen
Theatre Royal, Newcastle

Richard Armstrong & Anthony Hose/
David Pountney/Maria Björnson/Victor
Lockwood/Terry Gilbert (choreographer)

28 Feb   ***The Marriage of Figaro*** Mozart
29 performances
MacRobert Centre, Stirling
Eden Court, Inverness
King's Theatre, Edinburgh
His Majesty's Theatre, Aberdeen
Theatre Royal, Newcastle
Theatre Royal, Glasgow
Plus venues in Kirkcaldy, Dundee,
Doncaster, Darlington, Barrow, Crewe,
Wolverhampton

Roderick Brydon & Peter Stanger/Toby
Robertson/Alan Barrett/Victor
Lockwood/Jim Hastie (choreographer)

Note: The performance on 23 June at Eden Court, Inverness
was attended by HRH The Prince of Wales.

4 Mar * ***The Magic Flute*** Mozart
16 performances
Adam Smith Theatre, Kirkcaldy
Empire Theatre, Sunderland
RNCM, Manchester
Empire Theatre, Liverpool
Theatre Royal, York
King's Theatre, Edinburgh
Plus venues in Dundee, Doncaster, Darlington, Crewe

David Frame/David Pountney/David Fielding/Maria Björnson (costumes)/Victor Lockwood

29 Mar * ***Macbeth*** Verdi
12 performances
Empire Theatre, Sunderland
Opera House, Manchester
Empire Theatre, Liverpool
King's Theatre, Edinburgh
His Majesty's Theatre, Aberdeen
Theatre Royal, Newcastle
Theatre Royal, Glasgow

James Conlon & Alexander Gibson/David Pountney/Ralph Koltai/Nick Chelton

8 April * ***The Turn of the Screw*** Britten
7 performances
RNCM, Manchester
Theatre Royal, York
Teatr Wielki, Lodz
Palace of Culture, Warsaw
Staatstheater, Stuttgart
Gärtnerplatz, Munich

Roderick Brydon/Anthony Besch – Jeremy Sutcliffe (revival)/John Stoddart/Charles Bristow

19 April * ***Don Pasquale*** Donizetti
12 performances
Theatre Royal, York
King's Theatre, Edinburgh
Perth Theatre
His Majesty's Theatre, Aberdeen
Theatre Royal, Newcastle

David Frame/Peter Ebert/Peter Rice/Charles Bristow

30 April * ***Die Meistersinger von Nürnberg*** Wagner
9 performances
King's Theatre, Edinburgh
His Majesty's Theatre, Aberdeen
Theatre Royal, Newcastle
Theatre Royal, Glasgow

Alexander Gibson/David Pountney/Maria Björnson/Charles Bristow & Victor Lockwood

6 Sep ***Mary Queen of Scots*** Musgrave
(World Premiere)
8 performances
King's Theatre, Edinburgh (EIF)
Theatre Royal, Newcastle
Grand Theatre, Wolverhampton
Theatre Royal, Glasgow

Thea Musgrave & Leonard Hancock/Colin Graham/Robin Don & Colin Graham/Alex Reid (costumes)/Charles Bristow

2 Nov * ***Otello*** Verdi
5 performances
Theatre Royal, Glasgow

Alexander Gibson/Anthony Besch – Graham Vick (revival)/Ralph Koltai/Alex Reid (costumes)/Charles Bristow

16 Nov * ***Ariadne auf Naxos*** R Strauss
4 performances
Theatre Royal, Glasgow

Norman del Mar/Peter Foster/Anthony Besch – Peter Rice (revival)/John B Read & Victor Lockwood/Jim Hastie (choreographer)

18 Dec * ***Albert Herring*** Britten
1 performance
Theatre Royal, Glasgow

Note: 'A Farewell Performance for Mr and Mrs P Hemmings'.

30 Nov * ***The Golden Cockerel*** Rimsky-Korsakov
7 performances
Theatre Royal, Glasgow

Bryden Thomson & Alexander Gibson/David Pountney/Sue Blane/Maria Björnson (costumes)/Charles Bristow/Jim Hastie (choreographer)

21 Dec * ***Falstaff*** Verdi
2 performances
Theatre Royal, Glasgow

Alexander Gibson/Peter Ebert – John Lawson Graham (revival)/Peter Rice/Charles Bristow/Jim Hastie (choreographer)

1978

3 Jan * ***Falstaff*** Verdi
4 performances
Theatre Royal, Glasgow
Theatre Royal, Newcastle

Alexander Gibson/Peter Ebert – John Lawson Graham (revival)/Peter Rice/Charles Bristow/Jim Hastie (choreographer)

3 Jan ***Magical Musical Wardrobe***
6 performances
Theatre Royal, Glasgow

4 Jan ***The Marriage of Figaro*** Mozart
2 performances
Theatre Royal, Glasgow

Roderick Brydon/Toby Robertson/Alan Barrett/Victor Lockwood/Jim Hastie (choreographer)

13 Jan * ***The Rape of Lucretia*** Britten
9 performances
MacRobert Centre, Stirling
Empire Theatre, Liverpool
Grand Theatre, Leeds
His Majesty's Theatre, Aberdeen
King's Theatre, Edinburgh
Opéra de Lausanne
Opernhaus, Zurich
Stadtische Buhnen Theater, Frankfurt

Alexander Gibson/Anthony Besch – Graham Vick (revival)/John Stoddart/Victor Lockwood

25 Jan * ***Madama Butterfly*** Puccini
7 performances
Theatre Royal, Glasgow
King's Theatre, Edinburgh

Alexander Gibson/Peter Ebert – Nicholas Hytner (revival)/David Wilby/Victor Lockwood

8 Feb ***The Bartered Bride*** Smetana
14 performances
Theatre Royal, Glasgow
Empire Theatre, Liverpool
Grand Theatre, Leeds
His Majesty's Theatre, Aberdeen
King's Theatre, Edinburgh

Roderick Brydon & David Frame/David Pountney/Sue Blane/Maria Björnson (costumes)/Victor Lockwood/Peter Darrell (choreographer)

1 Mar ***Seraglio*** Mozart
20 performances
Theatre Royal, Glasgow
Empire Theatre, Liverpool
Grand Theatre, Leeds
His Majesty's Theatre, Aberdeen
King's Theatre, Edinburgh
Perth Theatre (2 visits)
Dundee College of Education
Theatre Royal, Newcastle
Theatre Royal, Glasgow

Gary Bertini, Peter Stanger & Alexander Gibson/David Pountney/David Fielding/Maria Björnson (costumes)/Victor Lockwood

27 April * ***Der Rosenkavalier*** R Strauss
8 performances
Theatre Royal, Newcastle
King's Theatre, Edinburgh
Theatre Royal, Glasgow

Walter Weller & Alexander Gibson/Anthony Besch/John Stoddart/Charles Bristow

6 May * ***The Turn of the Screw*** Britten
6 performances
King's Theatre, Edinburgh
Opernhaus, Zurich
Stadtische Buhnen Theater, Frankfurt
Eden Court, Inverness

Roderick Brydon & Leonard Hancock/Anthony Besch/John Stoddart/Charles Bristow

8 May * *A Midsummer Night's Dream* Britten
7 performances
King's Theatre, Edinburgh
Opernhaus, Zurich
His Majesty's Theatre, Aberdeen
Empire Theatre, Liverpool
Theatre Royal, Newcastle

Leonard Hancock & Roderick Brydon/
Toby Robertson/Robin Archer/Victor
Lockwood/Jim Hastie (choreographer)

16 May * *Die Meistersinger von Nürnberg*
Wagner
2 performances
King's Theatre, Edinburgh

Alexander Gibson/David Pountney/
Maria Björnson/Charles Bristow & Victor
Lockwood/Jim Hastie (choreographer)

30 May * *Mary Queen of Scots* Musgrave
1 performance
Staatsoper, Stuttgart

Thea Musgrave/Colin Graham/Robin
Don & Colin Graham/Alex Reid
(costumes)/Charles Bristow/
Peter Darrell (choreographer)

20 June *Hansel and Gretel* Humperdinck
15 performances
Theatre Royal, Glasgow (2 visits)
Eden Court, Inverness
His Majesty's Theatre, Aberdeen
Perth Theatre

Alexander Gibson & David Frame/Peter
Ebert/Sue Blane/Maria Björnson
(costumes)/Victor Lockwood

20 July *Dido and Aeneas* Purcell
5 performances
Théâtre de l'Archevêché
(Aix-en-Provence Festival)

Charles Mackerras/John Copley/Stefanos
Lazaridis/Jim Hastie (choreographer)

23 Aug * *Pelléas et Mélisande* Debussy
3 performances
King's Theatre, Edinburgh (EIF)

Alexander Gibson/Colin Graham/
John Fraser/Charles Bristow

5 Sep * *La bohème* Puccini
5 performances
His Majesty's Theatre, Aberdeen
Theatre Royal, Newcastle
Empire Theatre, Liverpool

Robin Stapleton/Peter Ebert/
Peter Rice/Charles Bristow

7 Sep * *Die Fledermaus* J Strauss
5 performances
His Majesty's Theatre, Aberdeen
Theatre Royal, Newcastle
Empire Theatre, Liverpool
Theatre Royal, Glasgow

Brian Priestman & Alexander Gibson/
David Pountney – Graham Vick (revival)/
David Fielding/Alex Reid (costumes)/
Charles Bristow

Note: The performance on 22 Dec at the Theatre Royal,
Glasgow was a special performance for the STUC.

4 Oct *Simon Boccanegra* Verdi
5 performances
Theatre Royal, Glasgow

Henry Lewis/Peter Ebert/Peter Rice/
Mario Vanarelli (costumes)/
Victor Lockwood

18 Oct * *Jenůfa* Janáček
5 performances
Theatre Royal, Glasgow

Alexander Gibson & Anthony Hose/
David Pountney/Maria Björnson/Victor
Lockwood/Terry Gilbert (choreographer)

4 Nov * *The Catiline Conspiracy* Hamilton
4 performances
Theatre Royal, Glasgow

Roderick Brydon/Anthony Besch/
Luciana Arrighi/Charles Bristow

15 Nov **Triple Bill**
4 performances
Theatre Royal, Glasgow

Savitri Holst
Charles Mackerras/Graham Vick/
Russell Craig/Victor Lockwood

Fanny Robin Harper
Edward Harper/Graham Vick/
Russell Craig/Victor Lockwood

Dido and Aeneas Purcell
Charles Mackerras/John Copley/
Stefanos Lazaridis/Robert Bryan/
Jim Hastie (choreographer)

1979

2 Jan * *Der Rosenkavalier* R Strauss
2 performances
Theatre Royal, Glasgow

Alexander Gibson/Anthony Besch/
John Stoddart/Charles Bristow

Note: The performance on 4 Jan marked Michael Langdon's
'farewell to the operatic stage'.

3 Jan * *Die Fledermaus* J Strauss
6 performances
Theatre Royal, Glasgow

Brian Priestman & Alexander Gibson/
David Pountney – Graham Vick (revival)/
David Fielding/Alex Reid (costumes)/
Charles Bristow & Victor Lockwood/
Jim Hastie (choreographer)

17 Jan * *A Midsummer Night's Dream* Britten
4 performances
Theatre Royal, Glasgow

Roderick Brydon/Toby Robertson/
Robin Archer/Victor Lockwood/
Jim Hastie (choreographer)

31 Jan * *La bohème* Puccini
10 performances
Theatre Royal, Glasgow
Grand Theatre, Wolverhampton
New Theatre, Oxford
King's Theatre, Edinburgh
His Majesty's Theatre, Aberdeen

Alexander Gibson & David Frame/
Peter Ebert/Peter Rice/Charles Bristow

8 Mar * *Simon Boccanegra* Verdi
10 performances
Grand Theatre, Wolverhampton
New Theatre, Oxford
His Majesty's Theatre, Aberdeen
Theatre Royal, Newcastle
Empire Theatre, Liverpool

Roderick Brydon & Henry Lewis/Peter
Ebert/Peter Rice/Mario Vanarelli
(costumes)/Victor Lockwood

24 Mar * *Hansel and Gretel* Humperdinck
1 performance
New Theatre, Oxford

Alexander Gibson/Peter Ebert/
Maria Björnson/Victor Lockwood

4 April *Kátya Kabanová* Janáček
8 performances
Theatre Royal, Glasgow
King's Theatre, Edinburgh
Theatre Royal, Newcastle

Richard Armstrong & Wyn Davies/
David Pountney/Maria Björnson/
Victor Lockwood

18 April *Rigoletto* Verdi
13 performances
Theatre Royal, Glasgow
King's Theatre, Edinburgh
Theatre Royal, Newcastle
His Majesty's Theatre, Aberdeen

Alexander Gibson & Peter Stanger/
David Alden/David Fielding/Alex Reid
(costumes)/Robert Bryan

21 May *The Two Widows* Smetana
2 performances
Perth Theatre (Perth Festival)

Albert Rosen/David Pountney/
Sue Blane/Victor Lockwood

14 June   *Fiddler on the Roof* Bock
34 performances
Theatre Royal, Glasgow (3 visits)
Eden Court, Inverness
King's Theatre, Edinburgh
His Majesty's Theatre, Aberdeen

Guy Woolfenden & Peter Stanger/Peter
Ebert/Michael Knight/Mark Negim
(costumes)/Victor Lockwood/
Royston Maldoom (choreographer)

Note: The performance on 1 Nov at the Theatre Royal, Glasgow
was attended by Her Majesty The Queen and HRH The Duke
of Edinburgh.

29 Aug   * *The Golden Cockerel* Rimsky-Korsakov
7 performances
King's Theatre, Edinburgh (EIF)
Theatre Royal, Newcastle
Empire Theatre, Liverpool

Henry Lewis/David Pountney/
Sue Blane/Maria Björnson (costumes)/
Charles Bristow

1 Sep   *Eugene Onegin* Tchaikovsky
6 performances
King's Theatre, Edinburgh (EIF)
Theatre Royal, Glasgow
Alexander Gibson/David Pountney/Roger
Butlin/Deirdre Clancy (costumes)/Nick
Chelton/Terry Gilbert (choreographer)

3 Sep   * *The Turn of the Screw* Britten
3 performances
King's Theatre, Edinburgh (EIF)
Empire Theatre, Liverpool

Roderick Brydon/Anthony Besch –
Jeremy Sutcliffe (revival)/
John Stoddart/Charles Bristow

3 Oct   * *Pelléas et Mélisande* Debussy
5 performances
Theatre Royal, Glasgow

Roderick Brydon/Colin Graham –
John Lawson Graham (revival)/
John Fraser/Charles Bristow

17 Oct   *Orfeo ed Euridice* Gluck
9 performances
Theatre Royal, Glasgow
Sadler's Wells, London
Theatre Royal, Newcastle

Alexander Gibson/Peter Ebert/
Ingrid Rosell/Charles Bristow/
Peter Darrell (choreographer)

14 Nov   *Don Giovanni* Mozart
11 performances
Theatre Royal, Glasgow
Sadler's Wells, London
Theatre Royal, Newcastle

Alexander Gibson/David Pountney/
Maria Björnson/Nick Chelton

1980

3 Jan   *Eugene Onegin* Tchaikovsky
3 performances
Theatre Royal, Glasgow

Alexander Gibson/David Pountney/Roger
Butlin/Deirdre Clancy (costumes)/Nick
Chelton/Terry Gilbert (choreographer)

16 Jan   * *The Two Widows* Smetana
6 performances
Theatre Royal, Glasgow
Theatre Royal, Newcastle

Guy Woolfenden/David Pountney/
Sue Blane/Victor Lockwood

7 Feb   * *The Bartered Bride* Smetana
15 performances
Theatre Royal, Newcastle
Theatre Royal, Glasgow
Opera House, Buxton
Sadler's Wells, London
King's Theatre, Edinburgh

Albert Rosen & Peter Stanger/
David Pountney/Sue Blane/
Maria Björnson/Victor Lockwood/
Peter Darrell (choreographer)

Note: The performance on 7 Feb at the Theatre Royal,
Newcastle marked the debut of the Scottish Opera Orchestra.

6 Mar   * *Rigoletto* Verdi
13 performances
Opera House, Buxton
Theatre Royal, Glasgow
Playhouse, Edinburgh
His Majesty's Theatre, Aberdeen

Alexander Gibson & Peter Stanger/
David Alden/David Fielding/Alex Reid
(costumes)/Robert Bryan

2 April   * *Mary Queen of Scots* Musgrave
4 performances
Sadler's Wells, London
Theatre Royal, Newcastle

Meredith Davies/Colin Graham/
Robin Don & Colin Graham/Alex Reid
(costumes)/Charles Bristow/
Peter Darrell (choreographer)

16 April   * *Peter Grimes* Britten
8 performances
King's Theatre, Edinburgh
Theatre Royal, Newcastle
Theatre Royal, Glasgow

Alexander Gibson & Leonard Hancock/
Anthony Besch – Michael Follis (revival)/
Alix Stone/John B Read

7 May   *L'elisir d'amore* Donizetti
15 performances
Theatre Royal, Glasgow
Perth Theatre (Perth Festival)
His Majesty's Theatre, Aberdeen
Theatre Royal, Newcastle
MacRobert Centre, Stirling
Empire Theatre, Liverpool
Playhouse, Edinburgh

Roderick Brydon & Richard Honner/
Graham Vick/Russell Craig/
Victor Lockwood

22 May   * *A Midsummer Night's Dream* Britten
4 performances
Perth Theatre (Perth Festival)
Basel Theater, Basel
Opéra de Lausanne

Roderick Brydon/Toby Robertson/
Robin Archer/Victor Lockwood/
Jim Hastie (choreographer)

28 May   * *Orfeo ed Euridice* Gluck
2 performances
Opéra de Lausanne

Alexander Gibson/Peter Ebert/
Ingrid Rosell/Charles Bristow/
Peter Darrell (choreographer)

12 June   * *Fiddler on the Roof* Bock
3 performances
Playhouse, Edinburgh

Guy Woolfenden/Peter Ebert/
Michael Knight/Mark Negim
(costumes)/Victor Lockwood

27 Aug   *The Cunning Little Vixen* Janáček
3 performances
King's Theatre, Edinburgh (EIF)
His Majesty's Theatre, Aberdeen

Richard Armstrong & Wyn Davies/
David Pountney/Maria Björnson/Nick
Chelton/Stuart Hopps (choreographer)

28 Aug   *Wozzeck* Berg
9 performances
King's Theatre, Edinburgh (EIF)
Theatre Royal, Newcastle
Theatre Royal, Glasgow

Alexander Gibson/David Alden/
David Fielding/Charles Bristow/
Stuart Hopps (choreographer)

1 Oct   * *The Marriage of Figaro* Mozart
12 performances
Theatre Royal, Glasgow
Empire Theatre, Liverpool
Playhouse, Edinburgh
Theatre Royal, Newcastle

Gyorgy Fischer/Toby Robertson/
Alan Barratt/Victor Lockwood

15 Oct **_Tosca_** Puccini
14 performances
Theatre Royal, Glasgow
Empire Theatre, Liverpool
Playhouse, Edinburgh
Theatre Royal, Newcastle

Alexander Gibson/Anthony Besch/
Peter Rice/Mark Henderson

4 Nov **_The Barber of Seville_** Rossini
4 performances
MacRobert Centre, Stirling
Dundee College of Education

Ian Robertson/John Lawson Graham/
Alex Reid/Victor Lockwood

9 Dec * **_La bohème_** Puccini
2 performances
Theatre Royal, Glasgow

Jacques Delacôte/Peter Ebert – John
Lawson Graham (revival)/Peter Rice/
Charles Bristow

1981

6 Jan * **_La bohème_** Puccini
12 performances
Theatre Royal, Glasgow
Playhouse, Edinburgh
Empire Theatre, Liverpool
Opera House, Buxton

Jacques Delacôte & Richard Honner/
Peter Ebert – John Lawson Graham
(revival)/Peter Rice/Charles Bristow

7 Jan * **_Lucia di Lammermoor_** Donizetti
17 performances
Theatre Royal, Glasgow
Theatre Royal, Newcastle
Playhouse, Edinburgh
Eden Court, Inverness
Empire Theatre, Liverpool
Opera House, Buxton

Henry Lewis/John Lawson Graham/
Henry Bardon/Alix Stone (costumes)/
Charles Bristow

22 Jan **_The Barber of Seville_** Rossini
12 performances
Carnegie Hall, Dunfermline
Theatre Royal, Newcastle
Playhouse, Edinburgh
Adam Smith Theatre, Kirkcaldy
Eden Court, Inverness
Empire Theatre, Liverpool
Opera House, Buxton
Perth Theatre

Meredith Davies & Ian Robertson/
John Lawson Graham/Alex Reid/
Victor Lockwood

11 Mar **_La traviata_** Verdi
17 performances
Theatre Royal, Glasgow
Playhouse, Edinburgh (2 visits)
Grand Opera House, Belfast
Theatre Royal, Newcastle
Empire Theatre, Liverpool

Alexander Gibson & Peter Stanger/
David William/Michael Annals/
Alex Reid (costumes)/Victor Lockwood/
Stuart Hopps (choreographer)

15 April **_The Makropoulos Case_** Janáček
9 performances
Theatre Royal, Glasgow
Theatre Royal, Newcastle
Playhouse, Edinburgh

Richard Armstrong/David Pountney/
Maria Björnson/Nick Chelton

6 May * **_Eugene Onegin_** Tchaikovsky
14 performances
Theatre Royal, Glasgow
Theatre Royal, Newcastle
Playhouse, Edinburgh
Grand Opera House, Belfast

Alexander Gibson & Roderick
Brydon/David Pountney/Roger Butlin/
Deirdre Clancy (costumes)/Nick
Chelton/Terry Gilbert (choreographer)

2 July * **_A Midsummer Night's Dream_** Britten
3 performances
Kongresshaus, Villach, Austria
Monastery Garden, Ljubljana

Leonard Hancock/Toby Robertson – John
Lawson Graham (revival)/Robin Archer/
Victor Lockwood

3 July * **_The Rape of Lucretia_** Britten
2 performances
Kongresshaus, Villach, Austria
Monastery Garden, Ljubljana

Leonard Hancock/Anthony Besch – John
Lawson Graham (revival)/John Stoddart/
Victor Lockwood

1 Sep **_The Beggar's Opera_** Gay
21 performances
King's Theatre, Edinburgh (EIF)
Theatre Royal, Newcastle
Dominion Theatre, London
Theatre Royal, Glasgow

Guy Woolfenden/David William/
Michael Annals/Alex Reid (costumes)/
Spike Gavin/Geraldine Stephenson
(choreographer)

9 Sep **_The Pearl Fishers_** Bizet
11 performances
Theatre Royal, Newcastle
Capitol Theatre, Aberdeen
Empire Theatre, Liverpool
Theatre Royal, Glasgow

Ian Robertson/Steven Pimlott/
Stefanos Lazaridis/Mark Henderson/
Eleanor Fazan (choreographer)

28 Oct * **_Die Fledermaus_** J Strauss
13 performances
Theatre Royal, Glasgow (2 visits)
Theatre Royal, Newcastle
Empire Theatre, Liverpool
Playhouse, Edinburgh

Jacques Delacôte, Richard Honner
& Alexander Gibson/David Pountney –
John Lawson Graham (revival)/
David Fielding/Alex Reid (costumes)/
Victor Lockwood

25 Nov * **_Così fan tutte_** Mozart
5 performances
Theatre Royal, Glasgow

Gyorgy Fischer/Anthony Besch/
John Stoddart/Charles Bristow

1982

13 Jan **_L'Egisto_** Cavalli
23 performances
Theatre Royal, Glasgow
Playhouse, Edinburgh
Theatre Royal, Newcastle
Grand Opera House, Belfast
Dominion Theatre, London
Apollo Theatre, Oxford
Schlosstheater, Schwetzingen
Alte Oper, Frankfurt
La Fenice, Venice

Roderick Brydon & Raymond Leppard/
John Cox/Allen Charles Klein

15 Jan **_The Pearl Fishers_** Bizet
26 performances
Carnegie Hall, Dunfermline
Grand Opera House, Belfast
Playhouse, Edinburgh (2 visits)
Apollo Theatre, Oxford
Gaiety Theatre, Ayr
Eden Court, Inverness
Theatre Royal, Newcastle (2 visits)
Capitol Theatre, Aberdeen
Empire Theatre, Liverpool
Theatre Royal, Glasgow

Ian Robertson/Steven Pimlott/Stefanos
Lazaridis/Mark Henderson/Eleanor
Fazan & Tony Ellis (choreographers)

4 Feb * **_Così fan tutte_** Mozart
5 performances
Playhouse, Edinburgh
Theatre Royal, Newcastle

Gyorgy Fischer/Anthony Besch/
John Stoddart/Charles Bristow

3 Mar * **_Tosca_** Puccini
15 performances
Theatre Royal, Glasgow
Dominion Theatre, London
Playhouse, Edinburgh
Apollo Theatre, Oxford
Theatre Royal, Newcastle

Alexander Gibson/Anthony Besch/
Peter Rice/Mark Henderson

21 April   * ***The Cunning Little Vixen*** Janáček
7 performances
Theatre Royal, Glasgow
Theatre Royal, Newcastle

Wyn Davies & Richard Honner/David
Pountney/Maria Björnson/Nick
Chelton/Stuart Hopps (choreographer)

24 July   ***Manon Lescaut*** Puccini
15 performances
King's Theatre, Edinburgh (EIF)
Theatre Royal, Newcastle
Empire Theatre, Liverpool
His Majesty's Theatre, Aberdeen
Theatre Royal, Glasgow

Alexander Gibson & Peter Stanger/
John Cox/Allen Charles Klein/
Alix Stone (costumes)/Robert Bryan

15 Sep   * ***Seraglio*** Mozart
15 performances
Theatre Royal, Newcastle
Empire Theatre, Liverpool
His Majesty's Theatre, Aberdeen
MacRobert Centre, Stirling
Theatre Royal. Glasgow
Playhouse, Edinburgh

Ian Robertson/David Pountney/
David Fielding/Maria Björnson
(costumes)/Victor Lockwood

25 Sep   * ***A Midsummer Night's Dream*** Britten
9 performances
Empire Theatre, Liverpool
Theatre Royal, Newcastle
Theatre Royal, Glasgow

Steuart Bedford/Toby Robertson – John
Lawson Graham (revival)/Robin Archer/
Victor Lockwood/Nigel Nicholson
(choreographer)

1983

12 Jan   ***The Magic Flute*** Mozart
19 performances
Theatre Royal, Glasgow (2 visits)
Playhouse, Edinburgh
Dominion Theatre, London
Grand Theatre, Leeds
Theatre Royal, Newcastle
Grand Opera House, Belfast
Empire Theatre, Liverpool

Alexander Gibson & Ian Robertson/
Jonathan Miller/Philip Prowse/
Robert Bryan

26 Jan   * ***A Midsummer Night's Dream*** Britten
2 performances
Playhouse, Edinburgh
Steuart Bedford/Toby Robertson – John
Lawson Graham (revival)/Robin Archer/
Victor Lockwood/Nigel Nicholson
(choreographer)

4 Feb   * ***The Pearl Fishers*** Bizet
4 performances
Dominion Theatre, London
Grand Theatre, Leeds
Empire Theatre, Liverpool
Ian Robertson & Richard Honner/
Steven Pimlott/Stefanos Lazaridis/Mark
Henderson/Tony Ellis (choreographer)

2 Mar   * ***Die Meistersinger von Nürnberg***
Wagner
11 performances
Theatre Royal, Glasgow
Empire Theatre, Liverpool
Theatre Royal, Newcastle
Playhouse, Edinburgh

Alexander Gibson & Ian Robertson/
David Pountney – John Lawson Graham
(revival)/Maria Björnson/Charles Bristow
& Victor Lockwood/Michela Hardy
(choreographer)

27 April   ***Werther*** Massenet
10 performances
Theatre Royal, Glasgow
Empire Theatre, Liverpool
Theatre Royal, Newcastle
Playhouse, Edinburgh

Roderick Brydon/Rhoda Levine/
John Conklin/Robert Bryan

20 Aug   ***Death in Venice*** Britten
9 performances
Theatre Royal, Glasgow (2 visits)
King's Theatre, Edinburgh (EIF)
Theatre Royal, Newcastle
Empire Theatre, Liverpool

Roderick Brydon/François Rochaix/
Jean-Claude Maret/Jean-Philippe Roy

14 Sep   * ***The Golden Cockerel*** Rimsky-Korsakov
6 performances
Theatre Royal, Newcastle
Grand Opera House, Belfast
Empire Theatre, Liverpool
Theatre Royal, Glasgow

Alexander Gibson/David Pountney –
Jeremy Sutcliffe (revival)/Sue Blane/
Maria Björnson/Alan Campbell/
Nigel Nicholson (choreographer)

Note: A further six children's matinee performances with piano
accompaniment were given during the run.

19 Oct   ***Idomeneo*** Mozart
8 performances
Theatre Royal, Glasgow (2 visits)
Theatre Royal, Newcastle

Gyorgy Fischer/John Cox/Roger Butlin/
Robert Bryan

16 Nov   * ***Hansel and Gretel*** Humperdinck
8 performances
Theatre Royal, Glasgow (2 visits)
Theatre Royal, Newcastle

Stephen Barlow/Peter Ebert – Stefan
Janski (revival)/Sue Blane/Maria
Björnson/Alan Campbell/
Nigel Nicholson (choreographer)

16 Dec   ***My Fair Lady*** Loewe
14 performances
Theatre Royal, Glasgow

Ian Robertson/Peter Lichtenfels/Adrian
Vaux/Tim Goodchild (costumes)/Alan
Campbell/Kedzie Penfield (choreographer)

1984

18 Jan   * ***L'elisir d'amore*** Donizetti
11 performances
Theatre Royal, Glasgow
Theatre Royal, Newcastle
Empire Theatre, Liverpool
Playhouse, Edinburgh

Ian Robertson/Graham Vick/
Russell Craig/Victor Lockwood

30 Jan   * ***La bohème*** Puccini
11 performances
Theatre Royal, Glasgow (2 visits)
Theatre Royal, Newcastle
Playhouse, Edinburgh

Norman del Mar & Richard Honner/
Peter Ebert – John Lawson Graham
(revival)/Peter Rice/Alan Campbell

15 Mar   * ***L'Egisto*** Cavalli
9 performances
Theatre Royal, Glasgow
Empire Theatre, Liverpool
Theatre Royal, Newcastle

Peter Stanger/John Cox/Allen Charles
Klein/Nigel Nicholson (choreographer)

18 April   ***Turandot*** Puccini
11 performances
Theatre Royal, Glasgow
Empire Theatre, Liverpool
Theatre Royal, Newcastle
Playhouse, Edinburgh

Alexander Gibson/Tony Palmer/Kenneth
Carey/Barbara Lane (costumes)/
Nick Chelton/Derrick Zieba (sound)

22 May   ***Double Bill***
9 performances
Perth Theatre (Perth Festival)
Gaiety Theatre, Ayr
MacRobert Centre, Stirling
Gardyne Theatre, Dundee
Carnegie Hall, Dunfermline
Eden Court, Inverness

The Marriage Contract Rossini
The Silken Ladder Rossini

Richard Honner/Graham Vick/
Russell Craig/Ian Sommerville

21 Aug   ***Orion*** Cavalli
13 performances
King's Theatre, Edinburgh (EIF)
His Majesty's Theatre, Aberdeen
Theatre Royal, Newcastle
Theatre Royal, Glasgow
Playhouse, Edinburgh

Raymond Leppard & Peter Stanger/
Peter Wood/John Bury/Robert Bryan/
Beryl Shaw (archery coach)

5 Sep   * *Fidelio* Beethoven
15 performances
Theatre Royal, Glasgow
His Majesty's Theatre, Aberdeen
Theatre Royal, Newcastle
Empire Theatre, Liverpool
Playhouse, Edinburgh
Grand Theatre, Leeds

Alexander Gibson/Peter Ebert – Andy Hinds (revival)/Hans-Ulrich Schmückle/John McMurray (costumes)/Alan Campbell

19 Sep   * *Rigoletto* Verdi
15 performances
Theatre Royal, Glasgow
His Majesty's Theatre, Aberdeen
Theatre Royal, Newcastle
Empire Theatre, Liverpool
Playhouse, Edinburgh
Grand Theatre, Leeds

Ian Robertson/David Alden/David Fielding/Alex Reid (costumes)/Alan Campbell

1985

9 Jan   *Capriccio* R Strauss
7 performances
Theatre Royal, Glasgow
His Majesty's Theatre, Aberdeen
Empire Theatre, Liverpool

Norman del Mar/John Cox/Jack Notman/Alan Campbell/Peter Darrell (choreographer)

23 Jan   * *The Bartered Bride* Smetana
15 performances
Theatre Royal, Glasgow
His Majesty's Theatre, Aberdeen
Empire Theatre, Liverpool
Grand Opera House, Belfast
Playhouse, Edinburgh
Theatre Royal, Newcastle

Stephen Barlow/David Pountney/Sue Blane/Maria Björnson (costumes)/Alan Campbell/Jim Hastie (choreographer)

13 Feb   *The Barber of Seville* Rossini
17 performances
Theatre Royal, Glasgow
His Majesty's Theatre, Aberdeen
Empire Theatre, Liverpool
Grand Opera House, Belfast
Playhouse, Edinburgh
Theatre Royal, Newcastle

Alexander Gibson & Richard Honner/Robert David MacDonald/Sue Blane/Gerry Jenkinson

17 April   *Don Giovanni* Mozart
7 performances
Theatre Royal, Glasgow
Theatre Royal, Newcastle

Alexander Gibson/Graham Vick/Stefanos Lazaridis/Clare Mitchell (costumes)/Nick Chelton/Terry Gilbert (choreographer)

8 May   *Orlando* Handel
11 performances
Theatre Royal, Glasgow
Theatre Royal, Newcastle

Richard Hickox/Christopher Fettes/Antony McDonald/Paul Pyant/Ian Spink (choreographer)

15 May   * *Double Bill*
2 performances
Theatre Royal, Glasgow

The Marriage Contract Rossini
The Silken Ladder Rossini

Richard Honner/Graham Vick/Russell Craig/Ian Sommerville

5 June   *Hedda Gabler* Harper (World Premiere)
5 performances
Theatre Royal, Glasgow

Diego Masson/Graham Vick/Russell Craig/Matthew Richardson

4 Sep   *La vie Parisienne* Offenbach
16 performances
Theatre Royal, Glasgow
Theatre Royal, Newcastle
His Majesty's Theatre, Aberdeen
King's Theatre, Edinburgh
Empire Theatre, Liverpool
Apollo Theatre, Oxford

Alexander Gibson/Graham Vick/Richard Hudson/Bruno Boyer/Bruno Tonioli (choreographer)

2 Oct   * *The Magic Flute* Mozart
9 performances
Theatre Royal, Glasgow
Theatre Royal, Newcastle
His Majesty's Theatre, Aberdeen
King's Theatre, Edinburgh
Empire Theatre, Liverpool

Janos Furst/Jonathan Miler – Keith Warner (revival)/Philip Prowse/Alan Campbell

23 Oct   *Oberon* Weber
12 performances
Theatre Royal, Glasgow
Theatre Royal, Newcastle
His Majesty's Theatre, Aberdeen
King's Theatre, Edinburgh
Empire Theatre, Liverpool
Apollo Theatre, Oxford

Alexander Gibson/Graham Vick/Russell Craig/Nick Chelton

1986

22 Jan   *Il trovatore* Verdi
11 performances
Theatre Royal, Glasgow
King's Theatre, Edinburgh
His Majesty's Theatre, Aberdeen
Theatre Royal, Newcastle

Graeme Jenkins/Graham Vick/Michael Yeargan/John Waterhouse

12 Feb   * *Werther* Massenet
8 performances
Theatre Royal, Glasgow
King's Theatre, Edinburgh
His Majesty's Theatre, Aberdeen
Theatre Royal, Newcastle

Kenneth Montgomery/Rhoda Levine – Keith Warner (revival)/John Conklin/Alan Campbell

5 Mar   *The Rise and Fall of the City of Mahagonny* Weill
11 performances
Theatre Royal, Glasgow
King's Theatre, Edinburgh
His Majesty's Theatre, Aberdeen
Theatre Royal, Newcastle

Sian Edwards/David Alden/David Fielding/Alan Campbell

20 Mar   *The Tales of Hoffmann* Offenbach
11 performances
Gardyne Theatre, Dundee
Loreburn Hall, Dumfries
Town Hall, Elgin
Gaiety Theatre, Ayr
MacRobert Centre, Stirling
Carnegie Hall, Dunfermline

Simon Halsey/Matthew Richardson/Kenny Miller/Matthew Richardson

16 April   * *The Turn of the Screw* Britten
8 performances
Theatre Royal, Glasgow
King's Theatre, Edinburgh
Empire Theatre, Liverpool
Theatre Royal, Newcastle

Ronald Zollman/Anthony Besch/John Stoddart/Alan Campbell

30 April   *The Marriage of Figaro* Mozart
11 performances
Theatre Royal, Glasgow
King's Theatre, Edinburgh
Empire Theatre, Liverpool
Theatre Royal, Newcastle

Gyorgy Fischer/John Cox/John Byrne/Paul Pyant/Ian Spink (choreographer)

14 May   * *Tosca* Puccini
13 performances
Theatre Royal, Glasgow
King's Theatre, Edinburgh
Empire Theatre, Liverpool
Theatre Royal, Newcastle
Eden Court, Inverness

Alexander Gibson/Anthony Besch/Peter Rice/Alan Campbell

30 Sep　　*Carmen* Bizet
14 performances
Theatre Royal, Glasgow
Empire Theatre, Liverpool
King's Theatre, Edinburgh
His Majesty's Theatre, Aberdeen
New Tyne Theatre, Newcastle

John Mauceri & Sian Edwards/
Graham Vick/Michael Yeargan/Nick
Chelton/Sean Walsh (choreographer)

10 Oct　　*Intermezzo* R Strauss
8 performances
Theatre Royal, Glasgow
Empire Theatre, Liverpool
King's Theatre, Edinburgh
His Majesty's Theatre, Aberdeen
New Tyne Theatre, Newcastle

Stephen Barlow/John Cox/
Martin Battersby/Alan Campbell/
Imogen Claire (choreographer)

21 Oct　　*Iolanthe* Gilbert and Sullivan
14 performances
Theatre Royal, Glasgow
Empire Theatre, Liverpool
King's Theatre, Edinburgh
His Majesty's Theatre, Aberdeen
New Tyne Theatre, Newcastle

Wyn Davies/Keith Warner/
Marie-Jeanne Lecca/Nick Chelton/
Sean Walsh (choreographer)

1987

27 Jan　　*The Flying Dutchman* Wagner
12 performances
Theatre Royal, Glasgow
His Majesty's Theatre, Aberdeen
King's Theatre, Edinburgh
Tyne Theatre, Newcastle

Alexander Gibson/John Cox/Eugene
Lee/Donna Kress (costumes)/Nick
Chelton/Imogen Claire (choreographer)

4 Feb　　* *The Marriage of Figaro* Mozart
11 performances
Theatre Royal, Glasgow
His Majesty's Theatre, Aberdeen
King's Theatre, Edinburgh
Theatre Royal, Newcastle

Graeme Jenkins/John Cox/John Byrne/
Paul Pyant/Ian Spink (choreographer)

25 Feb　　*From the House of the Dead* Janáček
7 performances
Theatre Royal, Glasgow
His Majesty's Theatre, Aberdeen
King's Theatre, Edinburgh
Tyne Theatre, Newcastle

Richard Armstrong/David Pountney/
Maria Björnson/Chris Ellis

28 April　　*Madama Butterfly* Puccini
13 performances
Theatre Royal, Glasgow
Tyne Theatre, Newcastle
Empire Theatre, Liverpool
King's Theatre, Edinburgh

Alexander Gibson/Nuria Espert/
Ezio Frigerio/Franca Squarciapino
(costumes)/Bruno Boyer

7 May　　* *The Barber of Seville* Rossini
10 performances
Theatre Royal, Glasgow
Tyne Theatre, Newcastle
Empire Theatre, Liverpool
King's Theatre, Edinburgh

Richard Hickox/Robert David
MacDonald/Sue Blane/Alan Campbell

21 May　　*Billy Budd* Britten
8 performances
Theatre Royal, Glasgow
Tyne Theatre, Newcastle
Empire Theatre, Liverpool
King's Theatre, Edinburgh

John Mauceri & Peter Stanger/
Graham Vick/Chris Dyer/Nick Chelton

15 Sep　　*Aida* Verdi
17 performances
Theatre Royal, Glasgow
Playhouse, Edinburgh
His Majesty's Theatre, Aberdeen
Tyne Theatre, Newcastle

John Mauceri & John Pryce-Jones/
Gilbert Deflo/William Orlandi/Bruno
Boyer/Ilka Doubek (choreographer)

25 Sep　　*Seraglio* Mozart
11 performances
Theatre Royal, Glasgow
Playhouse, Edinburgh
His Majesty's Theatre, Aberdeen
Tyne Theatre, Newcastle

Yan Pascal Tortelier/Richard Jones/
David Fielding/Maria Björnson
(costumes)/Victor Lockwood

21 Oct　　*Lulu* Berg
8 performances
Theatre Royal, Glasgow
Playhouse, Edinburgh
His Majesty's Theatre, Aberdeen
Tyne Theatre, Newcastle

John Mauceri/John Cox/John Bury/
Elizabeth Bury (costumes)/John Bury

11 Dec　　* *La vie Parisienne* Offenbach
10 performances
Theatre Royal, Glasgow

John Pryce-Jones & Peter Stanger/
Graham Vick – John Wells (revival)/
Richard Hudson/Alan Campbell/
Michele Hardy (choreographer)

1988

26 Jan　　* *The Pearl Fishers* Bizet
12 performances
Theatre Royal, Glasgow
His Majesty's Theatre, Aberdeen
Playhouse, Edinburgh
Theatre Royal, Newcastle

Peter Robinson/Steven Pimlott –
Stephen Lawless (revival)/
Lez Brotherstone/Paul Pyant/
Eleanor Fazan (choreographer)

6 Feb　　*Così fan tutte* Mozart
8 performances
Theatre Royal, Glasgow
Theatre Royal, Newcastle

Graeme Jenkins/Richard Jones/
Nigel Lowery/Christopher Toulmin

25 Feb　　* *Eugene Onegin* Tchaikovsky
10 performances
Theatre Royal, Glasgow
His Majesty's Theatre, Aberdeen
Playhouse, Edinburgh
Theatre Royal, Newcastle

Alexander Gibson & John Pryce-Jones/
David Pountney – Ceri Sherlock (revival)/
Roger Butlin/Alan Campbell/Terry Gilbert
(choreographer)

19 April　　* *Death in Venice* Britten
5 performances
Theatre Royal, Glasgow

Richard Bernas/François Rochaix – David
Walsh (revival)/Jean-Claude Maret/Alan
Campbell/Ilka Doubek (choreographer)

10 May　　*La bohème* Puccini
14 performances
Theatre Royal, Glasgow
Theatre Royal, Newcastle
Empire Theatre, Liverpool
Playhouse, Edinburgh

John Mauceri & John Pryce-Jones/
Elijah Moshinsky/Michael Yeargan/
Robert Bryan

19 May　　*Candide* Bernstein
14 performances
Theatre Royal, Glasgow
Theatre Royal, Newcastle
Empire Theatre, Liverpool
Playhouse, Edinburgh

John Mauceri & Justin Brown/
Jonathan Miller & John Wells/
Richard Hudson/David Cunningham/
Anthony van Laast (choreographer)

21 Sep　　*The Midsummer Marriage* Tippett
7 performances
Theatre Royal, Glasgow
Theatre Royal, Newcastle
Playhouse, Edinburgh
His Majesty's Theatre, Aberdeen

John Pryce-Jones/Tim Albery/Tom
Cairns & Antony McDonald/Ian
Sommerville/Ian Spink (choreographer)

5 Oct * **The Magic Flute** Mozart
13 performances
Theatre Royal, Glasgow
Theatre Royal, Newcastle
Playhouse, Edinburgh
His Majesty's Theatre, Aberdeen
Alhambra Theatre, Bradford

Yoram David/Jonathan Miller – David Walsh
(revival)/Philip Prowse/Alan Campbell

18 Oct **Die Fledermaus** J Strauss
14 performances
Theatre Royal, Glasgow
Theatre Royal, Newcastle
Playhouse, Edinburgh
His Majesty's Theatre, Aberdeen
Alhambra Theatre, Bradford

Jacek Kasprzyk/Simon Callow/
Bruno Santini/David Cunningham/
Stuart Hopps (choreographer)

17 Nov * **Così fan tutte** Mozart
6 performances
MacRobert Centre, Stirling
Eden Court, Inverness
Gardyne Theatre, Dundee

Justin Brown & Robert Dean/
Richard Jones – Tim Hopkins (revival)/
Nigel Lowery

16 Dec * **Iolanthe** Gilbert and Sullivan
12 performances
Theatre Royal, Glasgow

Grant Llewellyn & Robert Dean/
Keith Warner/Marie-Jeanne Lecca/
Alan Campbell/Sean Walsh

1989

17 Jan * **La bohème** Puccini
12 performances
Theatre Royal, Glasgow
His Majesty's Theatre, Aberdeen
Playhouse, Edinburgh
Apollo Theatre, Oxford
Theatre Royal, Newcastle

John Pryce-Jones/Elijah Moshinsky –
Kate Brown (revival)/Michael Yeargan/
Robert Bryan

27 Jan **Das Rheingold** Wagner
11 performances
Theatre Royal, Glasgow
His Majesty's Theatre, Aberdeen
Playhouse, Edinburgh
Apollo Theatre, Oxford
Theatre Royal, Newcastle

John Mauceri/Richard Jones/Nigel
Lowery/David Lovett & Nigel Lowery/
Matthew Hamilton & Richard Jones
(movement directors)

8 Feb **Don Giovanni** Mozart
11 performances
Theatre Royal, Glasgow
His Majesty's Theatre, Aberdeen
Playhouse, Edinburgh
Apollo Theatre, Oxford
Theatre Royal, Newcastle

John Mauceri & Justin Brown/David
Walsh/Katherine Hysing/Eleonore
Kleiber (costumes)/Torkel Blomkvist/
Elaine Bryce (choreographer)

23 Mar **Oedipus Rex** Stravinsky
5 performances
Theatre Royal, Glasgow

Graeme Jenkins/Stefanos Lazaridis &
Michael Hunt/David Cunningham

Note: *Oedipus Rex* shared a double bill with Scottish Ballet's
production of Stravinsky's *Petrushka*.

25 Apr **La traviata** Verdi
13 performances
Theatre Royal, Glasgow
Empire Theatre, Liverpool
Theatre Royal, Newcastle
Playhouse, Edinburgh
Eden Court, Inverness

John Mauceri & John Pryce-Jones/
Nuria Espert/Ezio Frigerio/Franca
Squarciapino (costumes)/Bruno Boyer/
Salvador Távora Triano (choreographer)

23 May **Street Scene** Weill
9 performances
Theatre Royal, Glasgow
Empire Theatre, Liverpool
Theatre Royal, Newcastle
Playhouse, Edinburgh

John Mauceri & David Drummond/
David Pountney/David Fielding/Paul
Pyant/David Toguri (choreographer)

19 Sep **The Merry Widow** Lehár
13 performances
Theatre Royal, Glasgow
Playhouse, Edinburgh
Theatre Royal, Newcastle
His Majesty's Theatre, Aberdeen

John Pryce-Jones & Martin André/Di
Trevis/Bunny Christie/Gerry Jenkinson/
Jane Gibson (movement director)

5 Oct * **The Marriage of Figaro** Mozart
14 performances
Theatre Royal, Glasgow
Playhouse, Edinburgh
Theatre Royal, Newcastle
His Majesty's Theatre, Aberdeen
Eden Court, Inverness

Justin Brown/John Cox/John Byrne/
Michael Wilson/Ian Spink (choreographer)

18 Oct * **Jenůfa** Janáček
7 performances
Theatre Royal, Glasgow
Playhouse, Edinburgh
Theatre Royal, Newcastle
His Majesty's Theatre, Aberdeen

Roderick Brydon & Robert Dean/
David Pountney – Sally Day (revival)/
Maria Björnson/John Waterhouse/
Terry Gilbert (choreographer)

29 Dec * **Die Fledermaus** J Strauss
2 performances
Theatre Royal, Glasgow

John Mauceri/Simon Callow/
Bruno Santini/David Cunningham/
Stuart Hopps (choreographer)

1990

3 Jan * **Die Fledermaus** J Strauss
3 performances
Theatre Royal, Glasgow
Playhouse, Edinburgh
Empire Theatre, Liverpool
Theatre Royal, Newcastle

John Mauceri/Simon Callow/
Bruno Santini/David Cunningham/
Stuart Hopps (choreographer)

24 Jan **Double Bill**
8 performances
Theatre Royal, Glasgow
Playhouse, Edinburgh
Empire Theatre, Liverpool
Theatre Royal, Newcastle

Oedipus Rex Stravinsky
Duke Bluebeard's Castle Bartók

Vachtang Matchavariani/
Stefanos Lazaridis/David Cunningham

13 Feb **La forza del destino** Verdi
11 performances
Theatre Royal, Glasgow
Playhouse, Edinburgh
Empire Theatre, Liverpool
Theatre Royal, Newcastle

John Mauceri/Elijah Moshinsky/
Michael Yeargan/David Cunningham

18 Apr * **Madama Butterfly** Puccini
14 performances
Theatre Royal, Glasgow
His Majesty's Theatre, Aberdeen
Theatre Royal, Newcastle
Playhouse, Edinburgh

John Mauceri/Nuria Espert/Ezio Frigerio/
Franca Squarciapino (costumes)/Alan
Campbell

25 Apr **Salome** R Strauss
9 performances
Theatre Royal, Glasgow
His Majesty's Theatre, Aberdeen
Theatre Royal, Newcastle
Playhouse, Edinburgh

John Mauceri/André Engel/Nick Rieti/
Elizabeth Neumuller (costumes)/André
Diot/Françoise Grès (choreographer)

10 May
Così fan tutte Mozart
10 performances
Theatre Royal, Glasgow
His Majesty's Theatre, Aberdeen
Theatre Royal, Newcastle
Playhouse, Edinburgh

Peter Hirsch/Jürgen Gosch/Nina Ritter

14 May
The Threepenny Opera Weill
17 performances
Tramway, Glasgow
Royal Lyceum Theatre, Edinburgh
Gardyne Theatre, Dundee
MacRobert Centre, Stirling
Eden Court, Inverness
Town Hall, Elgin
Gaiety Theatre, Ayr
Festival Theatre, Pitlochry
Plus venues in Blackpool, Swindon,
Bury St Edmunds, Basildon

Stuart Hutchinson/Lucy Bailey/
Simon Vincenzi/David Lawrence

30 Aug
* *Tosca* Puccini
16 performances
Theatre Royal, Glasgow
His Majesty's Theatre, Aberdeen
Playhouse, Edinburgh
Theatre Royal, Newcastle

Alexander Gibson & Robert Dean/
Anthony Besch/Peter Rice/Alan Campbell

18 Sep
The Trojans Berlioz
10 performances
Theatre Royal, Glasgow
His Majesty's Theatre, Aberdeen
Playhouse, Edinburgh
Theatre Royal, Newcastle
Royal Opera House, London

John Mauceri/Tim Albery/Tom Cairns &
Antony McDonald/Peter Mumford

Note: Seven of the 10 performances were given with Parts I
and II across consecutive evenings.

Note: The performance on 5 Dec at the Royal Opera House
was attended by HRH The Duchess of Gloucester.

17 Oct
The Vanishing Bridegroom Weir
(World Premiere)
9 performances
Theatre Royal, Glasgow
His Majesty's Theatre, Aberdeen
Playhouse, Edinburgh
Theatre Royal, Newcastle
Royal Opera House, London

Alan Hacker/Ian Spink/
Richard Hudson/Simon Corder

1991

16 Jan
* *La bohème* Puccini
14 performances
Theatre Royal, Glasgow
Apollo Theatre, Oxford
Alhambra Theatre, Bradford
Playhouse, Edinburgh
Theatre Royal, Newcastle

Marco Guidarini/Elijah Moshinsky –
David Walsh (revival)/Michael Yeargan/
Robert Bryan

29 Jan
Fidelio Beethoven
14 performances
Theatre Royal, Glasgow
Apollo Theatre, Oxford
Alhambra Theatre, Bradford
Playhouse, Edinburgh
Theatre Royal, Newcastle

Roderick Brydon & Robert Dean/Stephen
Wadsworth/Derek McLane/Dunya
Ramicova (costumes)/Peter Kaczorowski

8 Feb
* *The Cunning Little Vixen* Janáček
10 performances
Theatre Royal, Glasgow
Apollo Theatre, Oxford
Alhambra Theatre, Bradford
Playhouse, Edinburgh
Theatre Royal, Newcastle

Justin Brown/David Pountney – John
Lloyd Davies (revival)/Maria Björnson/
Nick Chelton/Stuart Hopps
(choreographer)

16 April
Falstaff Verdi
11 performances
Theatre Royal, Glasgow
His Majesty's Theatre, Aberdeen
Theatre Royal, Newcastle
Playhouse, Edinburgh

John Mauceri & Justin Brown/Ian Judge/
Mark Thompson/Robert Bryan

16 May
Regina Blitzstein (European Premiere)
5 performances
Theatre Royal, Glasgow
Theatre Royal, Newcastle

John Mauceri/Robert Carsen/
Michael Levine/Jean Kalman/
Daniel Pelzig (choreographer)

3 Sep
La clemenza di Tito Mozart
9 performances
Theatre Royal, Glasgow
His Majesty's Theatre, Aberdeen
Hippodrome, Birmingham
Theatre Royal, Newcastle

Nicholas McGegan & Martin André/
Stephen Wadsworth/Thomas Lynch/
Dunya Ramicova (costumes)/
Peter Kaczorowski

13 Sep
* *Madama Butterfly* Puccini
16 performances
Theatre Royal, Glasgow
Grand Opera House, Belfast
His Majesty's Theatre, Aberdeen
Hippodrome, Birmingham
Theatre Royal, Newcastle
Playhouse, Edinburgh

Alexander Gibson & Robert Dean/
Nuria Espert – Katherine Twaddle
(revival)/Ezio Frigerio/Franca
Squarciapino (costumes)/Alan Campbell

19 Oct
Die Walküre Wagner
7 performances
Theatre Royal, Glasgow
Hippodrome, Birmingham
Theatre Royal, Newcastle

John Mauceri/Richard Jones/
Nigel Lowery/Pat Collins/
Matthew Hamilton (choreographer)

29 Oct
* *Carmen* Bizet
16 performances
Theatre Royal, Glasgow
Grand Opera House, Belfast
His Majesty's Theatre, Aberdeen
Hippodrome, Birmingham
Theatre Royal, Newcastle
Playhouse, Edinburgh

Marco Guidarini & Robert Dean/Graham
Vick – Paul Maloney (revival)/Michael
Yeargan/Alan Campbell/Seán Walsh
(choreographer)

1992

22 Jan
* *The Marriage of Figaro* Mozart
12 performances
Theatre Royal, Glasgow
Alhambra Theatre, Bradford
Playhouse, Edinburgh
Theatre Royal, Newcastle

Justin Brown & Christopher McCracken/
John Cox – Sally Day (revival)/John Byrne/
Paul Pyant/Caroline Pope
(choreographer)

6 Feb
* *La traviata* Verdi
13 performances
Theatre Royal, Glasgow
Alhambra Theatre, Bradford
Playhouse, Edinburgh
Theatre Royal, Newcastle

Takuo Yuasa & Robert Dean/Nuria Espert
– Katherine Twaddle (revival)/Ezio
Frigerio/Franca Squarciapino (costumes)/
Alan Campbell/Terry Gilbert
(choreographer)

19 Feb
* *Billy Budd* Britten
5 performances
Theatre Royal, Glasgow
Theatre Royal, Newcastle

Richard Armstrong/Graham Vick – Paul
Maloney (revival)/Chris Dyer/Nick Chelton

22 April
Don Giovanni Mozart
16 performances
Theatre Royal, Glasgow
Eden Court, Inverness
Theatre Royal, Newcastle
Playhouse, Edinburgh
His Majesty's Theatre, Aberdeen

Robert Dean & Timothy Lole/
Tom Cairns/Ian Sommerville/
Aletta Collins (choreographer)

21 May *Aida* Verdi
12 performances
Theatre Royal, Glasgow
Eden Court, Inverness
Theatre Royal, Newcastle
Playhouse, Edinburgh
His Majesty's Theatre, Aberdeen

John Mauceri & Christopher Gayford/
Gilbert Deflo/William Orlandi/Alan
Campbell/Lise la Cour (choreographer)

20 Aug *The Oprichnik* Tchaikovsky
1 performance
Usher Hall, Edinburgh (EIF)

Note: A concert performance conducted by Mark Ermler.

9 Sep *Così fan tutte* Mozart
11 performances
Theatre Royal, Glasgow
His Majesty's Theatre, Aberdeen
Theatre Royal, Newcastle
King's Theatre, Edinburgh

Justin Brown & Robert Dean/
Graham Devlin/Ben Ormerod

29 Sep *Il trovatore* Verdi
10 performances
Theatre Royal, Glasgow
His Majesty's Theatre, Aberdeen
Theatre Royal, Newcastle
King's Theatre, Edinburgh

Richard Armstrong & Paul Wynne
Griffiths/Mark Brickman/Tim Hatley/
Ben Ormerod

21 Oct *Julius Caesar* Handel
7 performances
Theatre Royal, Glasgow
His Majesty's Theatre, Aberdeen
Theatre Royal, Newcastle
King's Theatre, Edinburgh

Samuel Bächli/Willy Decker/
John Macfarlane/Chris Ellis

17 Dec *The Magic Flute* Mozart
6 performances
Theatre Royal, Glasgow

Nicholas McGegan & Robert Dean/Martin
Duncan/Ken Lee/Heather Carson/
Linda Dobell (movement director)

1993
14 Jan *La bohème* Puccini
15 performances
Theatre Royal, Glasgow
King's Theatre, Edinburgh
Theatre Royal, Newcastle

Marco Guidarini/Caroline Sharman/
Michael Yeargan/Robert Bryan

23 Jan *The Magic Flute* Mozart
10 performances
Theatre Royal, Glasgow
King's Theatre, Edinburgh
Theatre Royal, Newcastle

Nicholas McGegan & Robert Dean/
Martin Duncan/Ken Lee/Heather
Carson/Linda Dobell (movement director)

21 April *Norma* Bellini
11 performances
Theatre Royal, Glasgow
His Majesty's Theatre, Aberdeen
King's Theatre, Edinburgh
Theatre Royal, Newcastle

John Mauceri/Ian Judge/John Gunter/
Deirdre Clancy (costumes)/Simon Tapping

5 May *Eugene Onegin* Tchaikovsky
13 performances
Theatre Royal, Glasgow
Eden Court, Inverness
His Majesty's Theatre, Aberdeen
King's Theatre, Edinburgh
Theatre Royal, Newcastle

Robert Dean & Timothy Lole/David
Pountney – James Ross (revival)/Roger
Butlin/Deirdre Clancy (costumes)/
Alan Campbell/Karen Rabinowitz
(choreographer)

18 May *The Makropoulos Case* Janáček
7 performances
Theatre Royal, Glasgow
His Majesty's Theatre, Aberdeen
King's Theatre, Edinburgh
Theatre Royal, Newcastle

John Mauceri/David Pountney – Sally Day
(revival)/Maria Björnson/Nick Chelton

16 Aug *I due Foscari* Verdi
12 performances
King's Theatre, Edinburgh (EIF) (2 visits)
Theatre Royal, Glasgow
Theatre Royal, Newcastle
His Majesty's Theatre, Aberdeen

Richard Armstrong/Howard Davies/
Ashley Martin-Davis/Alan Burrett/
Stuart Hopps (choreographer)

22 Sep *Tosca* Puccini
14 performances
Theatre Royal, Glasgow
King's Theatre, Edinburgh
Theatre Royal, Newcastle
His Majesty's Theatre, Aberdeen

Alexander Gibson & Timothy Lole/Anthony
Besch/Peter Rice/Alan Campbell

14 Oct *Kátya Kabanová* Janáček
8 performances
Theatre Royal, Glasgow
King's Theatre, Edinburgh
Theatre Royal, Newcastle
His Majesty's Theatre, Aberdeen

Richard Armstrong/Mark Brickman/
Richard Aylwin/Alan Burrett

27 Oct *Salome* R Strauss
8 performances
Theatre Royal, Glasgow
King's Theatre, Edinburgh
Theatre Royal, Newcastle
His Majesty's Theatre, Aberdeen

Richard Armstrong/André Engel – Rennie
Wright (revival)/Nick Rieti/Elizabeth
Neumuller (costumes)/Clive Pleasance/
Nicola Bowie (choreographer)

1994
20 Jan *The Magic Flute* Mozart
10 performances
Theatre Royal, Glasgow
His Majesty's Theatre, Aberdeen
Theatre Royal, Newcastle
King's Theatre, Edinburgh

Nicholas McGegan & Timothy Lole/
Martin Duncan/Ken Lee/Paul Pyant

15 Feb *The Turn of the Screw* Britten
6 performances
Tramway, Glasgow

Timothy Lole/David Leveaux/
Vicki Mortimer/Alan Burrett

12 April *Peter Grimes* Britten
8 performances
Theatre Royal, Glasgow
Centro Cultural de Belém, Lisbon
Theatre Royal, Newcastle

Richard Armstrong/Joachim Herz/
Reinhart Zimmermann/Eleonore
Kleiber (costumes)/Chris Ellis/
Linda Dobell (choreographer)

6 May *Tristan und Isolde* Wagner
12 performances
Theatre Royal, Glasgow (2 visits)
Centro Cultural de Belém, Lisbon
Theatre Royal, Newcastle (2 visits)
Festival Theatre, Edinburgh (2 visits)

Richard Armstrong/Yannis Kokkos &
Peter Watson/Michael Spray/
Kate Flatt (choreographer)

Note: The performance on 25 June marked the opening of the
Festival Theatre, Edinburgh.

15 Aug *Fidelio* Beethoven
12 performances
Festival Theatre, Edinburgh (EIF) (2 visits)
Theatre Royal, Glasgow
Theatre Royal, Newcastle

Richard Armstrong & Stephen Clarke/Tim
Albery/Stewart Laing/Peter Mumford

5 Oct *L'elisir d'amore* Donizetti
11 performances
Theatre Royal, Glasgow
His Majesty's Theatre, Aberdeen
Eden Court, Inverness
Theatre Royal, Newcastle
King's Theatre, Edinburgh

Marco Guidarini/Giles Havergal/
Russell Craig/Michael Calf/Terry John
Bates (choreographer)

7 Oct   ***Mary Stuart*** Donizetti
11 performances
Theatre Royal, Glasgow
Theatre Royal, Newcastle
Festival Theatre, Edinburgh

Richard Armstrong & Timothy
Lole/Stefanos Lazaridis/Stefanos
Lazaridis/Sue Willmington (costume)/
Davy Cunningham/Denni Sayers
(choreographer)

28 Oct   * ***Madama Butterfly*** Puccini
10 performances
Theatre Royal, Glasgow
Theatre Royal, Newcastle
Festival Theatre, Edinburgh

Alexander Gibson & Stephen Clarke/
Nuria Espert – Dafydd Burne-Jones
(revival)/Ezio Frigerio/Franca Squarciapino
(costumes)/Michael P Wilson

1995

7 Jan   * ***Iolanthe*** Gilbert and Sullivan
10 performances
Theatre Royal, Glasgow

Stephen Clarke & David Jones/Keith
Warner – Seán Walsh (revival)/Marie-
Jeanne Lecca/Nick Chelton

24 Jan   ***The Marriage of Figaro*** Mozart
14 performances
Theatre Royal, Glasgow
His Majesty's Theatre, Aberdeen
Festival Theatre, Edinburgh
Theatre Royal, Newcastle

Nicholas McGegan & Timothy Lole/
David Leveaux/Vicki Mortimer/Paul
Pyant/Wayne McGregor (choreographer)

Note: The performance on 19 May at the Theatre Royal,
Glasgow was attended by HRH The Duchess of Gloucester.

28 April   * ***La forza del destino*** Verdi
8 performances
Theatre Royal, Glasgow
Festival Theatre, Edinburgh
Theatre Royal, Newcastle

Richard Armstrong & Stephen Clarke/
Elijah Moshinsky – Roberto Goldschlager
(revival)/Michael Yeargan/Davy
Cunningham

11 May   ***Life with an Idiot*** Schnittke
6 performances
Theatre Royal, Glasgow

Richard Armstrong/Jonathan Moore/
David Blight/Paule Constable/
Caroline Ward (movement director)

27 May   * ***Madama Butterfly*** Puccini
4 performances
Theatre Royal, Glasgow
Theatre Royal, Newcastle
His Majesty's Theatre, Aberdeen

Alexander Gibson & Stephen Clarke/
Dafydd Burne-Jones/Ezio Frigerio/
Franca Squarciapino (costumes)/
Michael P Wilson

14 Aug   ***The Jacobin*** Dvořák
9 performances
Festival Theatre, Edinburgh (EIF) (2 visits)
Theatre Royal, Glasgow
Theatre Royal, Newcastle

Richard Armstrong & Stephen Clarke/
Christine Mielitz/Reinhart Zimmermann/
Eleonore Kleiber (costumes)/Chris Ellis/
Elaine Tyler-Hall (choreographer)

6 Sep   ***Don Giovanni*** Mozart
Theatre Royal, Glasgow
9 performances
Theatre Royal, Newcastle
Festival Theatre, Edinburgh

Nicholas McGegan & Dominic Wheeler/
John Cox/Peter Howson/Geraint
Pughe/Charles Linehan (choreographer)

25 Oct   ***La belle Hélène*** Offenbach
10 performances
Theatre Royal, Glasgow
Theatre Royal, Newcastle
Festival Theatre, Edinburgh

Emmanuel Joel/Patrice Caurier &
Moshe Leiser/Christian Rätz/Agostino
Cavalca (costumes)/Hervé Audibert

1996

12 Jan   ***Hansel and Gretel*** Humperdinck
13 performances
Theatre Royal, Glasgow
His Majesty's Theatre, Aberdeen
Eden Court, Inverness
Festival Theatre, Edinburgh

Guido Ajmone-Marsan & David Jones/
Mark Tinkler/Richard Aylwin/Paul Pyant

24 Jan   * ***La traviata*** Verdi
18 performances
Theatre Royal, Glasgow
His Majesty's Theatre, Aberdeen
Eden Court, Inverness
Festival Theatre, Edinburgh
Theatre Royal, Newcastle

Richard Armstrong & Stephen Clarke/
Nuria Espert – Peter Watson (revival)/
Ezio Frigerio/Franca Squarciapino
(costumes)/Michael P Wilson

Note: The performance on 13 June at the Festival Theatre,
Edinburgh was attended by HRH The Duchess of Gloucester.

2 April   ***Alceste*** Gluck
8 performances
Theatre Royal, Glasgow
Theatre Royal, Newcastle
Festival Theatre, Edinburgh

Nicholas McGegan & Dominic Wheeler/
Yannis Kokkos/Patrice Trottier/Richild
Springer (movement director)

14 May   ***Turandot*** Puccini
10 performances
Theatre Royal, Glasgow
Theatre Royal, Newcastle
Festival Theatre, Edinburgh

Richard Armstrong & Stephen Clarke/
Christopher Alden/Paul Steinberg/
Heather Carson

23 Aug   ***Inés de Castro*** MacMillan
(World Premiere)
7 performances
Festival Theatre, Edinburgh (EIF) (2 visits)
Theatre Royal, Glasgow
Theatre Royal, Newcastle

Richard Armstrong & Stephen Clarke/
Jonathan Moore/Chris Dyer/
Paule Constable

3 Oct   ***Idomeneo*** Mozart
6 performances
Theatre Royal, Glasgow
Festival Theatre, Edinburgh

Antoni Ros Marbá/David McVicar/
Ace McCarron

12 Oct   ***The Pearl Fishers*** Bizet
3 performances
Theatre Royal, Glasgow
Festival Theatre, Edinburgh
Theatre Royal, Newcastle

Note: Concert performances conducted by Stephen Clarke.

6 Nov   * ***Il trovatore*** Verdi
10 performances
Theatre Royal, Glasgow
Festival Theatre, Edinburgh
Theatre Royal, Newcastle

Richard Armstrong & David Jones/
Mark Brickman – Karen Howard (revival)/
Tim Hatley/Ben Ormerod

1997

15 Jan   * ***La bohème*** Puccini
17 performances
Theatre Royal, Glasgow
Festival Theatre, Edinburgh
Theatre Royal, Newcastle
His Majesty's Theatre, Aberdeen
Eden Court, Inverness

Stephen Clarke & Richard Armstrong/
Elijah Moshinsky – Daniel Slater (revival)/
Michael Yeargan/Simon Mills

12 Feb   ***Die Fledermaus*** J Strauss
18 performances
Theatre Royal, Glasgow
Festival Theatre, Edinburgh
His Majesty's Theatre, Aberdeen
Theatre Royal, Newcastle
Eden Court, Inverness

Nicholas Braithwaite & David Jones/Giles
Havergal/Kenny Miller/Hugh Vanstone/
Terry John Bates (choreographer)

23 April   ***Samson and Delilah*** Saint-Saëns
12 performances
Theatre Royal, Glasgow
Festival Theatre, Edinburgh
Theatre Royal, Newcastle

Frédéric Chaslin & David Jones/Antony
McDonald/Wolfgang Göbbel/Philippe
Giraudeau (movement director)

28 May   * *The Cunning Little Vixen* Janáček
9 performances
Theatre Royal, Glasgow
Theatre Royal, Newcastle
Festival Theatre, Edinburgh

Martin André & Stephen Clarke/David
Pountney – Stuart Hopps (revival)/
Maria Björnson/Nick Chelton

20 Aug   *Ariadne auf Naxos* R Strauss
3 performances
Festival Theatre, Edinburgh (EIF)

Richard Armstrong/Martin Duncan/Tim
Hatley/Jackie Galloway (costumes)/
Chris Ellis/Seán Walsh (choreographer)

Note: These performances were of the 1912 version.
Molière's play *Le bourgeois gentilhomme* was performed
before the opera.

16 Sep   * *Norma* Bellini
10 performances
Theatre Royal, Glasgow
Festival Theatre, Edinburgh
Alhambra Theatre, Bradford

Julian Smith/Ian Judge/John Gunter/
Deirdre Clancy (costumes)/
Davy Cunningham

30 Sep   *Rigoletto* Verdi
12 performances
Theatre Royal, Glasgow
Festival Theatre, Edinburgh
Alhambra Theatre, Bradford

Richard Armstrong & Derek Clark/
Kenny Ireland/Richard Aylwin/Andy
Philips/Nicola Bowie (choreographer)

15 Oct   * *Peter Grimes* Britten
7 performances
Festival Theatre, Edinburgh
Theatre Royal, Glasgow
Alhambra Theatre, Bradford

Richard Armstrong & Stephen Clarke/
Joachim Herz – Elaine Kidd (revival)/
Reinhart Zimmermann/Eleonore Kleiber
(costumes)/Victor Lockwood

12 Dec   * *Tosca* Puccini
7 performances
Theatre Royal, Glasgow
Festival Theatre, Edinburgh

Guido Ajmone-Marsan/Anthony Besch/
Peter Rice/Alan Campbell

1998

3 Jan   * *Tosca* Puccini
4 performances
Festival Theatre, Edinburgh

Guido Ajmone-Marsan & David Jones/
Anthony Besch/Peter Rice/Alan Campbell

5 Feb   *Così fan tutte* Mozart
10 performances
Theatre Royal, Glasgow
Festival Theatre, Edinburgh
Eden Court, Inverness

Nicholas McGegan & Derek Clark/Stewart
Laing/Aldona Cunningham/Zerlina Hughes

18 Feb   Double Bill
3 performances
Theatre Royal, Glasgow
Festival Theatre, Edinburgh

Snatched by the Gods Vir
Broken Strings Vir

Richard Farnes/Antony McDonald/
Philippe Giraudeau/Giuseppe di Iorio

20 Feb   *Samson* Handel
4 performances
Theatre Royal, Glasgow
Festival Theatre, Edinburgh
Eden Court, Inverness
Music Hall, Aberdeen

Note: Concert performances conducted by Derek Clark.

18 Mar   *Ariadne auf Naxos* R Strauss
8 performances
Theatre Royal, Glasgow
Festival Theatre, Edinburgh

Richard Armstrong/Martin Duncan/Tim
Hatley/Jackie Galloway (costumes)/
Chris Ellis/Seán Walsh (choreographer)

Note: These performances were of the 1916 version.

5 May   *The Queen of Spades* Tchaikovsky
8 performances
Theatre Royal, Glasgow
Empire Theatre, Sunderland
Festival Theatre, Edinburgh

Richard Armstrong/Yannis Kokkos/
Patrice Trottier/Suzanne Hywel
(choreographer)

23 May   * *La traviata* Verdi
12 performances
Theatre Royal, Glasgow
Empire Theatre, Sunderland
His Majesty's Theatre, Aberdeen
Festival Theatre, Edinburgh

Richard Armstrong & David Jones/Nuria
Espert – Peter Watson (revival)/Ezio
Frigerio/Franca Squarciapino (costumes)/
Michael P Wilson/Suzanne Hywel
(choreographer)

3 Sep   *Dalibor* Smetana
6 performances
Festival Theatre, Edinburgh (EIF)
Theatre Royal, Glasgow

Richard Armstrong/David Pountney/
Ralph Koltai/Sue Willmington
(costumes)/Davy Cunningham

16 Sep   * *The Magic Flute* Mozart
13 performances
Festival Theatre, Edinburgh
Theatre Royal, Glasgow
His Majesty's Theatre, Aberdeen

Richard Farnes & Derek Clark/Martin
Duncan/Ken Lee/Chris Ellis/Linda
Dobell (movement director)

17 Oct   * *Tristan und Isolde* Wagner
7 performances
Theatre Royal, Glasgow
Festival Theatre, Edinburgh

Richard Armstrong/Peter Watson/
Yannis Kokkos/Michael Spray

2 Dec   * *Hansel and Gretel* Humperdinck
10 performances
Theatre Royal, Glasgow
Festival Theatre, Edinburgh

Richard Armstrong & David Jones/
Mark Tinkler/Richard Aylwin/Paul Pyant

1999

6 Feb   *Der Rosenkavalier* R Strauss
5 performances
Theatre Royal, Glasgow
Festival Theatre, Edinburgh

Richard Armstrong/David McVicar/Michael
Vale/Tanya McCallin (costumes)/Tina
McHugh/Andrew George (choreographer)

20 Feb   *The Magic Fountain* Delius
4 performances
Theatre Royal, Glasgow
Festival Theatre, Edinburgh

Richard Armstrong/Aidan Lang/
Ashley Martin-Davis/Paul Pyant/
Andrew George (choreographer)

30 Mar   * *La bohème* Puccini
11 performances
Theatre Royal, Glasgow
Festival Theatre, Edinburgh
His Majesty's Theatre, Aberdeen
Eden Court, Inverness

Guido Ajmone-Marsan & Derek Clark/
Elijah Moshinsky – Tom Smith (revival)/
Michael Yeargan/Ace McCarron

5 May   *Aida* Verdi
10 performances
Festival Theatre, Edinburgh
Theatre Royal, Glasgow

Emmanuel Joel & Fergus Sheil/Antony
McDonald/George Souglides/Tania
Spooner (costumes)/Wolfgang Göbbel/
Philippe Giraudeau (movement director)

27 May   * *Inés de Castro* MacMillan
6 performances
Theatre Royal, Glasgow
Festival Theatre, Edinburgh

Richard Armstrong/Jonathan Moore/
Chris Dyer/Paule Constable

29 Aug   *Macbeth* Verdi
3 performances
Festival Theatre, Edinburgh (EIF)

Richard Armstrong/Luc Bondy/Rolf
Glittenberg/Rudy Sabounghi
(costumes)/Dominique Bruguière/
Lucinda Childs (choreographer)

22 Sep   *Kátya Kabanová* Janáček
6 performances
Theatre Royal, Glasgow
Festival Theatre, Edinburgh

Richard Armstrong/Rennie Wright/
Richard Aylwin/Davy Cunningham/
Maxine Brahan (choreographer)

22 Oct   *Carmen* Bizet
14 performances
Theatre Royal, Glasgow
His Majesty's Theatre, Aberdeen
Festival Theatre, Edinburgh
Empire Theatre, Sunderland

Nicholas Braithwaite & Derek Clark/Patrice
Caurier & Moshe Leiser/Christian Fenouillat/
Agostino Cavalca/Christopher Forey

6 Nov   *Friend of the People* Horne
(World Premiere)
6 performances
Theatre Royal, Glasgow
Festival Theatre, Edinburgh
Empire Theatre, Sunderland

Richard Farnes/Christopher Alden/
Allen Moyer/Joanna Parker (costumes)/
Heather Carson

10 Dec   * *The Marriage of Figaro* Mozart
12 performances
Theatre Royal, Glasgow
Festival Theatre, Edinburgh
Empire Theatre, Sunderland

Raymond Leppard & Derek Clark/
David Leveaux – Aidan Lang (revival)/
Vicki Mortimer/Deirdre Clancy
(costumes)/Paul Pyant/Maxine Brahan
(choreographer)

2000

4 Mar   *Parsifal* Wagner
5 performances
Festival Theatre, Edinburgh
Theatre Royal, Glasgow

Richard Armstrong/Silviu Purcarete/
Christophe Forey

29 Mar   * *Tosca* Puccini
8 performances
Theatre Royal, Glasgow
Festival Theatre, Edinburgh

Richard Farnes/Anthony Besch/
Peter Rice/Alan Campbell

2 May   *Macbeth* Verdi
10 performances
Theatre Royal, Glasgow
Theater an der Wien, Vienna
Festival Theatre, Edinburgh

Richard Armstrong/Luc Bondy/Rolf
Glittenberg/Rudy Sabounghi
(costumes)/Dominique Bruguière/
Lucinda Childs (choreographer)

13 May   * *Salome* R Strauss
7 performances
Theatre Royal, Glasgow
Festival Theatre, Edinburgh

Richard Armstrong/André Engel/Nick
Rieti/Elizabeth Neumuller (costumes)/
André Diot/Françoise Grès (choreographer)

21 Aug   *Das Rheingold* Wagner
8 performances
Festival Theatre, Edinburgh (EIF)
Theatre Royal, Glasgow

Richard Armstrong/Tim Albery/Hildegard
Bechtler/Ana Jebens (costumes)/Wolfgang
Göbbel/Vanessa Gray (movement director)

17 Oct   * *L'elisir d'amore* Donizetti
12 performances
Theatre Royal, Glasgow
His Majesty's Theatre, Aberdeen
Eden Court, Inverness
Festival Theatre, Edinburgh

Richard Farnes & Fergus Shiel/Giles
Havergal/Russell Craig/Gerry Jenkinson/
Terry John Bates (choreographer)

5 Dec   *Madama Butterfly* Puccini
10 performances
Theatre Royal, Glasgow
Festival Theatre, Edinburgh

Guido Ajmone-Marsan/David McVicar/
Yannis Thavoris/Paule Constable/Leah
Hausman (choreographer)

2001

28 Mar   * *Don Giovanni* Mozart
10 performances
Theatre Royal, Glasgow
Festival Theatre, Edinburgh
His Majesty's Theatre, Aberdeen
Eden Court, Inverness

Richard Armstrong & Derek Clark/John
Cox/Peter Howson/Davy Cunningham/
Leah Hausman (choreographer)

Note: The performance on 24 April at the Theatre Royal,
Glasgow was attended by HRH The Duchess of Gloucester.

5 May   * *Il trovatore* Verdi
10 performances
Theatre Royal, Glasgow
Festival Theatre, Edinburgh

Richard Armstrong & Stephen Clarke/
Mark Brickman – Peter Watson (revival)/
Tim Hatley/Davy Cunningham

Note: The performance on 19 June at the Festival Theatre,
Edinburgh was attended by HRH The Duke of Gloucester and
HRH The Duchess of Gloucester.

25 May   * *Inés de Castro* MacMillan
5 performances
Theatre Royal, Glasgow
Coliseu, Porto
Festival Theatre, Edinburgh

Richard Armstrong/Jonathan Moore/
Chris Dyer/Michael P Wilson

23 Aug   *Die Walküre* Wagner
8 performances
Festival Theatre, Edinburgh (EIF)
Theatre Royal, Glasgow

Richard Armstrong/Tim Albery/Hildegard
Bechtler/Ana Jebens (costumes)/Wolfgang
Göbbel/Vanessa Gray (movement director)

Note: The performance on 8 Sep at the Theatre Royal, Glasgow
was attended by HRH The Duchess of Gloucester.

17 Sep   * *La traviata* Verdi
16 performances
Theatre Royal, Glasgow
Festival Theatre, Edinburgh

Stephen Clarke & Richard Armstrong/
Nuria Espert – Peter Watson (revival)/
Ezio Frigerio/Franca Squarciapino
(costumes)/Chris Ellis/Lynne Hockney
(choreographer)

17 Oct   * *Così fan tutte* Mozart
15 performances
Theatre Royal, Glasgow
His Majesty's Theatre, Aberdeen
Festival Theatre, Edinburgh
Eden Court, Inverness

Vincent de Kort & Derek Clark/Stewart
Laing/Aldona Cunningham/Zerlina
Hughes/Linda Dobell (choreographer)

2002

28 Feb   *Monster* Beamish (World Premiere)
6 performances
Theatre Royal, Glasgow
Festival Theatre, Edinburgh
The Dome, Brighton

Diego Masson/Michael McCarthy/
Richard Aylwin/Ace McCarron

13 Mar   * *Der Rosenkavalier* R Strauss
6 performances
Theatre Royal, Glasgow
Festival Theatre, Edinburgh

Richard Armstrong/David McVicar/Tanya
McCallin (costumes)/Tina MacHugh/
Andrew George (choreographer)

Note: The performance on 16 April at the Festival Theatre,
Edinburgh was attended by HRH The Duchess of Gloucester.

25 April   * *Così fan tutte* Mozart
3 performances
Theatre Royal, Glasgow

Vincent de Kort/Stewart Laing/
Aldona Cunningham/Zerlina
Hughes/Linda Dobell (choreographer)

10 May   * *Madama Butterfly* Puccini
14 performances
Theatre Royal, Glasgow
Festival Theatre, Edinburgh
Eden Court, Inverness
His Majesty's Theatre, Aberdeen

Richard Armstrong & Derek Clark/
David McVicar – Leah Hausman (revival)/
Yannis Thavoris/Paule Constable/Leah
Hausman (movement director)

Note: The performance on 5 June at the Theatre Royal,
Glasgow was attended by HRH The Duchess of Gloucester.

25 Aug   *Siegfried* Wagner
7 performances
Festival Theatre, Edinburgh (EIF)
Theatre Royal, Glasgow

Richard Armstrong/Tim Albery/
Hildegard Bechtler/Ana Jebens
(costumes)/Peter Mumford/
Vanessa Gray (movement director)

1 Oct   * *Die Fledermaus* J Strauss
13 performances
Theatre Royal, Glasgow (2 visits)
Eden Court, Inverness
Festival Theatre, Edinburgh (2 visits)
His Majesty's Theatre, Aberdeen

Wyn Davies/Giles Havergal/
Kenny Miller/Gerry Jenkinson/
Terry John Bates (choreographer)

27 Nov   *Orfeo ed Euridice* Gluck
10 performances
Theatre Royal, Glasgow
Festival Theatre, Edinburgh
Regent Theatre, Stoke-on-Trent

Raymond Leppard/Lucinda Childs/
Claire Sternberg/Christophe Forey

2003

25 Jan   *Rigoletto* Verdi
11 performances
Theatre Royal, Glasgow
Festival Theatre, Edinburgh
Regent Theatre, Stoke-on-Trent

Richard Armstrong/Rennie Wright/
Richard Aylwin/Davy Cunningham/
Maxine Braham (movement director)

5 April   *Götterdämmerung* Wagner
4 performances
Festival Theatre, Edinburgh

Richard Armstrong/Tim Albery/
Hildegard Bechtler/Ana Jebens
(costumes)/Peter Mumford/
Vanessa Gray (movement director)

Note: The performance on 8 Aug was billed as a Gateway performance as part of the EIF.

16 May   *The Magic Flute* Mozart
17 performances
Theatre Royal, Glasgow (3 visits)
Festival Theatre, Edinburgh (2 visits)
His Majesty's Theatre, Aberdeen
Eden Court, Inverness

Vincent de Kort/Jonathan Moore/
Rae Smith/Bruno Poet/Peter Brennan
(movement director)

11 Aug   *Der Ring des Nibelungen* Wagner
5 complete cycles
Festival Theatre, Edinburgh (EIF)
Theatre Royal, Glasgow
The Lowry, Manchester

Richard Armstrong/Tim Albery/Hildegard
Bechtler/Ana Jebens (costumes)/
Wolfgang Göbbel & Peter Mumford/
Vanessa Gray (movement director)

Note: The performances on 25, 26, 28, and 30 Aug at the Festival Theatre, Edinburgh were attended by HRH The Duchess of Gloucester.

3 Dec   * *Aida* Verdi
4 performances
Theatre Royal, Glasgow

Richard Armstrong/Antony McDonald/
George Souglides/Tania Spooner
(costumes)/Giuseppe di Iorio/Philippe
Giraudeau (movement director)

2004

13 Jan   * *Aida* Verdi
8 performances
Theatre Royal, Glasgow
Festival Theatre, Edinburgh
Theatre Royal, Newcastle

Richard Armstrong & Piers Maxim/
Antony McDonald/George Souglides/
Tania Spooner (costumes)/Giuseppe di
Iorio/Philippe Giraudeau (movement
director)

17 Jan   *The Magic Flute* Mozart
8 performances
Theatre Royal, Glasgow
Festival Theatre, Edinburgh
Empire Theatre, Liverpool

Vincent de Kort/Jonathan Moore/
Rae Smith/Bruno Poet/Peter Brennan
(movement director)

28 April   *La bohème* Puccini
17 performances
Theatre Royal, Glasgow
Eden Court, Inverness
Festival Theatre, Edinburgh

Richard Farnes/Stewart Laing/
Christopher Kondek (video)/Claire
Murphy (costumes)/Heather Carson/
Wayne McGregor (movement director)

Note: The performance on 22 June at the Festival Theatre, Edinburgh was attended by HRH The Duchess of Gloucester.

14 May   *The Minotaur* Evans (World Premiere)
18 performances
Theatre Royal, Glasgow
Festival Theatre, Edinburgh
Dundee Rep
His Majesty's Theatre at Hilton, Aberdeen
Eden Court, Inverness

Oliver Rundell/Mark Hathaway/
Finlay McLay/Iain Piercy (film
animation)/Davy Cunningham/
Steinvor Palsson (choreographer)

Note: *The Minotaur* was billed as 'An opera for children in two acts'.

18 Aug   *Oberon* Weber
1 performance
Usher Hall, Edinburgh (EIF)

Note: A concert performance conducted by Richard Armstrong.

8 Oct   *Double Bill*
6 performances
Theatre Royal, Glasgow
Festival Theatre, Edinburgh

Erwartung Schoenberg
Duke Bluebeard's Castle Bartók

Richard Armstrong/André Engel/Nicky
Rieti/Chantal de la Coste-Messelière
(costumes)/André Diot

5 Nov   * *Tosca* Puccini
14 performances
Theatre Royal, Glasgow
Festival Theatre, Edinburgh

Guido Ajmone-Marsan & Derek Clark/
Anthony Besch – Aidan Lang (revival)/
Peter Rice/Robert B Dickson

2005

19 Jan   *The Knot Garden* Tippett
6 performances
Theatre Royal, Glasgow
Festival Theatre, Edinburgh

Richard Armstrong/Antony McDonald/
Giuseppe di Iorio

19 Feb   *Semele* Handel
7 performances
Theatre Royal, Glasgow
Festival Theatre, Edinburgh

Christian Curnyn/John La
Bouchardière/Giuseppe di Iorio/Magali
Gerberon (costumes)/Giuseppe di Iorio

13 Mar   *Andrea Chénier* Giordano
2 performances
Glasgow Royal Concert Hall
Usher Hall, Edinburgh

Note: Concert performances conducted by Richard Armstrong.

25 May   * *Fidelio* Beethoven
11 performances
Theatre Royal, Glasgow
Festival Theatre, Edinburgh

Richard Armstrong & Derek Clark/Tim
Albery/Simon Daw/Peter Mumford

23 Aug   *The Death of Klinghoffer* Adams
(UK Stage Premiere)
4 performances
Festival Theatre, Edinburgh

Edward Gardner/Anthony Neilson/
Miriam Buether/Chahine Yavroyan

2006

4 May   *Don Giovanni* Mozart
10 performances
Theatre Royal, Glasgow
Festival Theatre, Edinburgh

Richard Armstrong/Tim Albery/Tobias
Hoheisel/Peter Mumford/Ben Wright
(choreographer)

25 May   * *Carmen* Bizet
10 performances
Theatre Royal, Glasgow
Festival Theatre, Edinburgh

Gintaras Rinkevicius & Derek Clark/
Patrice Caurier & Moshe Leiser – Aidan
Lang (revival)/Christian Fenouillat/
Agostino Cavalca/Christophe Forey

4 Oct   * *Der Rosenkavalier* R Strauss
10 performances
Theatre Royal, Glasgow
Festival Theatre, Edinburgh

Richard Armstrong/David McVicar/
Tanya McCallin (costumes)/Clare
O'Donoghue/Andrew George
(choreographer)

Note: The performance on 25 Nov at the Festival Theatre, Edinburgh was attended by HRH The Duke of Gloucester and HRH The Duchess of Gloucester.

7 Nov   *Tamerlano* Handel
8 performances
Theatre Royal, Glasgow
Festival Theatre, Edinburgh

Christian Curnyn/John La Bouchardière/
Gideon Davey/Giuseppe di Iorio

2007

28 Mar   * *Madama Butterfly* Puccini
18 performances
Theatre Royal, Glasgow
Regent Theatre, Stoke-on-Trent
Festival Theatre, Edinburgh
His Majesty's Theatre, Aberdeen

Francesco Corti & Derek Clark/David
McVicar – Leah Hausman (revival)/Yannis
Thavoris/Robert B Dickson/Leah
Hausman (movement director)

16 May   *Lucia di Lammermoor* Donizetti
10 performances
Theatre Royal, Glasgow
Regent Theatre, Stoke-on-Trent
Festival Theatre, Edinburgh
His Majesty's Theatre, Aberdeen

Julian Smith & James Grossmith/John
Doyle/Liz Ascroft/Wayne Dowdeswell

3 Oct   *The Barber of Seville* Rossini
12 performances
Theatre Royal, Glasgow
His Majesty's Theatre, Aberdeen
Eden Court, Inverness
Festival Theatre, Edinburgh

Sergio La Stella & Derek Clark/Thomas
Allen/Simon Higlett/Mark Jonathan

19 Oct   *Seraglio* Mozart
9 performances
Theatre Royal, Glasgow
His Majesty's Theatre, Aberdeen
Eden Court, Inverness
Festival Theatre, Edinburgh

Jeremy Carnall & James Grossmith/
Tobias Hoheisel & Imogen Kogge/
Tobias Hoheisel/Andreas Grüter

2008

29 Feb   *Five:15 Operas Made in Scotland*
(World Premieres)
7 performances
Òran Mór, Glasgow
The Hub, Edinburgh

The King's Conjecture Williams &
MacLaverty Derek Clark/Ben Twist/
Andrew Storer/Michael McCarthy
(dramaturg)

The Queens of Govan Osborne, Khan
& Saadi Derek Clark/Michael McCarthy/
Andrew Storer/Michael McCarthy
(dramaturg)

Dream Angus Deazley, McCall Smith &
Twist Derek Clark/Ben Twist/Andrew
Storer/Kally Lloyd-Jones (choreographer)/
Michael McCarthy (dramaturg)

The Perfect Woman Cresswell & Butlin
Derek Clark/Frederic Wake-Walker/
Andrew Storer/Michael McCarthy
(dramaturg)

Gesualdo Armstrong & Rankin
Derek Clark/Michael McCarthy/Andrew
Storer/Michael McCarthy (dramaturg)

11 April   *A Night at the Chinese Opera* Weir
8 performances
Theatre Royal, Glasgow
His Majesty's Theatre, Aberdeen
Eden Court, Inverness
Festival Theatre, Edinburgh

Sian Edwards & James Grossmith/Lee
Blakeley/Jean-Marc Puissant/Jenny Cane/
Kally Lloyd-Jones (movement director)

13 May   *Falstaff* Verdi
13 performances
Theatre Royal, Glasgow
His Majesty's Theatre, Aberdeen
Eden Court, Inverness
Festival Theatre, Edinburgh

Peter Robinson & Derek Clark/
Dominic Hill/Tom Piper/Ben Ormerod/
Dominic Leclerc (movement director)

9 Aug   *The Two Widows* Smetana
6 performances
Festival Theatre, Edinburgh (EIF)
Theatre Royal, Glasgow

Francesco Corti/Tobias Hoheisel & Imogen
Kogge/Tobias Hoheisel/Peter Mumford/
Kally Lloyd-Jones (choreographer)

7 Oct   *The Secret Marriage* Cimarosa
9 performances
Theatre Royal, Glasgow
Eden Court, Inverness
His Majesty's Theatre, Aberdeen
Festival Theatre, Edinburgh

Garry Walker & James Grossmith/Harry
Fehr/Tom Rogers/Johanna Town/Kally
Lloyd-Jones (movement director)

30 Oct   *La traviata* Verdi
10 performances
Theatre Royal, Glasgow
Eden Court, Inverness
His Majesty's Theatre, Aberdeen
Festival Theatre, Edinburgh

Emmanuel Joel-Hornak & Derek Clark/
David McVicar/Tanya McCallin/Jennifer
Tipton/Andrew George (choreographer)

2009

23 Jan   *The Love of Three Oranges* Prokofiev
4 performances
Theatre Royal, Glasgow
Festival Theatre, Edinburgh

Timothy Dean/Lee Blakeley/
Emma Wee/John Clark

Note: A co-production with the Royal Scottish Academy of Music and Drama.

6 Feb   *La traviata* Verdi
6 performances
Theatre Royal, Glasgow
Grand Opera House, Belfast

Emmanuel Joel-Hornak & Derek Clark/
David McVicar/Tanya McCallin/Jennifer
Tipton/Andrew George (choreographer)

20 Feb   *Five:15 Operas Made in Scotland*
(World Premieres)
7 performances
Òran Mór, Glasgow
The Hub, Edinburgh

The Lightning-Rod Man Dixon & Parker
Derek Clark/Frederic Wake-Walker/
Andrew Storer/Michael McCarthy
(dramaturg)

Happy Story Fennessy & Bone
Derek Clark/Nicholas Bone/Andrew
Storer/Michael McCarthy (dramaturg)

White Williams & McCartney Derek
Clark/Frederic Wake-Walker/Andrew
Storer/Michael McCarthy (dramaturg)

Death of a Scientist Harris & Harris
Derek Clark/Michael McCarthy/Andrew
Storer/Michael McCarthy (dramaturg)

Remembrance Day MacRae & Welsh
Derek Clark/Michael McCarthy/Andrew
Storer/Michael McCarthy (dramaturg)

Note: The performance on 7 Mar at The Hub, Edinburgh was attended by HRH The Duchess of Gloucester.

29 Mar   *I Puritani* Bellini
1 performance
City Halls, Glasgow

Note: A concert performance conducted by Francesco Corti.

29 April   *Così fan tutte* Mozart
13 performances
Theatre Royal, Glasgow
Eden Court, Inverness
His Majesty's Theatre, Aberdeen
Festival Theatre, Edinburgh

Tobias Ringborg & James Grossmith/
David McVicar/Yannis Thavoris/Tanya
McCallin (costumes)/Franck Brigel

20 May   *Manon* Massenet
9 performances
Theatre Royal, Glasgow
Eden Court, Inverness
His Majesty's Theatre, Aberdeen
Festival Theatre, Edinburgh

Francesco Corti & Derek Clark/Renaud
Doucet/André Barbe/Guy Simard/
Renaud Doucet (choreographer)

23 Sep * ***The Elixir of Love*** Donizetti
11 performances
Theatre Royal, Glasgow
Eden Court, Inverness
His Majesty's Theatre, Aberdeen
Festival Theatre, Edinburgh

Francesco Corti & James Grossmith/Giles
Havergal/Russell Craig/Gerry Jenkinson/
Terry John Bates (choreographer)

21 Oct ***The Italian Girl in Algiers*** Rossini
9 performances
Theatre Royal, Glasgow
Eden Court, Inverness
His Majesty's Theatre, Aberdeen
Festival Theatre, Edinburgh

Wyn Davies & Derek Clark/Colin McColl/
Tony Rabbit/Nic Smillie (costumes)/
Tony Rabbit/Kally Lloyd-Jones
(movement director)

2010

22 Jan ***War and Peace*** Prokofiev
(World Premiere of the original version)
4 performances
Theatre Royal, Glasgow
Festival Theatre, Edinburgh

Timothy Dean/Irina Brown/Chloe
Lamford/Johanna Town/Kally Lloyd-
Jones (movement director)

Note: A co-production with the Royal Scottish Academy of
Music and Drama.

25 Feb * ***La bohème*** Puccini
19 performances
Theatre Royal, Glasgow
Festival Theatre, Edinburgh
His Majesty's Theatre, Aberdeen
Eden Court, Inverness
Grand Opera House, Belfast
Grand Canal Theatre, Dublin

Francesco Corti & Derek Clark/Stewart
Laing/Christopher Kondek (video)/
Theo Clinkard (costumes)/Heather
Carson/Ian Spink (movement director)

Note: A special preview performance was given on 23 February
for readers of *The Sun* newspaper.
Note: The performance on 20 April at the Festival Theatre,
Edinburgh was attended by HRH The Duke of Gloucester and
HRH The Duchess of Gloucester.

8 April ***The Adventures of Mr Brouček*** Janáček
4 performances
Theatre Royal, Glasgow
Festival Theatre, Edinburgh

Martin André/John Fulljames/Alex
Lowde/Finn Ross (video)/Lucy Carter/
Ben Wright (choreographer)

15 May ***Five:15 Operas Made in Scotland***
(World Premieres)
9 performances
Elphinstone Hall, University of Aberdeen
Traverse Theatre, Edinburgh
Òran Mór, Glasgow

Zen Story Young & Spence
Derek Clark/Michael McCarthy/Andrew
Storer/Catherine Deverell (costumes)/
Michael McCarthy (dramaturg)

Sublimation Fells & Strachan
Derek Clark/Matthew Richardson/
Andrew Storer/Catherine Deverell
(costumes)/Pippa Murphy (sound)/
Kally Lloyd-Jones (choreographer)/
Michael McCarthy (dramaturg)

The Money Man Cresswell & Butlin
Derek Clark/Matthew Richardson/
Andrew Storer/Catherine Deverell
(costumes)/Michael McCarthy
(dramaturg)

74° North Mealor, Stollery &
Davidson Derek Clark/Michael
McCarthy/Andrew Storer/Catherine
Deverell (costumes)/Pippa Murphy
(sound)/Michael McCarthy (dramaturg)

The Letter Khodosh & MacLaverty
Derek Clark/Irina Brown/Andrew
Storer/Catherine Deverell (costumes)/
Kally Lloyd-Jones (movement director)
Michael McCarthy (dramaturg)

23 Aug ***La fanciulla del West*** Puccini
1 performance
Usher Hall, Edinburgh (EIF)

Note: A concert performance conducted by Francesco Corti.

29 Oct ***The Marriage of Figaro*** Mozart
14 performances
Theatre Royal, Glasgow
Eden Court, Inverness
His Majesty's Theatre, Aberdeen
Festival Theatre, Edinburgh

Francesco Corti & James Grossmith/
Thomas Allen/Simon Higlett/Mark
Jonathan/Kally Lloyd-Jones (choreographer)

2011

21 Jan * ***The Cunning Little Vixen*** Janáček
4 performances
Theatre Royal, Glasgow
Festival Theatre, Edinburgh

Timothy Dean/David Pountney – Elaine
Tyler-Hall (revival)/Maria Björnson/Ian
Jones/Elaine Tyler-Hall (choreographer)

Note: A co-production with the Royal Scottish Academy of
Music and Drama.

15 Feb ***Orlando*** Handel
Theatre Royal, Glasgow
5 performances
Festival Theatre, Edinburgh

Paul Goodwin/Harry Fehr/Yannis
Thavoris/Andrzej Goulding
(projections)/Anna Watson

26 Mar ***Intermezzo*** R Strauss
5 performances
Theatre Royal, Glasgow
Festival Theatre, Edinburgh

Francesco Corti/Wolfgang Quetes/
Manfred Kaderk/Matthias Hönig

11 May ***Rigoletto*** Verdi
16 performances
Theatre Royal, Glasgow
Festival Theatre, Edinburgh
His Majesty's Theatre, Aberdeen
Eden Court, Inverness
Grand Opera House, Belfast
Grand Canal Theatre, Dublin

Tobias Ringborg & Derek Clark/
Matthew Richardson/Jon Morrell/Tony
Rabbit/Kally Lloyd-Jones (choreographer)

Note: A special preview performance was given on 9 May for
readers of *The Sun* newspaper.

29 Aug ***The Seven Deadly Sins*** Weill
5 performances
HMV Picture House, Edinburgh
O2 ABC, Glasgow

Jessica Cottis/Kally Lloyd-Jones/
Janis Hart/Grahame Gardner/
Kally Lloyd-Jones (choreographer)

Note: A co-production with Company Chordelia. Part of The
Edinburgh Festival Fringe.

21 Oct * ***The Barber of Seville*** Rossini
12 performances
Theatre Royal, Glasgow
Eden Court, Inverness
His Majesty's Theatre, Aberdeen
King's Theatre, Edinburgh

Francesco Corti & James Grossmith/
Thomas Allen/Simon Higlett/
Robert B Dickson

2012

20 Jan ***Betrothal in a Monastery*** Prokofiev
4 performances
Theatre Royal, Glasgow
Festival Theatre, Edinburgh

Timothy Dean/Rodula Gaitanou/
Jamie Vartan/Simon Corder/
Kally Lloyd-Jones (choreographer)

Note: A co-production with the Royal Conservatoire of Scotland.

4 Feb ***Hansel and Gretel*** Humperdinck
7 performances
Theatre Royal, Glasgow
Festival Theatre, Edinburgh

Emmanuel Joel-Hornak/Bill Bankes-
Jones/Tim Meacock/Mark Doubleday/
Kally Lloyd-Jones (choreographer)

17 Mar ***The Rake's Progress*** Stravinsky
7 performances
Theatre Royal, Glasgow
Festival Theatre, Edinburgh

Sian Edwards/David McVicar/
John Macfarlane/David Finn/
Andrew George (choreographer)

4 May * ***Tosca*** Puccini
14 performances
Theatre Royal, Glasgow
Eden Court, Inverness
Festival Theatre, Edinburgh
His Majesty's Theatre, Aberdeen

Francesco Corti & Derek Clark/Anthony
Besch – Jonathan Cocker (revival)/
Peter Rice/Robert B Dickson

5 June **Double Bill**
1 performance
City Halls, Glasgow

Cavalleria rusticana Mascagni
Pagliacci Leoncavallo

Note: A concert performance to mark the 50th anniversary of
Scottish Opera, conducted by Francesco Corti.

29 Aug *New Opera Made in Scotland*

The Lady from the Sea Armstrong
& Strachan (World Premiere)
4 performances
King's Theatre, Edinburgh (EIF)
Theatre Royal, Glasgow

Derek Clark/Harry Fehr/Yannis
Thavoris/Finn Ross (video)/Warren
Letton/Kally Lloyd-Jones (movement
director)/Michael McCarthy (dramaturg)

Clemency MacMillan &
Symmons Roberts
(Scottish Premiere)
4 performances
King's Theatre, Edinburgh (EIF)
Theatre Royal, Glasgow

Derek Clark/Katie Mitchell – Dan
Ayling (revival)/Alex Eales/John Bright
(costumes)/Warren Letton/ Joseph Alford
(movement director)

In the Locked Room Watkins & Harsent
(World Premiere)
5 performances
Traverse Theatre, Edinburgh (EIF)
Theatre Royal, Glasgow

Michael Rafferty/Michael McCarthy/
Samal Blak/Ace McCarron/
Michael McCarthy (dramaturg)

Ghost Patrol MacRae & Welsh
(World Premiere)
5 performances
Traverse Theatre, Edinburgh (EIF)
Theatre Royal, Glasgow

Michael Rafferty/Matthew Richardson/
Samal Blak/Tim Reid (video)/Ace
McCarron/Michael McCarthy &
Matthew Richardson (dramaturgs)

17 Oct ***The Magic Flute*** Mozart
17 performances
Theatre Royal, Glasgow
His Majesty's Theatre, Aberdeen
Eden Court, Inverness
Festival Theatre, Edinburgh
Grand Opera House, Belfast

Ekhart Wycik & Derek Clark/Thomas
Allen/Simon Higlett/Mark Jonathan/
Kally Lloyd Jones (movement director)

2013

25 Jan ***A Midsummer Night's Dream*** Britten
5 performances
Theatre Royal, Glasgow
Eden Court, Inverness
King's Theatre, Edinburgh

Timothy Dean/Olivia Fuchs/Niki
Turner/Tim Reid (video)/Warren Letton/
Mandy Demetriou (choreographer)

Note: A co-production with the Royal Conservatoire of Scotland.

15 Feb ***Werther*** Massenet
7 performances
Theatre Royal, Glasgow
Festival Theatre, Edinburgh

Francesco Corti/Pia Furtado/
Helen Goddard/Oliver Fenwick

4 April ***The Flying Dutchman*** Wagner
6 performances
Theatre Royal, Glasgow
Festival Theatre, Edinburgh

Francesco Corti/Harry Fehr/Tom Scutt/
Ian William Galloway (video)/Kally Lloyd-
Jones (movement director)

15 May ***The Pirates of Penzance***
Gilbert and Sullivan
58 performances
Theatre Royal, Glasgow
His Majesty's Theatre, Aberdeen
Festival Theatre, Edinburgh
Eden Court, Inverness
Opera House, Manchester
Hippodrome, Bristol
Theatre Royal, Newcastle
New Theatre, Oxford
Wales Millennium Centre, Cardiff

Derek Clark, John Owen Edwards &
James Grossmith/Martin Lloyd-
Evans/Jamie Vartan/Colin Grenfell/
Steve Elias (choreographer)

Opera for All

26 Sep 1966–17 Mar 1967 – 76 performances
Così fan tutte Mozart/*Cinderella* Rossini/*Madam Butterfly* Puccini

16 Oct 1967–16 June 1968 – 87 performances
Don Giovanni Mozart/*The Barber of Seville* Rossini/*Madam Butterfly* Puccini

14 Oct 1968–18 June 1969 – 75 performances
Don Giovanni Mozart/*Don Pasquale* Donizetti/*Madam Butterfly* Puccini

21 Oct 1969–20 June 1970 – 76 performances
La traviata Verdi/*Don Pasquale* Donizetti/*Martha* Flotow

19 Oct 1970–3 July 1971 – 68 performances
La traviata Verdi/*Martha* Flotow/*Cinderella* Rossini
Note: The performance on 28 Oct at the Webster Theatre, Arbroath was attended by HRH Princess Margaret.

18 Oct 1971–4 Mar 1972 – 60 performances
Cinderella Rossini/*The Fair Maid of Perth* Bizet/*Lucia di Lammermoor* Donizetti

6 Nov 1972–29 June 1973 – 61 performances
Rigoletto Verdi/*Count Ory* Rossini/*Lucia di Lammermoor* Donizetti

5–23 Nov 1973 – 11 performances
La bohème Puccini

5 Nov 1974–17 Jan 1975 – 15 performances
The Barber of Seville Rossini

6–24 Jan 1976 – 11 performances
Die Fledermaus J Strauss

24 Jan–3 Feb 1977 – 6 performances
La bohème Puccini

Scottish Opera Go Round and Scottish Opera on Tour

2 Feb 1978 – 10 performances
Candide Bernstein
Stewart Robertson/Graham Vick

9 Mar 1978 – 36 performances
The Elixir of Love Donizetti
Stewart Robertson/Graham Vick/Russell Craig/Victor Lockwood/John M Querns (piano)

18 May 1978 – 16 performances
Peace (World Premiere) by Carl Davis and John Wells
Stewart Robertson/Graham Vick/Russell Craig/Victor Lockwood/John M Querns (piano)

13 Nov 1978 – 18 performances
Così fan tutte Mozart
Stewart Robertson/John Lawson Graham/Alex Reid/Victor Lockwood/John M Querns (piano)

19 Jan 1979 – 33 performances
Curtain Calls (World Premiere) by Graham Vick, based on Offenbach
Stewart Robertson/Graham Vick/John M Querns (piano)

18 May 1979 – 30 performances
La traviata Verdi
Graham Vick (director)/Russell Craig (designer)/Victor Lockwood (lighting designer)/John M Querns (piano)

26 Oct 1979–7 April 1982 – 37 performances
The Quest of the Hidden Moon (World Premiere) by Ian Robertson
Ian Robertson & Simon Halsey/Graham Vick/Alan Hatton/Peter Bentley/John M Querns, Joyce Fieldsend & Lesley Anne Sammons (piano)
Note: *The Telephone* by Menotti was presented before the first two performances.

13 Feb 1980 – 17 performances
Double Bill: *Susanna's Secret* Wolf-Ferrari & *The Telephone* Menotti
Graham Vick (director & designer)/Peter Bentley (lighting designer)/Lesley Anne Sammons & John M Querns (piano)

14 Jan 1981–15 April 1983 – 48 performances
Cinderella Rossini
Graham Vick (director)/Alexis Leighton (revival director)/Alex Reid/Alan Campbell/Lesley Anne Sammons, Peter Lockwood & Christopher Middleton (piano)

2 Sep 1981 – 35 performances
The Marriage of Figaro Mozart
Rebecca Meitlis (director)/Emma Purdy (set)/Sue Wilmington (costumes)/Peter Bentley (lighting)/Jim Hastie (choreographer)/Lesley Anne Sammons (piano)

16 Sep 1982–16 April 1983 – 24 performances
Madam Butterfly Puccini
John Lawson Graham (director)/Tony Whelan (designer)/Alan Campbell (lighting)/Peter Gray Lockwood (piano)

27 Jan 1983 – 10 performances
Don Giovanni Mozart
Declan Donnellan (director)/Nick Ormerod (designer)/Peter Gray Lockwood & Christopher Middleton (piano)

21 Feb 1985 – 20 performances
Carmen Bizet
Keith Warner (director & designer)/Peter Bentley (lighting)/Gerald Moore (piano)

5 Nov 1985 – 23 performances
Tosca Puccini
Keith Warner (director)/Marie-Jeanne Lecca (designer)/Victor Lockwood (lighting)/Lesley Anne Sammons (piano)

2 Sep 1986 – 19 performances
Jenůfa Janáček
Matthew Richardson (director)/Ashley Martin-Davies (designer)/Steven Goff (choreographer)/Brenda Hurley (piano)

19 Feb 1987 – 20 performances
Macbeth Verdi
Richard Jones (director)/Nigel Lowery (designer)/Brenda Hurley (piano)

14 Sep 1987 – 36 performances
La bohème Puccini
Paul Maloney (director)/Gregory Smith (designer)/Victor Lockwood (lighting)/Mark Dorrell (piano)

19 May 1988 – 10 performances
Jenůfa Janáček
Matthew Richardson (director)/Ashley Martin-Davies (designer)/Steven Goff (choreographer)/Brenda Hurley (piano)

27 Aug 1988 – 32 performances
Don Carlos Verdi
David Walsh (director)/Karen Tennent (designer)/Alan Campbell (lighting)/Mark Dorrell (piano)

26 Aug 1989 – 38 performances (including 11 with chamber orchestra)
Pagliacci Leoncavallo & *Cavalleria rusticana* Mascagni
Robert Dean/Mike Ashman/Bernard Culshaw/Alan Campbell/Mark Dorrell (piano)

23 Aug 1990 – 32 performances
Eugene Onegin Tchaikovsky
Mark Brickman (director)/Julian McGowan (designer)/Kevin Sleep (lighting)/Alex Collinson (piano)

20 Aug 1991 – 34 performances
Mary Stuart Donizetti
Ian Spink (director)/Richard Hudson (designer)/Simon Corder (lighting)/Christopher McCracken (piano)

25 Aug 1992 – 32 performances
Seraglio Mozart
Nick Broadhurst (director)/Simon Higlett (designer)/Vince Herbert (lighting)/Nicholas Bosworth (piano)

5 Mar 1993 – 10 performances
Seraglio Mozart
Martyn Brabbins/Nick Broadhurst/Simon Higlett/Vince Herbert

7 Sep 1993 – 15 performances
Orpheus and Eurydice Gluck
Anthony Fabian (director)/Charlotte Watts (designer)/Mark Jonathan (lighting)/Harry Bicket (piano)/Wayne McGregor (choreographer)

3 Mar 1994 – 10 performances
Orpheus and Eurydice Gluck
Anthony Fabian (director)/Charlotte Watts (designer)/Mark Jonathan (lighting)/Wayne McGregor (choreographer)

6 Sep 1994 – 18 performances
The Grand Duchess of Gerolstein Offenbach
Mark Tinkler (director)/Julian Crouch (designer)/John Linstrum (lighting)/Mark Dorrell (piano)

1 Sep 1995 – 20 performances
La bohème Puccini
Stewart Laing (director & designer)/Zerlina Hughes (lighting)/Jeremy Silver & Richard Peirson (piano)

3 Sep 1996 – 21 performances
Così fan tutte Mozart
James Robert Carson (director)/George Souglides (designer)/Giuseppe di Iorio (lighting)/Stephen Higgins & Richard Peirson (piano)

2 Sep 1997 – 21 performances
The Barber of Seville Rossini
Matthew Lloyd (director)/Fotini Dimou (designer)/Gerry Jenkinson (lighting)/David Munro (piano)

15 Sep 1998 – 18 performances
The Makropoulos Case Janáček
Antony McDonald (director & designer)/Wolfgang Göbbel (lighting)/David Munro (piano)

7 Sep 1999 – 21 performances
Don Pasquale Donizetti
Cynthia Buchan (director)/Matthew Wright (designer)/Jeanine Davies (lighting)/David Munro (piano)

19 Sep 2000 – 21 performances
Hansel and Gretel Humperdinck
Gordon Anderson (director)/Es Devlin (designer)/Mark Doubleday (lighting)/Wayne McGregor (movement director)/Kevin Thraves (piano)

4 Sep 2001 – 21 performances
La bohème Puccini
Caroline Sherman (director)/Simon Higlett (designer)/Paul Need (lighting)/Kally Lloyd-Jones (movement director)/Ian Shaw (piano)

9 Oct 2002 – 7 performances
La bohème Puccini
Derek Clark/Caroline Sherman/Simon Higlett/Paul Need/Kally Lloyd-Jones (movement director)

15 April 2003 – 11 performances
Eugene Onegin Tchaikovsky
John La Bouchardière (director)/Emma Donovan (designer)/Simon Mills (lighting)/Maxine Braham (choreographer)/Alistair Lilley (piano)

5 April 2004 – 8 performances
Eugene Onegin Tchaikovsky
Derek Clark/John La Bouchardière/Emma Donovan/Simon Mills/Maxine Braham (choreographer)

9 April 2005 – 8 performances
Hansel and Gretel Humperdinck
Derek Clark/Dafydd Burne-Jones/Es Devlin/Mark Doubleday/Laila Diallo (movement director)

31 Aug 2005 – 19 performances
Macbeth Verdi
Dominic Hill (director)/Tom Piper (designer)/Bruno Poet (lighting)/Laila Diallo (movement director)/Oliver Rundell (piano)

Small- and Medium-Scale Touring as Scottish Opera

1 April 2006 – 8 performances
La bohème Puccini
Derek Clark/Caroline Sherman/Simon Higlett/Paul Need/Kally Lloyd-Jones (movement director)

6 Sep 2006 – 19 performances
Die Fledermaus J Strauss
Lee Blakeley (director)/Adrian Linford (designer)/Jenny Cane (lighting designer)/Kally Lloyd-Jones (choreographer)/Oliver Rundell (piano)

3 April 2007 – 10 performances
Die Fledermaus J Strauss
Oliver Rundell/Lee Blakeley/Adrian Linford/Jenny Cane/Kally Lloyd-Jones (choreographer)

5 Sep 2007 – 19 performances
Cinderella Rossini
Harry Fehr (director)/Tom Rogers (designer)/Johanna Town (lighting)/Kally Lloyd-Jones (movement director)/Ian Ryan (piano)

1 April 2008 – 9 performances
Cinderella Rossini
Oliver Rundell/Harry Fehr/Tom Rogers/Johanna Town/Kally Lloyd-Jones (movement director)

31 July 2008 – 3 performances
Cinderella Rossini
Harry Fehr/Tom Rogers/Johanna Town/Kally Lloyd-Jones/Ian Ryan
Note: Part of The Edinburgh Festival Fringe.

4 Sep 2008 – 26 performances
The Merry Widow Lehár
Clare Whistler (director)/Dody Nash (designer)/Simon Mills (lighting)/Ruth Wilkinson & Ian Ryan (piano)

10 Sep 2009 – 24 performances
Kátya Kabanová Janáček
Kally Lloyd-Jones (director)/Adrian Linford (designer)/Johanna Town (lighting)/Ian Ryan (piano)

7 Sep 2010 – 13 performances
Carmen Bizet
Derek Clark/Ashley Dean/Cordelia Chisholm/Johanna Town/Joyce Deans (movement director)/Louise Davidson (choreographer)

14 Oct 2010 – 14 performances
Carmen Bizet
Ashley Dean/Cordelia Chisholm/Johanna Town/Joyce Deans/Louise Davidson/Susannah Wapshott (piano)

8 Sep 2011 – 25 performances (including 8 at the Young Vic, London)
Orpheus in the Underworld Offenbach
Oliver Mears (director)/Simon Holdsworth (designer)/Kevin Treacy (lighting)/Anna Morrissey (movement director)/Claire Haslin & Ruth Wilkinson (piano)

4 Oct 2011 – 8 performances (comprising 3 in Scotland and 5 in Northern Ireland)
Orpheus in the Underworld Offenbach
Derek Clark/Oliver Mears/Simon Holdsworth/Kevin Treacy/Anna Morrissey

20 Sep 2012 – 26 performances
La traviata Verdi
Annilese Miskimmon (director)/Nicky Shaw (designer)/Mark Jonathan (lighting)/Susannah Wapshott (piano)

7 Mar 2013 – 8 performances
La traviata Verdi
Derek Clark/Annilese Miskimmon/Nicky Shaw/Mark Jonathan

Essential Scottish Opera and Opera Highlights

Singers in order: soprano, mezzo-soprano, tenor, baritone, unless stated otherwise.

ESO 1993 – 4 Mar – 6 venues
Jacquelyn Fugelle/Yvonne Burnett/Ian Storey/
David Ellis/Piano: Martin Fitzpatrick

ESO 1994 – 25 Mar – 14 venues
Fiona Cameron/Claire Shearer/Iain Paton/Tom
McVeigh/Piano: Gareth Hancock

ESO 1995 – 4 Mar – 14 venues
Susannah Glanville (soprano)/Lisa Milne (soprano)/Ian
Storey/Andrew Hammond/Piano: Ian Shaw

ESO 1996 – 9 Mar – 16 venues
Claire Rutter/Claire Bradshaw/Richard Coxon/
Stephen Gadd/Piano: Ian Shaw

ESO 1997 – 12 April – 15 venues
Mary Callan Clarke/Louise Armit/David Newman/
Martin Higgins/Piano: Richard Pierson & Rachel
Andrist

ESO 1998 – 22 Feb – 15 venues
Franzita Whelan/Joanna Campion/Gordon Wilson/
Benjamin Bland/Piano: Stephen Higgins

ESO 1999 – 16 Feb – 16 venues
Ann Archibald/Michelle Walton/Ivan Sharpe/Simon
Kirkbride/Piano: Stephen Higgins

ESO 2000 – 29 Feb – 16 venues
Sarah Rhodes/Clare Shearer/Alfred Boe/Eddie Wade/
Piano: Ian Shaw

ESO 2001 – 3 Feb – 16 venues
Rachel Hynes/Kathryn Turpin/Roland Wood
(baritone)/Piano: Ian Shaw

ESO 2002 – 2 Feb – 16 venues
Rachel Hynes/Deborah Humble/Andrew Mackenzie-
Wicks/Pauls Putnins/Piano: John Cameron

ESO 2003 – 21 Jan – 20 venues
Benedikte Moes/Sarah Jillian Cox/Darren Abrahams/
John Mackenzie/Piano: Ian Shaw

ESO 2004 – 10 Feb – 20 venues
Elizabeth Cragg (soprano)/Adele Mason (soprano)/
Karen Cargill (mezzo-soprano)/Daniel Jordan
(bass-baritone)/Piano: Ian Shaw

ESO 2005 – 18 Jan – 15 venues
Claire Wild/Sandra Bundy/Mark Chaundy/Christopher
Dixon/Piano: Ian Shaw

ESO 2006 – 17 Jan – 15 venues
Edel Shannon/Julia Riley/Alexander Grove/Paul Carey
Jones/Piano: Ian Shaw

ESO 2007 – 16 Jan – 15 venues
Sarah Redgwick/Katherine Allen/Adriano Graziani/
Adam Miller/Piano: Ian Shaw

ESO 2008 – 15 Jan – 15 venues
Amanda Forbes/Catriona Barr/Blake Fischer/Anders
Ostberg/Piano: Ian Shaw

ESO 2009 – 27 Jan – 15 venues
Joanne Boag/Chloé de Backer/Joshua Ellicott/Samuel
Evans/Piano: Philip Voldman

Opera Highlights 2010 – 2 Feb – 21 venues
Miranda Sinani/Louise Collett/Adrian Ward/Robert
Tucker/Piano: Ruth Wilkinson

Opera Highlights 2011 – 1 Feb – 15 venues
Marie Claire Breen/Catherine Hopper/Nicholas Watts/
Njabulo Madlala/Piano: Alison Luz

Opera Highlights 2012 – 31 Jan – 15 venues
Anita Watson/Rosie Aldridge/Robert Anthony
Gardiner/Marcus Farnsworth & Riccardo Simonetti/
Piano: Susannah Wapshott

Opera Highlights 2013 – 17 Jan – 17 venues
Eleanor Dennis/Katie Grosset/Nicky Spence/
Duncan Rock & Gary Griffiths/Piano: Ruth Wilkinson
& Claire Haslin

Photograph Acknowledgements

Bob Anderson 18 bl, 21, 68 bl, 78, 114 tl, 134, 227 t

Courtesy of Ann Baird 189

Clive Barda 242, 243

Beaverbrook Newspapers 221

Keith Brame 87

Bryan & Shear Ltd 14 br, 33, 35 tr, 52 tl, 52 tr, 68 tl, 82 tl, 97 t, 114 tr, 118 t, 161, 206 t, 227 bl

Richard Campbell 9, 49, 173, 175 1st 10 photos, 211, 240

Bill Cooper 37, 38, 47 b, 51, 56 both, 59, 60, 63 all, 64, 66, 74–5, 81 all, 84, 85, 98, 99, 100, 105, 111 bl, 112, 113 bl, 121, 129, 145, 157, 158, 168 bl, 182, tl, 182 tr

Alan Crumlish 122, 181 tl

Stephen Cummiskey 241

Peter Devlin 106 bl, 172 tl, 182 tr

KK Dundas 6, 198, 199, 239, 244, 245 both, 250 both, 251, 253 l

David Farrell 14 t

Drew Farrell 111 tr, 130 bl, 130 br, 142 all, 170, 194, 215, 287

Tommy Ga-Ken Wan 90, 175 last 5 photographs, 193, 197 b, 201, 233, 253 r

Courtesy of Lady Gibson 13 tl

James Glossop 224, 246 both, 247, 248, 249 both

Courtesy of John Lawson Graham 148 br

Ronald Gunn 206 br

Mark Hamilton 77, 93 both, 111 tl, 111 br, 138 both, 146, 152, 182 bl, 182 br, 230 tr, 231, 252

Sean Hudson 181 bl, 230 tl

Tas Kyprianou 130 t

Liz Lees 203, 204, 208 all

Laurie Lewis 167

Courtesy of Claire Livingstone 213 tl

Nigel Luckhurst 52 bl, 52 br

Eamonn McGoldrick 187

John Mackay 178

G MacDominic 27

Alastair Muir 104

Scotsman Publications Ltd 35 tl, 188

Courtesy of the Scottish Government 197 t, 237 l, 237 r

Gordon Rule 68 br

Lewis Segal 84 l, 148 bl, 217 tr

Paul Shillabeer 13 br, 14 bl

Primrose Smith & Sons 18 tr

Phil Smyth 191

David Southern 17

Eric Thorburn 25, 35 b, 46, 47 t, 55, 83 tl, 83 br, 88, 91 br, 94, 97 bl, 97 br, 102 all, 106, 107 br, 108, 113 br, 118 b, 122, 125 tl, 125 tr, 132, 137, 141 l, 141 tr, 148 t, 151 tr, 151 b, 155, 163, 164, 168 r, 169, 172 tr, 177, 184, 210, 214 t, 217 tl, 218, 222, 225 tl, 227 br, 228 all, 234, 235, 236 bl, 236 r

The Times 213 b

Vista 206 bl

Alice Wilson 219 all

Reg Wilson 18 tl, 68 tr

Unknown 13 tr, 13 bl, 18 br, 23, 28, 31, 41, 42, 44, 70, 71, 73, 83 bl, 91 l, 114 b, 117, 125 tl, 125 tr, 126, 151 tl, 168 tl, 184 br, 213 tr, 214 b, 216, 223, 225 tr, 236 tl

Index of People

Where appropriate, page numbers refer to captions rather than to photographs

Index of Operas

Where appropriate, page numbers refer to captions rather than to photographs

Opposite: Act II, *The Two Widows*, directors Tobias Hoheisel and Imogen Kogge, 2008.